Managing Human Resources in Europe

Managing Human Resources in Europe provides an analysis of the most important themes in European human resource management (HRM) written by leading authorities based all over Europe.

Unrivalled by any other text it provides a thematic approach with distinctive country examples in each chapter and is characterized by a critical approach with special attention given to dilemmas, controversies, paradoxes and problems in the field.

This text is essential reading for all those studying or working in HRM in Europe allowing an exciting synthesis of theory and practice, illustrated with living case studies.

Henrik Holt Larsen is Professor in Human Resource Management at Copenhagen Business School, Denmark. **Wolfgang Mayrhofer** is Professor of Organisational Behaviour and Management at Vienna University of Economics and Business Administration, Austria.

Routledge Global Human Resource Management Series

Edited by Randall S. Schuler, Susan E. Jackson, Paul Sparrow and Michael Poole

Routledge Global Human Resource Management is an important new series that examines human resources in its global context. The series is organized into three strands: Content and issues in global human resource management (HRM); Specific HR functions in a global context; and comparative HRM. Authored by some of the world's leading authorities on HRM, each book in the series aims to give readers comprehensive, in-depth and accessible texts that combine essential theory and best practice. Topics covered include cross-border alliances, global leadership, global legal systems, HRM in Asia, Africa, Europe and the Americas, industrial relations, and global staffing.

Managing Human Resources in Cross-Border Alliances
Randall S. Schuler, Susan E. Jackson and Yadong Luo

Managing Human Resources in Africa
Edited by Ken N. Kamoche, Yaw A. Debrah, Frank M. Horwitz and Gerry Nkombo Muuka

Globalizing Human Resource Management
Paul Sparrow, Chris Brewster and Hilary Harris

Managing Human Resources in Asia-Pacific
Edited by Pawan S. Budhwar

International Human Resource Management 2nd edition
Policy and practice for the global enterprise
Dennis R. Briscoe and Randall S. Schuler

Managing Human Resources in Latin America
An agenda for international leaders
Edited by Marta M. Elvira and Anabella Davila

Global Staffing
Edited by Hugh Scullion and David G. Collings

Managing Human Resources in Europe
A thematic approach
Edited by Henrik Holt Larsen and Wolfgang Mayrhofer

Managing Human Resources in the Middle-East
Edited by Pawan S. Budhwar and Kamel Mellahi

Managing Global Legal Systems
International employment regulation and competitive advantage
Gary W. Florkowski

Global Industrial Relations
Edited by Michael J. Morley, Patrick Gunnigle and David G. Collings

Managing Human Resources in Europe

A thematic approach

Edited by
Henrik Holt Larsen and
Wolfgang Mayrhofer

Routledge
Taylor & Francis Group

LONDON AND NEW YORK

First published 2006 by Routledge
2 Park Square, Milton Park, Abingdon, Oxon OX14 4RN

Simultaneously published in the USA and Canada
by Routledge
270 Madison Ave, New York, NY10016

Routledge is an imprint of the Taylor & Francis Group

© 2006 editorial matter and selection Henrik Holt Larsen and Wolfgang Mayrhofer;
individual chapters, the contributors.

Typeset in Times and Franklin Gothic by BC Typesetting Ltd, Bristol
Printed and bound in Great Britain by
TJ International, Padstow, Cornwall

British Library Cataloguing in Publication Data
A catalogue record for this book is available from the British Library

Library of Congress Cataloging in Publication Data
Managing human resources in Europe: a thematic approach/[edited by]
Henrik Holt Larsen and Wolfgang Mayrhofer.
    p.   cm.
Includes bibliographical references and index.
ISBN 0–415–35100–6 (hard cover) – ISBN 0–415–35101–4 (soft cover)
1. Personnel management–Europe. 2. Personnel management.
I. Holt Larsen, Henrik. II. Mayrhofer, Wolfgang.
HF55492.E9M36 2006
658.3′094–dc22
2005018897

ISBN10: 0–415–35100–6 (hbk)
ISBN10: 0–415–35101–4 (pbk)

ISBN13: 978–0–415–35100–3 (hbk)
ISBN13: 978–0–415–35101–0 (pbk)

Contents

Illustrations

Figures

Tables

Contributors

Ruth Alas is Professor of Management, Chair of Management at Estonian Busines School, Estonia.

Torben Andersen is Associate Professor, PhD in Human Resource Management, Department of Marketing and Management, University of Southern Denmark.

Céline Auger is Research Assistant in Human Resource Management, EM LYON, France.

Chris Brewster is Professor of International Human Resource Management at Henley Management College, United Kingdom.

Dirk Buyens is Professor in Human Resource Management, Ghent University and Vlerick Leuven Gent Management School, Belgium.

Rita Campose e Cunha is Associate Professor of Human Resource Management and Organizational Behaviors at School of Economics and Business, Universidade Nova de Lisboa, Portugal.

Françoise Dany is Professor in Human Resource Management and Career Counselling, EM LYON, France.

Koen Dewettinck is Doctoral Researcher in Human Resource Management, Vlerick Leuven Gent Management School, Belgium.

Paul Gooderham is Professor of International Management at Norwegian School of Economics and Business Administration (NHH), Bergen, Norway.

Edeltraud Hanappi-Egger is Professor of Gender and Diversity in Organizations at Vienna University of Economics and Business Administration, Austria.

Bo Hansson is Researcher at IPF (The Institute for Personnel and Corporate Development) Uppsala University and Mälardalen University, Sweden.

Anne-Mette Hjalager is PhD, independent contract researcher/consultant at Aarhus Science Park, Denmark.

Ulf Johanson is Professor at School of Business, Mälardalen University, Sweden.

Rüdiger Kabst is Professor for Human Resource Management, Faculty of Economics and Business Administration, University of Giessen, Germany.

Birthe Kåfjord Lange is Research Scholar at the Department of Strategy and Management, Norwegian School of Economics and Business Administration.

Henrik Holt Larsen is Professor of Human Resource Management at Copenhagen Business School, Denmark.

Stephen Lee is Director, Centre for Voluntary Sector Management, Henley Management College, United Kingdom.

Margaret Linehan, Dr, is Senior Lecturer at Cork Institute of Technology, Cork, Ireland.

Christopher Mabey is Professor of Human Resource Management, Birmingham University Business School, UK.

Bo Månson, Drs, is researcher at the IPF Institute, University of Uppsala, Sweden.

Wolfgang Mayrhofer is Professor of Management and Organizational Behavior at Vienna University of Economics and Business Administration, Austria.

Irene Nikandrou is Lecturer of Management at Athens University of Economics and Business, Greece.

Odd Nordhaug is Professor of Administrative Science at Norwegian School of Economics and Business.

Nancy Papalexandris is Professor of Human Resource Management at Athens University of Economics and Business, Greece.

Erling Rasmussen, Dr, is Associate Professor, Department of Management & Employment Relations, The University of Auckland, New Zealand.

Eleni Stavrou-Costea is Assistant Professor of Management and Organizational Behavior at the University of Cyprus, Department of Public and Business Administration, Cyprus.

Stefan Strohmeier is Professor of Management Information Systems at Saarland University, Saarbruecken, Germany.

Ivan Svetlik is Professor of Human Resources and Social Policy at the University of Ljubljana, Faculty of Social Sciences, Slovenia.

Ton Wilthagen is Professor in Institutional and Legal Aspects of the Labour Market at the Faculty of Law and head of OSA's General Policy Research Programme, Tilburg University, the Netherlands.

Foreword

Routledge Global Human Resource Management is a series of books edited and authored by some of the best and most well-known researchers in the field of human resource management. This series is aimed at offering students and practitioners accessible, coordinated and comprehensive books in global human resource management (HRM). To be used individually or together, these books cover the main bases of comparative and international HRM. Taking an expert look at an increasingly important and complex area of global business, this is a groundbreaking new series that answers a real need for serious textbooks on global HRM.

Several books in this series are devoted to human resource management policies and practices in multinational enterprises. For example, some books focus on specific areas of global HRM policies and practices, such as global leadership development, global staffing and global labour relations. Other books address special topics that arise in multinational enterprises across the globe, such as managing HR in cross-border alliances, developing strategies and structures and managing legal systems for multinational enterprises. In addition to books on various HRM topics in multinational enterprises, several other books in the series adopt a comparative, and within region, approach to understanding global human resource management. These books on comparative human resource management can adopt two major approaches. One approach is to describe the HRM policies and practices found at the local level in selected countries in several regions of the world. This approach utilizes a common framework that makes it easier for the reader to systematically understand the rationale for the existence of various human resource management activities in different countries and easier to compare these activities across countries within a region. The second approach is to describe the HRM issues and topics that are most relevant to the companies in the countries of the region.

This book, *Managing Human Resources in Europe*, describes a wide variety of highly contemporary HRM issues and topics across European nations. Henrik Holt Larsen and Wolfgang Mayrhofer serve as editors of this book and authors of the opening and closing chapters that provide an excellent overview of the state of the art and state of the practice of HRM in Europe today. In their final chapter they offer some suggestions and possibilities for the future of European HRM. In the middle eleven chapters the thinking of more than twenty five authors is organized into four sections, each one taking a different perspective on HRM in Europe. In these four sections the authors describe the institutional context of European HRM, the organizational environment for European HRM, the roles and contributions of the HRM profession within Europe and the societal and economic macro trends within European HRM.

This Routledge series, Global Human Resource Management, is intended to serve the growing market of global scholars and professionals who are seeking a deeper and broader understanding of the role and importance of human resource management in companies as they operate throughout the world. With this in mind, all books in the series provide a thorough review of existing research and numerous examples of companies around the world. Mini-company stories and examples are found throughout the chapters. In addition, many of the books in the series include at least one detailed case description that serves as convenient practical illustrations of topics discussed in the book.

Because a significant number of scholars and professionals throughout the world are involved in researching and practicing the topics examined in this series of books, the authorship of the books and the experiences of companies cited in the books reflect a vast global representation. The authors in the series bring with them exceptional knowledge of the human resource management topics they address, and in many cases the authors have been the pioneers for their topics. So we feel fortunate to have the involvement of such a distinguished group of academics in this series.

The publisher and editor have also played a major role in making this series possible. Routledge has provided its global production, marketing and reputation to make this series feasible and affordable to academics and practitioners throughout the world. In addition, Routledge has provided its own highly qualified professionals to make this series a reality. In particular we want to indicate our deep appreciation for the work of our series editor, Francesca Heslop. She has been behind the series from the very beginning and has been invaluable in providing the needed support and encouragement to us and to the many authors in the series. She, along with the editorial assistant Emma Joyes, has helped make the process of completing this series an enjoyable one. For everything they have done, we thank them all.

Randall S. Schuler, Rutgers University and GSBA Zurich
Paul Sparrow, Manchester University
Susan E. Jackson, Rutgers University and GSBA Zurich
Michael Poole, Cardiff University

Preface

In a sense, the message of the present book can be summarized in the following paraphrase: 'On a clear day, you can see European Human Resource Management'. Given that human resource management (HRM) has developed as a theoretical construct and a practitioner field over the past two decades and that there is considerable evidence that European HRM has some unique characteristics, it makes sense to identify the distinct features of current European HRM. We identify such distinctive, unique features of European HRM and relate these to the generic HRM concept as this was coined in the US in the 1980s. We interpret the distinct European flavour of the HRM concept by incorporating a range of contextual factors, we see how HRM unfolds in various organizational types, we analyze the measurement of HR processes and we bridge HRM with organizational performance. By doing so, we hope to illustrate the significance of a European-based HRM concept which can guide researchers and practitioners in dealing with human resource issues in European organizations.

Apart from the first and the concluding chapters, all chapters fall into one of four overall subject headings. The first one relates to the institutional context for HRM and is called looking outside, because it describes the extra-organizational conditions under which the organization (has to) function(s). The second heading is called looking inside and refers to organizational features having an impact on the HRM processes. We focus here on three very different organizational types/ structures, i.e. multinationals, small and medium size organizations and not-for-profit organizations. In the third part, we analyze specific HRM methods by looking inside on the HR professionals and their role/impact on organizational features. In the fourth part we look beyond the organization by discussing societal and economic macro trends, e.g. diversity and virtualization of HRM. Combined, these four subject areas provide a broad and diverse basis for the analysis and interpretation of the European HRM arena.

Briefly presented, the content of the individual chapters is as follows. Chapter 1 sets the stage for the study of European HRM by looking at its elements, i.e. the generic

HRM concept and the characteristics of Europe providing the legitimacy to deal with the concept of European HRM. Moving from this to the first cluster of chapters (The institutional context, Chapters 2–4), Chapter 2 analyzes the impact of the European Union on HRM. In particular, the focus is on the issue of being a member of the EU vs. wanting to become a member. Deregulation is the title of Chapter 3, which among others discusses the relationship between flexibility and security. Within the overall developments of deregulation, there is a switch from the standard employment contract to a greater variety of different forms of employment and/or de facto attachment to the organization. Chapter 4 deals with this transition from industrial relations to employment relations.

The next cluster of Chapters (5–7) looks inside the organization, in particular the way in which HRM is embedded in organizational characteristics. The first chapter in this cluster (i.e. Chapter 5), sheds light on HRM systems and practices in multinational corporations. It focuses on MNC's strategy and the strategic role of the subsidiaries and on the strategic dimension of international HRM. Chapter 6 focuses on HRM in European SMEs (small and medium-sized enterprises) as these constitute more than 90 per cent of European companies, but 90 per cent of what we know about HRM applies to the other 10 per cent, i.e. large organizations. Besides size, another implicit assumption of theorising in HRM refers to not only large, but also large for-profit organizations. However, this is only part of the spectrum. A number of different organizational setups beyond the profit world like public agencies, not for profit organizations and NGOs have gained new attention. Chapter 7 looks at HRM beyond the for-profit world.

The third cluster of Chapters (8–10) looks at major challenges for the HR profession itself. The first issue reflects that HRM is increasingly viewed in economic terms. Therefore, HRM not only in theory but also in practice has to take a very strict cost-benefit-view on its activities. What gets measured gets taken seriously. Chapter 8 looks at this issue from an accounting and management control perspective. Linked with the need to prove an organizational unit's worth in financial terms is its direct contribution to organizational performance. HRM is one crucial success factor for organizational performance. Chapter 9 takes a universalistic as well as a contextual perspective on the link between HRM and organizational performance. HR work without HR departments is the topic of Chapter 10. Given the increased pressure on all units not directly adding value because of cost considerations involved in reducing organizational slack and keeping organizations lean – HRM departments and their work are under close scrutiny. The chapter discusses various roles that HR professionals can take.

The final part – Looking beyond – deals with societal and economic macro-trends. Chapter 11 shows the various dimensions of diversity and diversity management as well as its impact on the management of human resources. Chapter 12 deals with the virtualization of HRM: HR in network and loosely structured organizations.

The chapter builds on HR related aspects of boundaryless organizations and the increasing use of information technology as two important facets of virtualization.

The concluding chapter puts into a broader perspective the conclusions of the previous chapter and sums up the contribution of European HRM to the effectiveness of European organizations.

We want to thank all the co-authors of individual chapters for their immediate positive reaction to join the project and for their committed and skilful contribution to the final text. It has been an unusually smooth and delightful process to deal with this group of competent colleagues. We also want to thank Randall S. Schuler, Rutgers University, and Susan E. Jackson, GSBA Zürich, who on behalf of the series editors for the Routledge Global Human Resource Management series have shared their professionalism and insight with us and shown confidence and unflagging support throughout the entire writing process. Finally, we want to express our thanks to commissioning editor Francesca Heslop at Routledge for her unique combination of resoluteness, administrative talent and humour. In fact, we have been treated so positively and professionally by the co-editors, Randall, Susan and Francesca, that we did not have the heart to delay the submission of the manuscript even more than we did!

Henrik Holt Larsen
Wolfgang Mayrhofer
Copenhagen and Vienna, 2006

European HRM: a distinct field of research and practice

WOLFGANG MAYRHOFER AND HENRIK HOLT LARSEN

Setting the scene – HRM as an emerging concept

Why a book on European human resource management (HRM)? The justification is at least twofold. First, the concept of HRM has played a key role in management research and practice during the last decades. It is reflecting an increasing dependency by the organization on competent and committed employees. Second, the very large differences between the European countries in terms of size, geography, history, institutional structure and labour market characteristics makes Europe an interesting arena for studying HRM, and the European research in this field certainly reflects this diverse picture. On the other hand, despite the considerable differences in HRM context and practice between individual countries, there are also some generic European features – and (in certain areas) an increasing convergence – in European HRM practice. In addition, a broad-based debate about European HRM has developed in theory as well as in practice.

The individual chapters of this book analyze such specific features of European HRM. Before we go into these, however, we will discuss briefly core elements of the two underlying concepts, i.e. *HRM* and *Europe*.

HRM as a concept emerged in the USA during the early 1980s. Two now famous textbooks formulating specific frameworks (Beer *et al.* 1985; Fombrun *et al.* 1984) indicated a shift away from personnel management. Although these frameworks varied, both argued that HRM differed from personnel management in a number of significant ways. Most prominently, HRM involved more integration of personnel policies across functions and with the corporate strategy, gave a greater role to line managers, had a clear focus on the link between HRM and organizational performance, proposed a shift from collective to individual relationships and indicated a reorientation away from a primarily humanistic to a more organizationally oriented value system.

Roots for the development of HRM can be traced back at least to the early twentieth century (Gooderham *et al.* 2004). One root is Scientific Management and its emphasis on carefully selected, rewarded and managed individuals as a major resource in the process of production. A second root is the Human Relations movement focusing on the importance of social relationships in the workplace for individual well being and, implicitly at least, good performance. A third historical root is the emerging awareness of the importance of occupational psychology and health in the early twentieth century. Evidence of working conditions which could be damaging to the health of the employee created an understanding of the necessity of improving working conditions and minimizing health hazards on the job. Parts of occupational psychology and social work/welfare are linked to these issues. Finally, in the 1970s, the human capital pointed out, among others, that human labour is an asset rather than a cost and of crucial importance for organizational productivity.

The emergence of the concept of HRM created a partly heated discussion about the specifics of this concept and its relationship to personnel management (see, e.g. Armstrong 2000; Legge 2005; Süß 2004). This very intense debate over the content and consequences of HRM – sometimes even questioning the very justification of talking about a 'new concept' (i.e. HRM) in the first place – has been a significant feature of European HRM in Europe. At a fairly general level, however, there seems to be a fair degree of consensus about five major characteristics of the HRM concept.

First, HRM emphasizes the necessity of integrating HR activities across a variety of functions and with the organizational *strategic orientation* (Boxall & Purcell 2003; Greer 2001; Lengnick-Hall & Lengnick-Hall 1988). Arguably, this is maybe the core characteristic of HRM. The mutual relationship between business strategy and HRM and the beneficial aspects of integration have been increasingly acknowledged (see, e.g. Schuler & Jackson 2000). There is some evidence, however, that currently we see a 'two camp landscape' in HRM. In one group of organizations, HRM clearly is an integral part of the strategic processes, playing a role already in the early stages of the process and being a valued player. In a second group, HRM has an important role, but is clearly subordinate. It plays a role in strategic processes only at a later stage and has to realise what has been decided earlier on.

Second, *line managers* play a crucial role in the concept of HRM. Their importance has to be seen in light of the developments at the organizational level. Through a number of developments such as new organizational forms (Whittington *et al.* 1999), the delayering of organizations (Morden 1997) leading to less middle-managers or the increasing cost pressures especially for so called non-productive units, the size of HR departments relative to the number of employees has been reduced over the past decade (Mayrhofer *et al.* 2004). Thus, organizations are moving away from large, centralized (staff) units and assign more responsibility and resources to 'local' or 'front line' managers. In turn, this has a direct effect on the HR department: it has to think about new ways of supplying the necessary services, performing its functions and equipping line managers with the necessary skills and competencies to handle the new HR tasks that they are confronted with. At the same time, the role of HR departments partly changes. While they still, at least to some extent, provide technical expertise, their role as co-ordinating unit acting as a catalyst for HR efforts becomes more important. Line managers and human capacity outside the organization play a crucial role for fulfilling HR tasks.

Third, the link between HRM and organizational *performance* is heavily emphasized. There is a broad and sometimes passionate discussion about the performance effects of HRM activities. Basically, three different approaches exist concerning the effects of HR on organizational performance (Delery & Doty 1996). The universalistic or 'best practice' approach assumes that specific HR practices have a universal, additive and positive influence on organizational performance (e.g. Becker & Gerhart 1996). The contingency approach emphasizes the role of contingency factors when linking HR practices and organizational performance. Special attention is paid to organizational strategy. Likewise, the importance of factors outside of the HR area is highlighted (e.g. Gooderham *et al.* 1999). The configurational approach has a more HR internal view. It focuses on the importance of a pattern of mutually compatible HR practices for organizational performance (for an example, see Ichniowski *et al.* 1997). A steadily increasing number of studies exist that analyze various aspects of the link between HRM and organizational performance at the conceptual and empirical level (see, e.g. Bowen & Ostroff 2004; Gelade & Ivery 2003; Wright *et al.* 2003; Fey & Bjorkman 2001; Huselid *et al.* 1997; Youndt *et al.* 1996; Delaney & Huselid 1996). Despite different conceptual and methodological approaches, a common tendency emerges. At least under specific conditions and in certain combinations, HRM has a positive impact on firm performance, even though the size of the effects are often comparatively small.

Fourth, in the relationship between the individual and the organization, there is less emphasis on *collective* forms of interaction and representation. Individual negotiations of work contracts or the decay of collective forms of representation such as trade unions or works councils are examples here.

Fifth, HRM also indicates a value laden focus shift: from the idea of balancing individual and organizational interests to a clear priority for improving organizational performance, regarding individual interests not as a value in itself but a restriction which has to be met when pursuing organizational goals. The focus shift turns the attention to the impact of HRM on organizational strategy, its customers or shareholders. Critics, especially from a European background, point towards a narrowness of perspective and the ignorance of other potential focuses, stakeholders and outcomes of HRM (see, e.g. Guest 1990; Legge 2005).

Universality questioned – the European focus

The current concept of HRM is the dominating paradigm in theory and practice. It has substituted personnel management and is discussed not only in the US, but worldwide. In this respect, Europe is no exception.

In other ways, Europe provides an arguably unique mixture of unifying and dividing elements. Heterogeneity and centrifugal forces do not come as a surprise when looking at a continent with an area of 9,839 million square kilometres (the US: roughly the same area, i.e. 9,809 million square kilometres), roughly 800 million inhabitants (the US: less than half, approximately 295 million), 45 nation states and more than 70 languages. History, culture and the economic and institutional situation contribute to a picture of diversity, too.

Historically, a long and often belligerent relationship between European countries led to a tradition of tension and rivalry. This does include large European states like the UK, France, Spain, Germany or Italy as well as tensions and war-like conflicts between smaller states or ethnic groups. Current examples for the latter include the struggle of the Hungarian minorities in Slovakia and Romania or, much more visible and forceful, the conflicts in Northern Ireland, Bosnia or the Basque country and the fierce ideological competition between Eastern and Western European countries with a very different political and economic background from 1945 until the fall of the iron curtain in 1990.

Culturally, major studies grouping countries according to basic cultural dimensions find great differences within Europe (see, e.g. Hofstede 1980; Trompenaars 1994). Findings indicate that regardless of inevitable differences even between closely related countries such as, e.g. Germany and Austria; cultural clusters, e.g. a Nordic, an Anglo-Saxon, a Romanic and a Germanic cluster with deep rooted cultural differences at the level of values/norms and basic assumptions can be identified.

Economically, large differences at the country and individual level exist. On the one hand, one can find countries with a comparatively high Gross Domestic Product (GDP) like Germany (2,712.3 billion dollars), the UK (1,402.6) or Italy (1,240.6). They stand in sharp contrast to countries comparable in terms of size with only a fraction of these values, such as Turkey (215.1) or Poland (179.9), not to mention smaller countries like the Slovak Republic with 26.2 billion dollars (Source: OECD main economic indicators, Feb. 2004; all figures for 2003). Looking at the individual level and per capita income, the situation is similar. Luxembourg, Norway, Switzerland, Denmark, Iceland, Austria, Ireland and the Netherlands have a purchasing power parity ranging from 27,470 (the Netherlands) to 51,060 (Luxembourg) international dollars (roughly speaking, the international dollar is a hypothetical currency unit reflecting the worth of local currency unit. It is calculated by using purchasing power parities and allows the comparison between countries and over time). Only the US (rank 3) and Canada (rank 9) join them in the top ten countries in the world. On the other hand, European countries like Albania (4,040), the Ukraine (4,650), Romania (6,290) and also countries now entering the European Union like Latvia (8,940) or Poland (10,130) are much further down this list (Source: World Development Indicators Database, World Bank, July 2003).

Institutionally, great heterogeneity exists. For example, European countries have a great variety of differences in labour related regulations and institutions. One can mention here the issues of labour law, especially in the area of protection of employees, the degree of regulation of the world of work or type of industrial relations and the role of trade unions and employers' associations. For example, the UK's weak employment protection laws tend to create more of a 'hire and fire'-like working environment than in most European countries (Morton & Siebert 2001).

The European Union has partly changed this picture. It created a more unified context for organizations to operate in (Brewster 1994a; Brewster 1994b). Nevertheless, national institutions and individual countries still play an important role. One might argue that in the area of management practices we see a European hybrid model emerging. It is based on the assumption that there are forces from the market, technology and institutional context that promote convergent developments. At the same time, the cultural and institutional context at the national level promotes a more differentiated European picture in the area of management practices. Findings for convergent as well as divergent tendencies of management practices in Europe might be interpreted as two sides of the same coin: management practices in Europe *simultaneously* become more alike in certain areas and stay or become different in other areas (Mayrhofer *et al.* 2002).

Given these European specifics and disregarding other important influencing factors in this respect, most notably the differences in scientific and epistemological traditions, it is little wonder that a more contextual paradigm has played a major role in discussing HRM in Europe. The universalistic paradigm is essentially linked to a nomothetic social science approach. It uses evidence to test generalizations of an abstract and law-like character. Much of the HRM discussion coined by the US debate implicitly or explicitly follows this epistemological and theoretical path. By contrast, the contextual paradigm focuses on understanding the differences between and within HRM in various contexts and determining factors of these differences. In addition, the often implicit assumption in much universalistic HRM research – the organizations' objectives and their strategies are 'good' either for the organization or for society – is not necessarily shared. Therefore, the importance of factors such as culture, ownership structures, management decision processes, labour markets, the role of the state and trade union organization play an important role.

Linked to these considerations, the notion of 'European HRM' was developed, arguably as a reaction to the hegemony of US conceptions of HRM (see, e.g. Brewster 1994; Sparrow & Hiltrop 1994; Brewster *et al.* 2000). The specifics of this concept of European HRM do not touch the core tasks and basic function of HRM. Of course, supplying organizations with the right number of people with the right qualifications at a specified time and location is still a key characteristic of HRM. However, there are arguments about how this can and should be done and what 'right' means in this context. Specifically, in the discussion about European HRM some of the basic assumptions behind the US version of HRM are questioned, and it is argued that they are not or only partly applicable in Europe. Put differently, there is evidence pointing in the direction of a distinctive European approach.

First, there are considerable differences between the US and Europe in the legal environment relevant for HRM. Of course, even within Europe large differences exist. For example, take countries with a lot of labour related regulations such as the German speaking area and comparatively less regulated countries like, e.g. Ireland or the UK. Yet, the density of labour regulations in Europe is higher than in the US (Grubb & Wells 1993).

Second, compared to the US, crucial actors in industrial relations have a different role in Europe (for the relationship between HRM and industrial relations see, e.g. Guest 1987). For example, trade unions and employers' associations play a more important role. Their influence in the political system, their importance for management decisions and the significance of collective bargaining and collective agreements are just three examples of this.

Third, when looking at specific aspects of HRM, important differences between Europe and the US can be found. Examples of this include skill level and available types of qualifications in the workforce (Mason & Finegold 1997), the role of human resource development professionals (Nijhof & de Rijk 1997), and managerial attitude towards employees' participation in decision making (McFarlin *et al.* 1992).

Fourth, and maybe especially telling, is the direct encounter of US and European views of HRM in European subsidiaries of US multinationals. The subsidiaries of US multinationals are different from indigenous organizations or multinationals from other countries. By and large, the latter adapt more to the local European environment. US multinationals, however, not only seem to have a rather ethnocentric approach to international HRM with little re-transfer of best practices from their overseas operations. They are also proactive in searching to by-pass local conditions that they see as constraints (Ferner 1997; Gooderham *et al.* 1998).

Beyond these basic differences, an empirical look at the situation in Europe offers additional insight. Key points are the existence of country clusters of HRM in Europe and, in terms of longitudinal developments, an absence of change in various areas of HRM and some evidence of converging HR practices.

Depending on the dimensions used, various authors (e.g. Filella 1991; Brewster *et al.* 1997) find different clusters of economic activities in general and, specifically, HRM. Whether it is Anglo vs. the rest of Europe, the differentiation between Nordic, Germanic, Anglo and Southern clusters or a focus on single regions such as Nordic or central European, the message is clear: within Europe clusters of countries with different patterns of HR activities can be found.

The accepted wisdom is ubiquitous change because of global as well as local change drivers being taken for granted. Therefore, European HRM should be no exception, as *prima facie* plausibility and singular, eclectic evidence both seem to confirm such a view. However, empirical data question this. For European HRM, absence of change and prevalence of stability at the country level seem to be the rule rather than the exception. When looking at the developments in European countries, a great number of HR practices have remained remarkably stable over the past years. Only in a few HR areas such as the size of the HR department relative to the number of employees, or the use of performance related compensation systems there is a trend towards directional convergence, i.e. a move in the same direction (for a more detailed view see Mayrhofer *et al.* 2004).

Current topics – key themes in European HRM

Given that HRM has developed as a new concept over the past two decades and that there is considerable evidence that European HRM has some unique characteristics, it makes sense to go one step further and ask whether there are specific themes that characterize current European HRM. 'Specific' in this context can mean two things. First, it can address an issue that is primarily or exclusively discussed in Europe. The role of the European Union is one such example. Second, it can mean that certain aspects of the issue, have some typical European 'flavour'. Given this, we can identify four core themes in European HRM. The first one relates to the institutional context and is called *looking outside* because it describes the extra-organizational conditions under which organizations (have to) function. The second category is called *looking inside* and refers to organizational features having an impact on the HRM processes. We focus on three very different organizational types/structures, i.e. small and medium-sized organizations, not-for-profit organizations and multinationals. Third, we analyze specific HRM methods by *looking inside* on the HR professionals and their role/impact on organizational features. Fourth, we *look beyond* the organization by discussing societal and economic macro-trends, e.g. diversity and virtualization of HRM. Combined, these four spotlights provide a broad and diverse basis for the analysis and interpretation of the European HRM arena.

Looking outside – the institutional context

As has been outlined above, there is strong evidence that the wider institutional context of HRM in Europe is unique. This is especially true for the effects that the European Union has, but also applies to the specific situation of regulation/deregulation in many European countries and the changes that occur in the system of industrial relations. Three chapters relate to these specifics.

Impact of the European Union on HRM: being a member vs. wanting to become a member

One of the most significant developments in Europe is the current and future development of the European Union (EU). This is true for the countries who have been long term members of the EU as well as for those countries that have joined the EU recently or will be joining in the near future. In addition, most of the recent or future members have a joint characteristic: they belong to those transition economies that have to cope with the change from a centrally planned economy to a market economy.

HRM is affected by these developments, too. First, the major freedoms within the EU influence all major functional areas of HR work since recruitment, selection, training and development, appraisal, compensation and industrial relations are in one way or other influenced by the greater labour market that is available, by new means of comparison, by reacting to those comparisons etc. Second, especially the countries in transition economies who either are already within the EU or are preparing to join have to cope with their often markedly different tradition of doing HR work.

Ivan Svetlik and Ruth Alas discuss the impact of European Union on HRM using two recent access countries – Estonia and Slovenia – as an example. They show how the efforts of joining the EU affects HRM.

Deregulation: between freedom and anxiety

Degrees of (de)regulation, i.e. the guidance of individual and organizational behaviour by a set of norms and regulations at various legal levels vary greatly in Europe. Overall, however, there seems to be a tendency towards deregulation despite some paradoxical effects like the EU propelling deregulation by central institutions producing regulations about deregulation. This development has significant impact on HRM. Examples of that are the greater variety of forms of employment, working time regulations or the enhanced freedom of labour movement within the EU. Especially interesting are the developments and their effects on HRM in those countries which historically belong to the group of highly regulated countries and currently experience a sharp swing such as, e.g. Belgium.

Koen Dewettinck, Dirk Buyens, Céline Auger, Françoise Dany and Ton Wilthagen draw on this issue by discussing the relationship between flexibility and security in Belgium, France and the Netherlands. They analyse 'flexicurity' in a truly unique setting where, as in the case of Belgium, the national and cultural environment do not parallel each other.

The power game: from industrial relations to employment relations

Within the overall developments of deregulation, the 'new workforce' with its different qualification and career aspiration profile, the switch from the standard employment contract to a greater variety of different forms of employment and/or de facto attachment to the organization, the role of trade unions and, more general, of industrial relations is changing. This is not only true at the supra-national and national level, but also at the organizational level.

HRM is affected by these developments in a number of ways. First, organizational governance and HR activities where traditionally trade unions in Europe played an important and sometimes crucial role become different when the role of such an important stakeholder changes. Second, HR cannot any longer rely on agreements that are negotiated at a national level or have de facto such an impact. Thus, the arrangements at the organizational, site or even individual level gain importance, emphasizing a more active role of HR in this area and reflecting the tension between collectivism and individualism in this area.

Erling Rasmussen and Torben Andersen pick up these themes and look at the overall situation in Europe. Specifically, they deal with the situation in Denmark and the UK and focus on three crucial areas where there is an especially close connection between HRM and employment relations: employee communication, increased flexibility in remuneration and working time.

Looking inside – embeddedness in the organization

Not only the external, but also the internal institutional setting is important for theorizing about organizations in general and human resources in specific. More often than not, writings about HRM do not make clear in which organization HRM is embedded, thus assuming an ideal type of 'average organization' as the implicit model. However, at least three different types of organizations constitute a major element of the European landscape of organizations: small and medium-sized enterprises, not-for-profit-organizations and multinational corporations and their subsidiaries. Three chapters look specifically at HR issues in these types of organizations.

HRM and SME: 90 per cent of what we know about HRM applies to 10 per cent of the companies

The implicit point of reference in many writings about HRM – and, in fact, in much of theorizing about organizing – is the large organization with its functional differentiation, the relatively large number of organizational members and the relatively elaborated specialization. Yet, in terms of sheer numbers these organizations are a clear minority in Europe. Small and medium-sized enterprises (SMEs) constitute the majority of organizations. Therefore, it is surprising that this type of organization is not included in scientific research much more often.

In HRM, the situation is not different from the rest of the disciplines. Outspoken or latent, much of HR writing relates to the large organization. However, HR departments, functional specialists etc, are rarely found at the lower end of SMEs and have a different make up in the larger SMEs. Nevertheless, HRM has to take place. Thus, it is interesting to analyze how HRM is done in SMEs in different European countries.

Eleni Stavrou-Costea and Bo Manson draw the attention to HRM in small and medium-sized enterprises in Europe. They focus on classical HRM areas such as staffing or training and development and on flexibility issues and discuss their specifics in this type of organization.

Here, there and everywhere? HRM beyond the for-profit world

Besides size, another implicit assumption of theorizing in management in general and HRM in specific refers to the governance structure and the embeddedness of organizations: organizations are not only large, but also large-for-profit organizations. However, this is only part of the spectrum. Partly through the new discussion about the civil society, a number of different organizational types beyond the profit world like public agencies, not-for-profit organizations and NGOs have gained new attention.

HRM in such organizations has to deal with some marked differences. To mention just a few one can name a different employee structure with a larger proportion of people working on an honorary basis, a different set of organizational goals which guide HR strategy and practice or the often heavily egalitarian and flat structure of such organizations provide a specific context for HR. This is especially true if these organizations operate across national borders.

Chris Brewster and Stephen Lee look at the situation in Europe's not-for-profit international organizations. They consist of Inter-Governmental Organizations (IGOs), such as the European Commission and the many United Nations (UN) agencies and programs, and Non-Governmental Organizations (NGOs) which are as diverse as the Boy Scouts and Girl Guides, Churches and Church aid charities and the European Football Federation (UEFA).

Bridge over troubled water: the role of multinationals in the development of European HRM

'Development aid' (export of HQ practice to subsidiaries) or learning from abroad (i.e. HQ learns from the subsidiaries)? European as well as extra-European multinational corporations (MNCs) and their subsidiaries play an important role in the economic development of Europe. Frequently they are regarded as motors and central hubs from which not only economic impulses emerge, but also new management techniques are spread. Portfolio techniques in former times or the balanced scorecard models are just two examples where MNCs through their subsidiaries contributed to the fast distribution.

In HRM, the situation is similar. MNCs and their subsidiaries often develop and disseminate new HR tools and concepts. This is especially true for transition economies where companies are eager to pick up new solutions for their problems. However, one can argue that this is often not a one-sided relationship in terms of 'development aid', i.e. export of HQ practice to subsidiaries. Likewise, learning from abroad, i.e. HQ learns from the subsidiaries, can occur.

Paul Gooderham and Odd Nordhaug shed light on HRM systems and practices in multinational corporations. They focus on MNC's strategy and the strategic role of the subsidiaries and on the strategic dimension of international HRM.

Looking at oneself – the roles and contribution of HRM

Not only the external and internal context, but also the HR function itself and its role within the organization is widely discussed in European HRM. Three chapters deal with this issue, focusing in turn on the roles that HR professionals can take, measuring HR performance and the link between HRM and organizational performance.

An endangered species: HR work without HR departments

Given the increased pressure on all units not directly adding value because of cost considerations, reducing organizational slack, and keeping organizations lean – HRM departments and their work are under close scrutiny. There are already some examples of organizations outsourcing their complete HR department or at least different parts of their HR work. At the same time, the organizational workforce no longer consists of employees with traditional contracts, but encompasses very different types of relationships to the organization.

For HRM, this is a new situation requiring new answers. Becoming smaller but maintaining or even increasing HRM's contribution to the overall organizational success is a crucial task. Likewise, different types of models beyond the traditional 'HR department and its specialists' approach develop. They include outsourced HR departments, new types of sharing responsibilities between line management and HR specialists, including the integration of large parts of HR work into the tasks of line management. In addition, HR has to satisfy many stakeholders: management, employees, internal and external customers are the most prominent examples. These stakeholders often have markedly different interests. Within these partly contradictory expectations HRM and HR professionals have to define their role, especially as translators and bridge builders between different stakeholders.

Christopher Mabey, Anne-Mette Hjalager and Birthe Kåfjord Lange discuss various roles that HR professionals can take and illustrate these roles with examples from the UK, Denmark and Norway. They show typical roles for HR professionals and the consequences for HR work.

What gets measured gets taken seriously: micro-economics and HRM

Today's acid test for the management of HR is quite clear: is it *worth* it? As the language of business ultimately is money, worth in this sense means directly contributing to the financial performance of the organization. This is no surprise in light of increased cost pressure and competitiveness and the need to show the contribution of various areas to the overall organizational performance. Combined with an increasing importance of the economic logic in various segments of society this leads to two major effects in HRM.

First, HRM increasingly is viewed in economic terms. The terminological change from personnel management to HRM is just one indicator for the growing importance of looking at all resources including people from an economic angle. Therefore, HRM, not only in theory but also in practice, has to take a very strict cost-benefit-view on its activities. Second, a new need of documenting activities and 'proving' contributions arises. In HRM, this leads to a growing importance of the formal evaluation of HR activities, a new significance of HR costing and accounting.

Ulf Johanson and Bo Hansson look at this issue from an accounting and management control perspective, using empirical examples from the UK, Sweden and Spain. They show the great variety of possible forms of measurement as well as the difficulties linked with such an endeavour.

HRM and organizational performance

Linked with the need to prove an organizational unit's worth in financial terms is its direct contribution to organizational performance. Given the overall competitive situation of organizations, this does not come as a surprise.

HRM is one crucial success factor for organizational performance – at the latest since the 1980s this seems to be a dictum rarely questioned. Employees are regarded as a valuable resource, soft skills are becoming increasingly important, the effective and efficient use of human resources are critical for overall performance. A number of studies focus on the relationship between organizational success and HRM, some of them analyzing isolated HR practices like selection or compensation. For the past ten years, however, the attention has shifted to specific combinations of various HR practices and their impact on organizational performance. Such success relevant combinations are termed 'high performance', 'human-capital-enhancing', 'high-commitment' or 'sophisticated work practices'. The relevance of HR practices for organizational performance leads to the question whether such practices are common to all organizations and all countries. This chapter discusses the issue of the link between HRM and organizational performance in Europe.

Irene Nikandrou, Rita Campos e Cunha and Nancy Papalexandris take a universalistic as well as a contextual perspective on the link between HRM and organizational performance. They demonstrate the worth of both of these models when looking at a great variety of European countries.

Looking beyond – societal and economic macro-trends

Beyond the external and internal institutional context a number of broad, macro-economic and/or societal developments influence organizations in general and HRM specifically. Two of these developments have particular relevance for HRM: diversity and virtualization. Hence, two chapters deal with these trends.

Diversity: neither fad nor fashion, but necessity

Free movement within the EU, the internationalization of business processes and general societal developments like changing values, birth rates, roles of women in society etc, have made the workforce of companies more diverse. Instead of clear and stable role patterns with related expectations, workforce diversity will increase in terms of gender, ethnicity, age, disability, age, religion, sexual orientation etc.

This increased diversity creates new issues for HRM. Take the issue of working in a culturally mixed work group in an otherwise comparatively homogenous

environment. For instance, in many Austrian governmental authorities that up to now consisted of Austrian nationals only working together with colleagues of 'the same kind', the issue of multicultural leadership has become an issue because of the European Union and its demands on some of the processes that governmental authorities nowadays face like joint work groups with people from different countries, intercultural negotiations or the like.

Margaret Linehan and Edeltraud Hanappi-Egger analyze the situation in Ireland, Austria and Germany and show the various dimensions of diversity and diversity management as well as its impact on the management of human resources. They argue that promoting and supporting diversity and diversity management is a crucial task for HRM when contributing to organizational performance.

Virtualization of HRM: HR in network and loosely structured organizations

One of today's mega-trends is virtualization. The decoupling of processes/actions and the underlying material basis, especially through the means of information technology, has an impact on many aspects of the organization and organizing. Two major aspects have special importance. First, organizing itself goes beyond traditional arrangements using organizational forms labeled virtual, boundaryless, fractal, network or heterarchical. Second, the Internet and intranets provide a great number of possibilities for changing organizational processes. This reaches from core processes like integrated computer aided design down to operational processes like processing the reimbursement of travel expenses online.

In HRM, virtualization has a number of consequences. Examples contain different types of processes like various virtual forms of training measures or e-learning, virtual recruitment through company web-pages or new opportunities of communicating with employees through interest groups, regular e-mails or virtual bulletin boards as well as different types of 'objects' of HR like, e.g. call centres.

Rüdiger Kabst and Stefan Strohmeier deal with HR related aspects of boundaryless organizations and the increasing use of information technology as two important facets of virtualization. They relate these issues to the theoretical discussion about neo-institutionalism and show the scope of electronic HRM.

Concluding remark

Why a book on European HRM? Ideally, this chapter has made the answer clear. HRM as well as Europe has unique characteristics; the dynamic of the research discourse and the output in this area has greatly increased; finally, in a time of global business activities, an in-depth understanding of a key organizational success factor – human resources – in a major region of the world – Europe – is essential. The chapters in this book hopefully contribute to such an understanding.

References

Armstrong, M. 2000. The name has changed but has the game remained the same? *Employee Relations*, 22(6): 576–593.

Becker, B. & Gerhart, B. 1996. The impact of human resource management on organizational performance: progress and prospects. *Academy of Management Journal*, 39(4): 779–801.

Beer, M., Spector, B., Lawrence, P. R., Mills, D. Q. & Walton, R. E. 1985. *Human Resource Management*. New York, London: Free Press.

Bowen, D. E. & Ostroff, C. 2004. Understanding HRM-firm performance linkages: the role of the 'strength' of the HRM system. *Academy of Management Review*, 29(2): 203–221.

Boxall, P. & Purcell, J. 2003. *Strategy and Human Resource Management*. Houndsmills: Palgrave Macmillan.

Brewster, C. 1994. European HRM: reflection of, or challenge to, the American concept? In P. S. Kirkbride (ed.), *Human Resource Management in Europe*: 56–89. London *et al.*: Routledge.

Brewster, C. 1994a. Towards a 'European' model of human resource management. *Journal of International Business Studies*, 26(1): 1–24.

Brewster, C., Larsen, H. H. & Mayrhofer, W. 1997. Integration and assignment: a paradox in human resource management. *Journal of International Management*, 3(1): 1–23.

Brewster, C., Mayrhofer, W. & Morley, M. 2000. The concept of strategic European human resource management. In C. Brewster, W. Mayrhofer & M. Morley (eds.), *New Challenges for European Human Resource Management*: 3–33. London: Macmillan.

Delaney, J. T. & Huselid, M. A. 1996. The impact of human resource management practices on perceptions of organizational performance. *Academy of Management Journal*, 39(4): 949–969.

Delery, J. E. & Doty, H. 1996. Modes of theorizing in strategic human resource management: Tests of universalistic, contingency and configurational performance predictions. *Academy of Management Journal*, 39(4): 802–835.

Ferner, A. 1997. Country of origin effects and HRM in multinational companies. *Human Resource Management Journal*, 7(1): 19–38.

Fey, C. F. & Bjorkman, I. 2001. The effect of human resource management practices on MNC subsidiary performance in Russia. *Journal of International Business Studies*, 32(1): 59–75.

Filella, J. 1991. Is there a Latin model in the management of human resources? *Personnel Review*, 20(6): 14–23.

Fombrun, C. J., Tichy, N. & Devanna, M. A. 1984. *Strategic Human Resource Management*. New York *et al.*: John Wiley & Sons Ltd.

Gelade, G. A. & Ivery, M. 2003. The impact of human resource management and work climate on organizational performance. *Personnel Psychology*, 56(2): 383–404.

Gooderham, P., Morley, M., Mayrhofer, W. & Brewster, C. 2004. Human resource management: A universal concept? In C. Brewster, W. Mayrhofer & M. Morley (eds.), *European Human Resource Management – Convergence or Divergence?*: 1–26. London *et al.*: Butterworth-Heinemann.

Gooderham, P., Nordhaug, O. & Ringdal, K. 1998. When in Rome, do they do as the Romans? HRM practices of US subsidiaries in Europe. *Management International Review*, 38(2): 47–64.

Gooderham, P. N., Nordhaug, O. & Ringdal, K. 1999. Institutional and rational determinants of organizational practices: Human resource management in European firms. *Administrative Science Quaterly*, 44: 507–531.

Greer, C. R. 2001. *Strategic Human Resource Management. A general managerial approach* (2nd edn.). Upper Saddle River, NJ: Prentice Hall.

Grubb, D. & Wells, W. 1993. Employment regulation and patterns of work in EC countries. *OECD Economic Studies*, (21): 7–58.

Guest, D. E. 1987. Human resource management and industrial relations. *Journal of Management Studies*, 24(5): 503–521.

Guest, D. E. 1990. Human resource management and the American dream. *Journal of Management Studies*, 27(4): 377–397.

Hofstede, G. 1980. *Culture's Consequences*. Beverly Hills, CA: Sage.

Huselid, M. A., Jackson, S. E. & Schuler, R. S. 1997. Technical and strategic human resource management effectiveness as determinants of firm performance. *Academy of Management Journal*, 40(1): 171–188.

Ichniowski, C., Shaw, K. & Prennushi, G. 1997. The effects of human resource management practices on productivity: a study of steel finishing lines. *The American Economic Review*, 87(3): 291–313.

Legge, K. 2005. *Human Resource Management. Rhetorics and Realities*. Houndsmills, Basingstoke: Palgrave Macmillan.

Lengnick-Hall, C. A. & Lengnick-Hall, M. L. 1988. Strategic human resources management: a review of the literature and a proposed typology. *Academy of Management Review*, 13: 454–470.

Mason, G. & Finegold, D. 1997. Productivity, machinery and skills in the United States and Western Europe. *National Institute Economic Review*, 162(Oct.): 85–99.

Mayrhofer, W., Morley, M. & Brewster, C. 2004. Convergence, stasis, or divergence? In C. Brewster, W. Mayrhofer & M. Morley (eds.), *Human Resource Management in Europe. Evidence of Convergence?*: 417–436. London *et al.*: Elsevier/Butterworth-Heinemann.

Mayrhofer, W., Müller-Camen, M., Ledolter, J., Strunk, G. & Erten, C. 2002. The diffusion of management concepts in Europe – conceptual considerations and longitudinal analysis. *Journal of Cross-Cultural Competence & Management*, 3: 315–349.

McFarlin, D. B., Sweeney, P. D. & Cotton, J. L. 1992. Attitudes toward employee participation in decision-making: a comparison of European and American managers in a United States multinational company. *Human Resource Management*, 31(4): 363–383.

Morden, T. 1997. A strategic evaluation of re-engineering, restructuring, delayering and downsizing policies as flawed paradigm. *Management Decision*, 35(3): 240–266.

Morton, J. & Siebert, W. S. 2001. Labour market regimes and workers recruitment and retention in the European Union: plant comaparisons. *British Journal of Industrial Relations*, 39(4): 505–528.

Nijhof, W. J. & de Rijk, R. N. 1997. Roles, competences and outputs of HRD practitioners – a comparative study in four European countries. *Journal of European Industrial Training*, 21(6/7): 247–258.

Schuler, R. S. & Jackson, S. E. (eds.) 2000. *Strategic Human Resource Management*. Oxford *et al.*: Blackwell.

Sparrow, P. & Hiltrop, J. M. 1994. *European Human Resource Management in Transition*. Hempel Hempstead: Prentice Hall.

Süß, S. 2004. Weitere 10 Jahre später: Verhaltenswissenschaften und ökonomik. Eine chance für die personalwirtschaftslehre. *Zeitschrift für personalforschung*, 18(2): 222–242.

Trompenaars, F. 1994. *Riding the Waves of Culture. Understanding Diversity in Global Business*. Chicago, IL. *et al.*: Irwin.

Whittington, R., Pettigrew, A., Peck, S., Fenton, E. & Conyon, M. 1999. Change and complementarities in the new competitive landscape: a European panel study. *Organization Science*, 10(5): 583–600.

Wright, P. M., Gardner, T. M. & Moynihan, L. M. 2003. The impact of HR practices on the performance of business units. *Human Resource Management Journal*, 13(3): 21–36.

Youndt, M. A., Snell, S. A., Dean, J. W. J. & Lepak, D. P. 1996. Human resource management, manufacturing strategy, and firm performance. *Academy of Management Journal*, 39(4): 836–866.

Looking outside:
The institutional context

The European Union and HRM: impact on present and future members

2

IVAN SVETLIK AND RUTH ALAS

Introduction

The impact of European Union (EU) membership on human resource management (HRM) is by no means direct. One could say that EU influences certain segments of economic, political and social environments, such as labour market and employment policies, while cultural environments deliberately remain country specific. Organizations respond to the uncertainties coming from these environments, e.g. directives on protection of workers, working time, collective redundancies, European works councils, equal opportunities and labour legislation as well as on other instruments, such as employment guidelines and those fostering workers' participation, social dialogue and social protection by developing their HRM systems and practices (Leat 1998; Vaughan-Whitehead 2003). From this perspective, organizations' HRM systems and practices may have some common 'European features', although big differences have been observed between them in various analyses (Hall & Hall 1990; Hofstede 1991; Hollinshead & Leat 1995; Ignjatović & Svetlik 2003). As Gooderham *et al.* (2004: 22) claim market and pan-European forces are generating convergence in HRM practices among European firms, while deep seated and fundamental differences between European countries influence their divergent approaches.

The HRM convergence – divergence dilemma deserves special attention in the new EU member states and in the accessing ones. A decade long accession period has been used to harmonize their diverse institutional settings with the 'acquis communitaire'. This means that major changes in economic and political institutions have been introduced in a short period, thus creating a new organizations' environment that challenges HRM also. Therefore the impact of EU membership is expected to be more visible in the new countries than in the old ones. However, a lot of country specifics have been preserved, which keep HRM diverse. In the cluster analysis applied to the Cranet-E data 1999–2001 (Cranet-E), compiled on representative samples of medium-sized and large organizations in twenty-four European and some other countries, there were four new member states: the Czech Republic, Slovenia, Estonia, Cyprus and Bulgaria and Turkey, which are still in the process of accession. The HRM systems and practices of organizations from Slovenia and the Czech Republic have been identified as similar to the other countries of the Central Southern cluster: Germany, Austria, Italy, Spain and Portugal, while those of the rest have been placed in the Peripheral cluster together with Ireland and Greece (Ignjatović & Svetlik 2003). We expect that these differences depend mainly on historical, institutional and cultural factors. Big differences between the new as well as aspiring EU member countries in terms of HR issues dealt with, approaches to these issues and in terms of how HRM is shaped have been observed in other analyses also (Koubek & Vatchkova 2004; Alas & Svetlik 2004).

One could conceive the EU as a system composed of sub-systems – the member states. The differences between the member states cause tensions, which can be reduced by flows. In its Constitution, article 1–4, the EU assures free flow within its borders of persons, services, goods and capital and free entrepreneurship. This means that there should be no major institutional barriers to the flows. The flows are likely to occur when there are big enough differences: in saturation of markets, in resources and infrastructure available, in wages, prices of goods, services and capital, in the standard of living, in opportunities for entrepreneurship, quality of life etc. Therefore one could expect stronger flows of goods, services, capital and labour between the new and accessing countries on one hand and the old members of the EU on the other than between the old ones, at least in the first years after the accession since the differences between the old and new (as well as aspiring) EU countries are bigger than among themselves. Let us look at some of them.

Gross domestic product (GDP) per capita expressed in purchasing power standards in 2002 among the new and candidate EU countries only in Cyprus, Malta and Slovenia exceeded 70 per cent of the 25 EU countries' average, while non of the old EU member states fell below 70 per cent. Turkey, Romania and Bulgaria were at about 27–29 per cent, while the richest, Luxembourg, was at 210 per cent. A similar situation could be observed in the case of labour productivity per employed person, which only in Cyprus, Malta and Slovenia exceeded 70 per cent of EU-15 average in 2003 (Eurostat). The number of personal computers per 100 inhabitants in EU-15 in 2000 was 28.6, while in Bulgaria, Romania and Turkey it was below 5. Big differences were also observed in the numbers of Internet users, mobile phone subscribers etc. (Eurostat yearbook 2002). The unemployment rate in EU-15 countries in 2002 was 8.1 per cent on average, while in the new member states it was 14.5 per cent.

With the exception of southern Italy the regions with the highest rates of unemployment were in the new member countries, particularly Poland and Slovakia (Mlady 2004). In 2003 the active population of 25–64 years having achieved more than secondary education (ISCED 4 and more) in the new member states did not exceed 20 per cent, while in the old member states it was beyond 20 per cent with the exceptions of Austria, Luxembourg, Italy, Portugal and Greece. In some countries, such as Scandinavia it was even beyond 30 per cent (OECD 2003).

EU membership is gradually expected to lessen the differences in economic and social life between the member countries. However, this is a long-term process. In addition, EU membership brings to the new member states not only opportunities but also risks. Furthermore, some authors (Vaughan-Whitehead 2003) are afraid that new member states will endanger the 'social Europe'.

Let us hypothesise as to what the consequences of EU freedoms for the issues dealt with in the organizations by HRM and the HRM itself could be under conditions of significant differences between the new (including candidate) and the old EU countries. We will examine the consequences according to the three main freedoms written in the EU Constitution: free flow of goods and services, free flow of capital and free flow of labour. Needless to say their impacts are manifold due to their profound nature and therefore, in reality, individual consequences cannot always be ascribed to one or another only – one can speak about a multiple causality.

Free flow of goods and services

Free flow of goods and services increases the competitive pressure on home producers and simultaneously creates opportunities for their extension of markets abroad. In the last decade this has led to substantial restructuring of organizations in the new member states, especially in the private sector. One of the indicators of restructuring is the number of companies which have multiplied, and the number of big ones, which have fallen. In Slovenia for instance the number of vital economic units has increased more than five times in the last fifteen years. However, according to the statistical office of Slovenia there are only slightly more than 500 organizations, which employ over 200 workers. Together with the transition to a market economy this has had significant implications for HRM.

Box 2.1

Imperial Tobacco, which is the major owner of Tobačna Ljubljana has announced today reorganization of its European production plants in the framework of its permanent endeavours to improve the productivity and economic performance.

Imperial Tobacco has made a thorough analysis of its production capacities taking into consideration the influence of EU enlargement on its business in the accession countries. On this basis it has decided to stop the production of cigarettes in Slovenia, Slovakia and Hungary.

The group of Tobačna Ljubljana, which employs in Slovenia around 500 workers, of them about 260 in the production process, produced in the year 2003 5.8 billion cigarettes. It is envisaged that the production process will stop until May 2004. Sales and marketing activities will remain unchanged and thus the continuity of Tobačna Ljubljana will be guaranteed in the future.

Press release of Tobačna Ljubljana, 27 January 2004

The restructuring of organizations has lead, especially at the beginning of the transition, to several redundancies. Organizations wanted to reduce hidden unemployment. This was a special challenge for HR departments that were accustomed to the full employment and non-redundancy policies. In a very short period they had to single out redundant individuals and send them to the employment offices, to early retirement, to another organization, to self-employment or in the best possible case to retraining. Various approaches to reduction of the workforce, its re-deployment within the firm and to protection of key workers against their turnover have been invented, copied and tried out. As can be seen in Table 2.1, which is based on Cranet-E data, organizations from the new EU countries have used various measures for the reduction of the number of employees more often than those from the old ones. Less employee friendly measures, such as compulsory redundancies and avoidance of renewal of fixed term and temporary contracts have been used especially. Having solved the issue of surplus labour HR specialists have quite often been 'awarded' their own redundancy. Joining the EU may cause additional pressures with similar consequences.

The endeavours to make organizations slimmer in many cases affected HR departments. Some of their functions have been outsourced, e.g. training and selection tests, and some transferred over to managers. The question is to what extent this process could be described in terms of devolution (Brewster & Larsen 1992; Renwick & MacNeil 2002; Mesner-Andolšek & Štebe 2004), including the strengthening of the HRM strategic role, and to what extent it could be described as a simple reduction of HR professional activities. As the data in Table 2.2 indicate

Table 2.1 Organizations using various methods of employment reduction (%)

	Old EU+*	New EU+**
Reeruitment freeze	33.7	42.8
Early retirement	37.1	27.0
Voluntary redundancies	34.1	18.3
Compulsory redundancies	30.8	50.0
Redeployment	33.6	48.2
Outplacement	14.3	16.7
No renewal of fixed term/temporary contracts	33.4	44.1
Outsourcing	18.8	21.6

Source: Cranet-E 1999–2001

Notes·
* Old EU+ countries: Germany, Austria, Spain, Portugal, Italy, Greece, Ireland, Northern Ireland, Denmark, Finland, Norway, Sweden, Great Britain, Switzerland, Belgium, the Netherlands and France.
** New EU+ countries: Czech Republic, Slovenia, Bulgaria, Estonia, Cyprus and Turkey.

There is a statistically significant difference between the two groups of countries in the case of all presented indicators.

HRM function in the new EU countries is less professionalized and enjoys lower status than in the old ones. Organizations here have fewer HR departments or HR managers. HR managers are more frequently recruited from non-specialists either inside or outside organizations. They contribute to the implementation rather than to the creation of organizations' strategies and the responsibility for HR decisions is allocated to line managers rather than to HR departments. This is a kind of immature devolution of HR function characterized by high responsibility of line managers for HR without being trained and professionally supported for dealing with them, and by a rather weak HRM strategic role.

However, this process has also contributed to the development of a HR services market. Although organizations in the new EU countries use external HR services more seldom than those in the old ones (3.8–52.5 per cent and 19.4 69.0 per cent respectively) several new HR agencies have been founded anew or have come from abroad, e.g. Adecco, Hill International and others. They provide services to small organizations such as head hunting, training services etc. Cranet data for 2004 show that in Slovenia there is between 8.4 per cent and 54.9 per cent of big and medium-sized organizations which in the last three years have increased the utilization of external HRM services in different areas. The percentage of those, which have decreased the utilization of these services is negligible. In Estonia these numbers are 4.0 per cent (pensions) and 56.9 per cent (training).

Table 2.2 Indicators of the status of HRM presented as percentages of organizations

Indicators	Old EU+*	New EU+**
Organizations having HR departments/ managers	92.0	78.5
Organizations using external HR services for		
– pay and benefits	24.9	5.6
– recruitment and selection	50.6	24.3
– training and development	69.0	52.5
– workforce outplacement/reduction	19.4	3.8
HR manager recruited from non-specialists in organization	23.8	31.1
HR manager recruited from non-specialists outside	10.7	14.4
HR manager contributes to creation of organizational strategy	56.2	44.0
HR manager contributes to implementation of organizational strategy	10.8	17.5
Responsibility for HR decisions with line management for		
– pay and benefits	14.5	41.5
– recruitment and selection	14.1	22.8
– training and development	15.3	23.6
– industrial relations	12.2	40.2
– workforce expansion/reduction	19.8	42.8
Responsibility for HR decisions with HR department for		
– pay and benefits	14.5	4.5
– recruitment and selection	9.8	5.6
– training and development	9.9	8.3
– industrial relations	30.7	11.6
– workforce expansion/reduction	9.2	2.1

Source: Cranet-E 1999–2001

Notes:
* Old EU+ countries: Germany, Austria, Spain, Portugal, Italy, Greece, Ireland, Northern Ireland, Denmark, Finland, Norway, Sweden, Great Britain, Switzerland, Belgium, the Netherlands and France.
** New EU+ countries: Czech Republic, Slovenia, Bulgaria, Estonia, Cyprus and Turkey.

There is a statistically significant difference between the two groups of countries in the case of all presented indicators.

Free flow of capital

Free flow of capital leads to green field investments in the new member states and to buying of the existing firms, which is in parallel with the process of privatization. According to UNCTAD (2004) all the new EU member countries are classified as front runners on the basis of the ranks achieved on the 'inward FDI performance index and inward FDI potential index'. In combination with the intensified market pressures investments emphasize restructuring, which expresses itself in the creation of new organizations, their close downs, mergers, split-ups, take-overs and so on. It should not be forgotten that this also increases opportunities for home-based firms to invest abroad and to establish their subsidiaries. HRM is faced with a number of challenges on this basis.

Foreign firms quite often bring new organizational forms including new HRM practices. For instance they have been the first to start to recruit and hire new workers with the help of private employment agencies. This could be explained by their different practices and by the fact that in their new surroundings they haven't yet established networks which could be used in the recruitment procedures.

Table 2.3 shows that managers in the new EU countries are recruited much more often by word of mouth rather than by advertising in newspapers, as in the old EU countries. The informal recruitment of managers is nearly as important as advertising in the newspapers, which is not the case in the old countries. This could be ascribed to the higher importance of informal regulation, which is a characteristic of organizational culture in the majority of new EU countries (Koopman *et al.* 1999). The second explanation could be down to less developed labour market mechanisms, although organizations from the new countries rely much more on money than organizations from the old countries when recruitment and retention of employees is in question (see Table 2.3). Most of the new EU countries are also small in terms of the number of citizens, which makes specific labour market segments more transparent and manageable by means of informal networks.

Although foreign companies often count on cheaper labour in the new EU countries than is available in their home countries, they increase competition for skilled labour, such as for information and communication technology (ICT) and marketing. This pushes wages up and increases the employment dynamic including turnover in the new member states. Cranet-E data for 1999–2001 show that 10.5 per cent of big and medium-sized organizations from the old EU countries report an increase and 5.8 per cent a decrease in the number of employees in the three-year period before the survey. Relevant percentages for the organizations from the new EU countries are 27.2 per cent and 27.8 per cent respectively. In the period 1996–2002 hourly labour costs in the new EU countries increased between one third

Table 2.3 Recruitment and training practices presented in percentages of organizations

Indicators	*Old EU+**	*New EU+***
Recruitment of management by advertising in newspapers		
– senior management	42.2	18.5
– middle management	64.5	41.7
– junior management	60.4	40.5
Recruitment of managers by word of mouth		
– senior management	12.8	19.1
– middle management	18.6	32.4
– junior management	23.5	36.9
Increased pay for recruitment or retention purposes	44.7	63.5
No. of employees in/decreased by more than 5%	10.5/5.8	27.2/27.8
Proportion of employees in training	46.6	69.7
Average days of training of		
– management	5.8	9.2
– professionals/technicians	6.3	8.5
– clerical workers	4.0	6.0
– manual workers	3.8	3.8

Source: Cranet-E 1999–2001

Notes:
* Old EU+ countries: Germany, Austria, Spain, Portugal, Italy, Greece, Ireland, Northern Ireland, Denmark, Finland, Norway, Sweden, Great Britain, Switzerland, Belgium, the Netherlands and France.
** New EU+ countries: Czech Republic, Slovenia, Bulgaria, Estonia, Cyprus and Turkey.

There is a statistically significant difference between the two groups of countries in the case of all presented indicators.

and more than two times in Lithuania, while in the old EU countries they hardly increased by one third (Eurostat).

Foreign firms are expected to bring new production programmes and new technologies, for which the knowledge and skills of the existing employees may not be adequate. In some cases major retraining and adjustments to the new organizational culture are needed. Big and medium-sized organizations from the old EU countries report that 46.6 per cent of their employees received training in the year before the interview, while the relevant percentage for the new EU countries' organizations is 69.7 per cent (Cranet-E, 1999–2001). This is how new EU countries' organizations try to compensate for relatively lower levels of education and training of their employees.

In cases of organizations' mergers and take-overs employees are usually exposed to significant turbulence and HRM assists in these processes. There are redundancies, (in)voluntary dismissals, changes of job associated with training, new posts, promotions and demotions, changes to the job structure, remuneration and appraisal systems etc. Quite often different organizational cultures are in opposition, and the special endeavours of HRM and general management are needed to smooth out the differences.

Firms go abroad for two reasons: to expand their markets, which are more accessible from their representative offices and subsidiaries abroad and to find cheaper resources needed for their production, especially cheaper labour. In this respect firms from the new member states try to follow the example set by the older and more established ones. They also face the same dilemma, i.e. whether or not to transfer their own practices into the new environments or to adjust them to meet the needs of local culture and other conditions (Greaves 2000). The knowledge of cultures is in great demand; recruitment and preparation of some key employees to be sent abroad, e.g. to China, India or Russia requires a lot of hard work for HRM departments. Equally critical is the establishment of HRM function abroad. There are not just the labour costs to consider, but also the productivity level and the quality of products and services for which adequate training of personnel and leadership are needed. Equally important is the question of how to reorganize the home-based firm when it becomes more knowledge intensive. The change in the educational and qualification structure of employees, their retraining and redeployment, and the change in HR managerial styles are usually in question.

The case of Iskratel illustrates how firms in the new countries could cope with the challenges of free flow of goods, services and capital. It shows that like their counterparts, the old countries, they restructure their home business activities, which are becoming more knowledge intensive, and shift labour intensive production to less developed countries, particularly to the south and the east. It is observed in particular that the structure of the employee hierarchy changes and that HRM activities intensify.

Free flow of labour

Free flow of labour, although substantially restricted between the new and old EU member states for some years in the future, represents an additional challenge for the organizations and their HRM. It poses the questions: how strong flows could be expected from the new to the old member states and vice versa; how could big immigration be expected from non-member states to the new member states? What will the relation between the flow of labour and the flow of capital be?

PRACTICAL EXAMPLE FROM SLOVENIA

Branka Strniša

Iskratel's human-resources activities in the transition period

About Iskratel

Iskra is a Slovenian company and was founded in 1947. It began to develop the technology of stepping and crossbar telephone systems. In 1970 Iskra purchased a license for the Metaconta 10C system from a Belgium company, and in 1982 its engineers developed an original digital switching system known as SI2000, which is suitable for building private telephone exchanges and small-capacity exchanges. Modern day Iskratel was established in 1989 as a joint venture between Iskra and Siemens A.G. In addition to capital, the two partners brought to the new company their respective digital technologies. Iskratel's solutions are increasingly used for constructing new generation networks, which provide broadband access technologies, such as ADSL, as well as media crossover between the classical, circuit-switched networks and the packet-switched networks.

Iskratel's services include an advisory service, planning and constructing of networks, technical support and maintenance service for its customers. Its key markets are Commonwealth of Independent States, Slovenia, Eastern Europe and the Balkans. It is also successfully expanding to other parts of the world.

Human-resources management strategy

As a high-technology company we depend on the knowledge, innovation and initiative of our employees; we encourage their professional development, as well as enhancing their managerial and marketing roles. We encourage our employees to be independent and ready to take responsibility for the successful operation of the company by including a lot of Iskratel's specialists in the decision-making processes. Such a human-resources policy ensures the development of individuals' careers and the promotion of successful and motivated employees, encouraged to realize and test new ideas and give suggestions in practice. The reliability of such a strategy is reflected in increased efficiency and added value per employee.

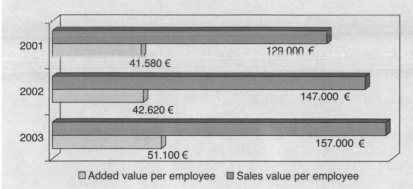

□ Added value per employee   ■ Sales value per employee

Figure 2.1 Iskratel: added value and turnover per employee (in Euro)

Staff recruitment

The Iskratel group employs 1,537 staff. Of these, 408 are in Iskratel-owned companies abroad and the rest in Slovenia in Iskratel and Iskratel Electronics. From 1994 the number of employees in Slovenian production units has been reduced from 414 to 306 and the number of employees in the development area has increased from 303 to 491.

At Iskratel we combine the experience and knowledge of our senior specialists with the fresh ideas and new skills of young members of staff, who bring a dynamic and innovative spirit to the company. We continually need an inflow of young colleagues, who also represent, primarily in the development branch of the company, the largest proportion of newly employed staff. We attract new employees by announcing job vacancies in daily newspapers, organizing open days with the aim of promoting the company, co-operating with university faculties and employment agencies, making use of the Internet, etc.

During the selection procedure we use team discussions and assess the candidates in terms of their mental abilities, personal skills, social awareness and motivation for work. The selection is based on the health, social, professional, mobility and development potentials of the candidates. For all the newly employed members we prepare an induction programme managed by individual mentors.

For several years we have been co-operating with the Faculty of Electrical Engineering and the Faculty of Computer and Information Science, where we encourage students to use their theoretical knowledge and practical skills in real-life environments. Iskratel's scholarship-awarding policy mainly aims at co-operating with gifted young technologists, who we try to involve in our current projects during their university study. As Iskratel is strongly development oriented, students of technical sciences find it an attractive employer. In 2003, sixty-six students were recipients of Iskratel's scholarships.

continued

The education, training and development of human resources

Iskratel focuses on development, and so we employ only the best-qualified specialists in telecommunications and management. In the past few years our human-resources policy has aimed at increasing the proportion of highly qualified personnel. In the 1990s Iskratel changed from a predominantly production-oriented company into a development-oriented company. As a result, in the past ten-year period the proportion of employees who have completed at least a two-year university course increased from 33 per cent in 1994 to 51 per cent in 2003. There are also 6 per cent of employees with Masters and PhD degrees. Most of our specialists completed their studies in electrical engineering; the other two largest groups are graduates of economics and organization studies.

Table 2.4 Education structure of Iskratel (%)

Education	1994	2003
Vocational education (2–3 years secondary)	34	18
Technical, general education (4 years secondary)	31	25
University education (2–4 years tertiary)	33	51
Masters and Ph.D.	2	6

Only by employing highly qualified specialists who follow and develop the newest knowledge in the area of telecommunications and management can we safeguard the successful operation of the company. We are setting up a process with which we will ensure the continuous training and education of our staff by efficiently identifying their training needs, as well as planning, realizing and assessing the training. On average, in the past five years, 1 per cent of our turnover has been allocated for training, with employees involved in training for an average of seven days per year.

In line with the philosophy of developing complete solutions, and integration trends in information and telecommunications technologies, we promote the integration of skills with respect to Iskratel's specialists by encouraging them to create our own training programmes with the purpose of transferring the development-related knowledge to the operational areas: servicing and sales. Iskratel's education and training activities include programmes for effective management, as well as expanding technical and interdisciplinary knowledge, and acquiring new marketing skills. We also encourage continuous practical training in specialist skills, computing and communications. As a highly export-oriented company, we also encourage our staff to learn foreign languages; as a result, more than 200 of our staff in the parent companies speak Russian, and most of the staff also use English in their day-to-day activities. In 2003 21 per cent of education and training was devoted to foreign languages, 56 per cent to vocational and technical and 23 per cent to general courses, seminars etc.

The development of human resources is focused on early identification and guidance of gifted, promising individuals with a technical background, who also show an interest in and a capability for various managerial areas, sales, etc. These individuals represent 17 per cent of the company's staff. The development of HR is also focused on managerial and sales staff, and, in particular on team enhancement. The programmes and procedures that are used for achieving these objectives are:

- the assessment of development potentials;
- the training of young, promising staff members;
- annual interviews;
- individual development plans.

A total of 45 per cent of employees are included in the process of detailed monitoring and development of human resources. The main motivational and planning tool used for managing promising and key staff members is the annual interview, which is the basic instrument of inter-hierarchal communication and is a two-way dialogue. The annual interview includes a review of achieved objectives and tasks, and the setting of new priority tasks – an agreement between a line manager and an employee; it is a commitment to carry out tasks and improve results.

The Iskratel Academy and the future

The participants of Iskratel's Academy have an opportunity to identify development potentials and implement them in specific projects. The aim of the academy is to disseminate basic managerial and interdisciplinary skills (project planning, management of processes and human resources, marketing, economy and finances, etc.), and to test these skills in practice – the preparation of an operating plan that can be used in the company. The academy encourages co-operation among various groups and operating fields; it sets up teamwork and promotes the skills of operational conduct. Each year twenty-four young staff members who have shown managerial capacities are involved in the academy's programme.

By identifying managerial potentials, Iskratel is setting up one of the most effective mechanisms for running the company. The Potential Evaluation Programme has been used, which includes self-improvement and independent learning by using personal plans, self-evaluation and evaluations made by others. Our aim is to increase the success and effectiveness of managers by allowing them to observe critically their own managerial style, and to determine the managerial style at any level of the company.

As Iskratel operates in the global telecommunications market, where competition is becoming tougher, we need to learn the most effective sales techniques. On the basis of a competence model regarding the sales staff, and the staff assessment, we open the Academy to sales staff. The programme they follow includes new technical knowledge and the latest sales techniques.

continued

In recent years Iskratel has changed from a production into a development-oriented company. In the following years we expect it to change again, i.e. to become a consulting and service company. The envisaged HR challenges are:

- related or joint working groups – composed of staff from all the companies of the Iskratel group, including companies operating abroad;
- joint monitoring of human resources, training, transfer of good practices and the setting up of competence centres;
- flexibility of human resources – currently staff turnover is less than 1 per cent, however, due to the opening of the borders in the EU we expect more staff turnover, and also more employees coming from abroad;
- human resources development requirements: the convergence of TC and IT skills, an entrepreneurial approach, good communication skills and flexibility with regard to the location of the job.

What do experiences from the past tell us? In the 1980s Spain, Portugal and Greece entered the EU. In the early 1990s migration flow from Spain remained as small as it was before. Although there was a rise in migration flow from Portugal, when taking into account reverse migration, the number of Portuguese and Spanish in other member states was actually reduced. The number of Greek nationals abroad in the EU did rise after the expiry of its transitional period in 1987, to reach 1.3 per cent of the population by 1995. But this growth did not exceed the growth in the presence of other EU nationals and was even smaller than the growth of the foreign population of non-EU origins (The Free Movement 2001). Eurostat (2000) analysis concluded that there has been no clear relationship between the changing patterns of population and labour stocks or migration, and the accession of Greece, Spain and Portugal.

It should be noted that migration flows in the old EU member states are fairly low in general. On average they account for 1.5 per cent of EU citizens and 3.3 per cent of non-EU citizens (Boeri *et al.* 2002). While the immigration from the non-EU countries could be well controlled, the low internal mobility could perhaps be explained by the mobility of capital, either private or via EU funds, and by high cultural diversity and rottenness of individuals in it. It seems that the majority of individuals prefer their language, primary networks and contacts, habits, institutional setting, welfare provision, natural surroundings etc., to higher wages and other opportunities on the labour market. There are also issues with recognition of qualifications, economic, financial, legal and administrative problems in the case of migration (MKW 2001). In other words, the push factors in their home surroundings, e.g. the economic crisis, low wages and unemployment, and the pull factors in the potential environment of migration, e.g. better wages and working conditions, would need to be stronger if one were to expect higher migration between the old EU member states. The question is if these differences are great enough between the old and the new member states in order to cause significant migration.

Current enlargement differs from previous ones because the income gap between accession countries and EU countries is bigger. For example, in Estonia the hourly salary is eight times lower than in the old EU countries and purchasing power is only 42 per cent of the purchasing power in the EU-15. Unemployment in the old EU countries is lower than in the new ones, where some regions in Poland, Slovakia and Bulgaria are particularly affected.

Cranet-E data show, however, that there are not great differences between the two groups of countries in terms of how difficult it is to attract or retain various groups of workers, from managers and experts to clerical and blue collar workers. In the new EU countries recruitment from abroad is used less frequently than in the old ones. In the case of international schemes for managers the opposite is true (see Table 2.4). One cannot expect big turbulence on this basis.

Although they vary considerably according to the underlying assumptions and the methodology various forecasts of labour movements due to enlargement lead to the following conclusions (The Free Movement 2001):

- the forecasts of long-run migration potential from the new countries to EU-15 countries is roughly 1 per cent of the EU-15 population;
- people from the new countries mostly will be willing to work abroad only for a limited period in order to earn money and then return home;
- the initial migration from the new countries into the EU-15 countries would be around 70,000 workers annually. This number would be 200,000 if it included those not working. Romania and Bulgaria would produce another initial flow of 50,000 workers annually;
- two-thirds of this flow would be expected to reach Germany;
- a study produced by a consortium of EU research institutes (Brücker and Boeri 2000) for the European Commission confirms that EU enlargement in 2004 would not significantly affect employment and wages in the EU.

The old EU countries that have set limits to free movement of labour from the new countries do not take into account that migration could have some positive sides:

- General development of the EU labour markets indicates a great need for migrants in the future. Most European countries, including candidate countries, are facing the problem of an ageing population. The average age in the EU will increase from 38.3 years in 1995 to 41.8 years in 2015 (European Commission 2000). The age group 0 to 25 years is going to decline and the number of retired people will grow significantly. It makes it difficult to maintain a sufficient workforce with the given demographic trend.
- Enlargement could reduce illegal activities in the border regions: people formally entering as tourists engage in short-term work aimed at generating income for repatriation to the country of permanent residence, so called 'trading tourism'.

Table 2.5 Indicators of organizations' employment flexibility presented in percentages of organizations

Indicators	Old EU+*	New EU+**
Recruitment from abroad	17.7	11.5
International schemes for managers	23.9	38.9
Increased use of flexible work arrangements in the last 3 years		
– weekend work	25.8	16.2
– shift work	23.9	14.6
– overtime	31.6	22.4
– annual hours contract	17.0	7.1
– part-time work	43.9	11.6
– job sharing	18.9	6.8
– flexi-time	36.8	18.4
– temporary/casual work	39.5	13.2
– fixed-term contracts	40.7	35.5
– homebased work	17.3	4.0
– tele-working	15.9	14.5
– subcontracting/outsourcing	36.6	27.8
Specification of jobs more detailed		
– for management	23.7	27.9
– for professionals/technicians	27.0	37.9
– for clerical workers	19.6	28.2
– for manual workers	14.0	22.3
Specification of jobs wider/flexible		
– for management	47.4	42.6
– for professionals/technicians	43.8	38.0
– for clerical workers	44.9	27.9
– for manual workers	34.3	20.1
Systematic analyses of training needs	73.3	59.9

Source: Cranet-E 1999–2001

Notes:
* Old EU+ countries: Germany, Austria, Spain, Portugal, Italy, Greece, Ireland, Northern Ireland, Denmark, Finland, Norway, Sweden, Great Britain, Switzerland, Belgium, the Netherlands and France.
** New EU+ countries: Czech Republic, Slovenia, Bulgaria, Estonia, Cyprus and Turkey.

There is a statistically significant difference between the two groups of countries in the case of all presented indicators.

- Some member states operate relatively large schemes of seasonal work, especially in agriculture, sometimes involving workers from very remote countries. Part of the predicted flow would be absorbed into this work without affecting the regular local labour markets
- The economic cycle may cause shortages and surpluses in specific sectors in the short run. In absence of free movement, such pressures may lead to illegal work.
- And finally, we should not forget that initially, the free movement of persons in the EU was stimulated in order to promote effective economic integration and to match better labour market needs with the supply of labour elsewhere. According to the study of the European Comission transnational mobility of European workers should be two–three times higher in order to achieve a 'healthy' level of labour mobility and to exploit the job potential of the Single European Market (MKW 2001).

A recent study in Estonia indicates that willingness to emigrate or work abroad has decreased (Narusk 2004). People have become more realistic about the possibilities in other countries and also more satisfied with life in Estonia. More than half of those who were willing to go abroad have changed their minds. This tendency could be seen in all age groups. Those who are eager to work abroad are young (72 per cent were between 15 and 19 years), male (59 per cent), with secondary education (60 per cent), or with unfinished university education and students. Estonians prefer Finland, Germany and Great Britan.

Until now, among Estonians, the most popular choice has been short time jobs in Finland (36 per cent). Sixty per cent of those going to Finland stayed less than three months there. Only 10 per cent of those who had worked abroad spent more than one year there. The main attracting factor was a higher wage.

Research indicates only a small impact on native unemployment of past immigration. But there is a risk of brain drain for the new EU countries. If too many young, skilled and well educated people leave a country, economic development and social security systems could be endangered. The mobility could increase in those segments where there is a high over-demand for labour in the old member states, such as in the ICT field. This would contribute to the wage drift and would cause difficulties in the new member states in terms of insufficient knowledge and skills capacity for the acceptance and utilization of new technologies, especially if such labour is not available in the non-member states. Such a brain drain could worsen the problem of insufficient education and training in the new EU countries in comparison to the old ones. Some HR managers openly support such a development as is demonstrated by the following interview:

Box 2.2 Ilona Lott, HR manager of Tallinna Vesi, owned by a British company: AS Tallinna Vesi/Tallinn Water

Tallinn Water is the biggest water company in Estonia. The company provides water and wastewater services in the City of Tallinn and in its surrounding areas. Tallinn Water operates two large facilities – Water Treatment Plant near Lake Ülemiste and Wastewater Treatment Plant in Paljassaare. The company serves more than 400,000 people. Tallinn Water was privatized in January 2001. There are 350 employees in the company.

Estonian companies should not be afraid of losing their 'brains'. It is natural that there will be some movement in both directions but whether it is permanent or more as a secondment for gaining some practical experience and knowledge, is another question.

Among the employees who have no higher education and who mainly perform skilled jobs, there is already current mobility and there will continue to be so in the future, as skilled handicraftsmen are valued highly in Western countries (Estonians are known for their good quality work). Mobility helps the higher educated to gain a wider range of experiences and knowledge, which are limited in a small country like Estonia.

In our company we have to review the HR practices because they have to be in accordance with the laws applied in the EU. There are some new issues for us, e.g. equal treatment of men and women.

There might be a new trend for foreign managers (good ones of course) to find work here to help us improve our standards. We have either 'old time' managers using an autocratic style or 'high-flying, young' managers who burn themselves out and lose interest quickly.

We could use the skills of foreign managers to build our business culture and improve the management of people in the organization in terms of higher commitment and higher satisfaction.

This issue could be addressed by HRM departments, either by strengthening the organization's internal labour markets or by widening the area and intensification of recruitment procedures. In the first case, remuneration, HR development and promotion systems will be accentuated in order to retain key workers, while in the second the accent will be on recruitment and induction of fluctuating newcomers. Cranet-E data (see Table 2.4) indicate that organizations from the new EU countries are more oriented towards their internal labour markets than their counterparts from the old EU countries. However, their internal labour markets are not particularly developed. In addition, they demonstrate lower flexibility.

Their utilization of flexible work arrangements is less frequent than in the old countries. Organizations in the new countries also tend towards more detailed rather than wider and more flexible specifications of jobs. They are less inclined to systematic analyses of training needs. This indicates more robust HRM policies, which will perhaps need some fine tuning in the future. It also indicates that organizations tend to create and protect internal labour markets rather than opening up opportunities to the external market.

If internal labour markets are so accentuated one would expect organizations to try to mobilise their existing human resources. Unfortunately this does not seem to be the case in the new countries' organizations. Although in some of them, e.g. Slovenia, the socialist tradition has been rich with various forms of participation, the general picture, which could be made on the basis of Cranet-E data is not promising (see Table 2.5). Organizations in the new countries neglect the vertical communication of managers to employees and of employees to managers. They are also far behind the organizations from the old countries with respect to involvement of employees in performance appraisal and with respect to the number of workers' representative bodies. Slovenia is an exception with 76.7 per cent of medium size and large organizations having joint consultative committee or works councils in comparison to the old EU countries, where this figure is 73.5 per cent. This indicates that organizations in the new countries haven't discovered the importance of human resources yet. In particular, their mobilization by means of involvement of employees in various work-related activities is low. The exception to this is training to which organizations from the new countries send more employees for more days than their counterparts from the old countries (see Table 2.3). Other studies also confirm a lack of workers' participation (Vaughan-Whitehead 2003).

Utilization of appraisal systems and the utilization of the appraisal results is also less frequent in the new countries. Organizations seem not to be aware of the contribution of human resources to the organizations' performance. Lower sensitivity for human resources is also reflected also in the lower levels of monitoring of special groups of employees in HRM practices. This may reflect the situation from the past, when a labour market did not exist or did not perform its evaluative function. If the market value of labour is not recognized its other values may not be observed either.

Home-based firms usually send top managers and some specialists to their subsidiaries. This could mean that the higher the share of foreign ownership the higher the percentage of top managers and experts from abroad in the new member countries. Their managers and experts will also go abroad in case of investments there. However, the flow of managers and experts is likely to follow the investment flows. One could expect a cascading logic meaning that foreign managers and experts will come to the new member states from the old ones, while theirs will be going to the less developed countries. This process will probably push wages up.

Table 2.6 Indicators of organizations' HRM practices presented in percentages of organizations

Indicators	Old EU+*	New EU+**
Increased communication of managers to employees in the last 3 years		
– through representative staff bodies	24.3	13.8
– verbally, direct to employees	50.5	27.1
– written direct to employees	47.2	28.5
– computer/electronic mail systems	71.7	59.5
– team briefings	49.9	29.0
Increased communication of employees to managers in the last 3 years		
– direct to senior managers	30.1	18.2
– through immediate superior	31.1	30.4
– through trade unions/works council	18.4	12.1
– through regular workforce meetings	29.8	19.3
– team briefings	39.1	21.3
– suggestion schemes	15.8	9.7
– attitude survey	26.9	15.1
Having workers' representative bodies	73.5	24.2
Having appraisal system for		
– management	70.7	50.7
– professionals/technicians	70.5	59.0
– clerical workers	65.4	52.2
– manual workers	55.4	50.0
Employees contribute to appraisal	56.9	29.0
Utilization of the appraisal system to determine		
– individual training needs	66.6	43.9
– organizational training needs	42.0	37.8
– promotion potential	47.1	37.4
– career development	48.1	28.2
– individual performance related pay	39.2	46.4
– organization of work	36.4	39.2
Monitoring special groups in HRM practices		
– disabled in recruitment	28.8	22.5
– disabled in training	12.0	3.2
– disabled in promotion	8.7	1.8
– women in recruitment	35.6	20.0
– women in training	21.0	9.7
– women in promotion	24.1	7.9

Source: Cranet-E 1999–2001

Notes:

* Old EU+ countries: Germany, Austria, Spain, Portugal, Italy, Greece, Ireland, Northern Ireland, Denmark, Finland, Norway, Sweden, Great Britain, Switzerland, Belgium, the Netherlands and France.

** New EU+ countries: Czech Republic, Slovenia, Bulgaria, Estonia, Cyprus and Turkey.

There is a statistically significant difference between the two groups of countries in the case of all presented indicators.

Another segment of the labour market where mobility of labour could be expected is the one for low demanding jobs. Already there are immigrant workers in public utilities, construction enterprises, agriculture and similar fields, not only in the old but also in the new EU countries. In 2003 there were around 40,000 foreign workers with work permits in Slovenia. This figure exceeded 5 per cent of all employees (ESS 2003). There could be some shifts in the flow of labour, e.g. in Slovenia, less from the Balkan non member states and more from Slovakia and Poland, or in Estonia, less from Russia and more from the neighbouring Baltic states. However, in the long run the demographic decline could cause a general shortage of labour, which will push home employees up the job ladder and attract immigrants from Asia and Africa to low paid jobs. This would be an increasing concern for HRM that could be addressed by specialised employment agencies, but also by the public training agencies on the one hand and companies' HRM on the other. There will not only be a shortage of technical skills, but, in many cases, a cultural gap that will have to be bridged.

Conclusions

In conclusion one could stress that there exist rather big differences between the old and the new EU member states in their economies and societies, although the differences between the new EU member states, including the candidate ones, should not be overlooked. These differences increase the dynamic in the HRM field in the new member states by means of privatization, foreign direct investments, organizational and technological restructuring and so on. Several organizations of the new countries follow the pattern of those from the old ones and set up their business units abroad. The dynamics in the HRM field are expressed in terms of employment flows into and out of organizations, into and out of the countries, unemployment, wage increase and labour force adjustments by means of education and training. However, in comparison to the organizations of the old member states the ones in the new member states remain highly oriented towards the internal labour markets and use less flexible employment arrangements.

The HRM heritage of the new countries has not been very rich. The HRM function does not enjoy high status in the organizations, it is prone to informal regulation, utilization of simple tools and methods and rather poor utilization of human resources in terms of direct involvement of employees in work and management activities. A kind of immature devolution of HRM has been indicated by high involvement of line managers in HRM, however, without their proper training and professional support and without sufficient strengthening of the HRM strategic role.

It seems that a rather robust HRM in the new EU countries needs its development and refinements. Apart from the involvement of line managers, focus on the education and training of employees and the development of the HRM services' market in terms of newly founded and incoming employment, training, head hunting and other agencies, it will have to strive for its strategic position. HRM will also have to improve and enrich professional methods, help develop employees' participation and follow the internationalization of organizations' activities by its own internationalization.

References

Alas, R. & Svetlik, I. 2004. Estonia and Slovenia: building modern HRM using a dualist approach. In C. Brewster, W. Mayrhofer, & M. Morley (eds.), *Human Resource Management in Europe: Evidence of Convergence?* Amsterdam *et al.*: Elsevier.

Boeri, T., Hanson, G. & McCormic, B. 2002. *Immigration Policy and the Welfare System.* Oxford: Oxford University Press.

Brewster, C. & Larsen, H. H. 1992. Human resource management in Europe: evidence from the countries. *The International Journal of Human Resource Management*, 3(3): 409–434.

Brücker, H. & Boeri, T. 2000. *The Impact of Eastern Enlargement on Employment and Labour Markets in the EU Member States.* Commissioned by the Employment and Social Affairs DG of the European Commission, Berlin and Milano, European Integration Consortium 2000.

Cranet-E. 1999–2001. *The Cranfield Network for the Study of Human Resource Management in Europe.* Cranfield University, School of Management.

ESS 2003. *Employment Service of Slovenia, Annual Report.*

European Commission 2000. *People in Europe. Demographic change: The regional dimension. Trends and policy issues.* http://europa.eu.int (accessed autumn 2004).

European Commission Information Note 2001. *The Free Movement of Workers in the Context of Enlargement.* http://europa.eu.int/comm/enlargement/docs/pdf/migration_enl.pdf (accessed autumn 2004).

Eurostat 2000. *Patterns and Trends in International Migration in Western Europe. Eurostat Studies and Research.* Luxembourg.

Eurostat 2004. http://europa.eu.int/comm/eurostat/newcronos/reference/display.do?screen = detailref&lan (accessed autumn 2004).

Eurostat Yearbook 2002. *The Statistical Guide to Europe*, pp. 426–427.

Gooderham, P., Morley, M., Brewster, C. & Mayrhofer, W. 2004. Human resource management: a universal concept? In C. Brewster, W. Mayrhofer & M. Morley (eds.), *Human Resource Management in Europe: Evidence of Convergence.* Amsterdam *et al.*: Elsevier.

Greaves, I. 2000. Cultural diversity: ignore, minimize, utilize? In I. Adigun & I. Svetlik (eds.), *Managing Cultural Diversity – implications for the EU integration. Conference proceedings.* University of Ljubljana, Faculty of Social Sciences.

Hall, E. T. & Hall, M. R. 1990. *Understanding Cultural Differences.* Yarmouth: Intercultural Press.

Hofstede, G. 1991. *Cultures and Organizations: Software of the Mind.* London: McGraw Hill.

Hollinshead, G. & Leat, M. 1995. *Human Resource Management: An International and Comparative Perspective on the Employment Relationship.* London *et al.*: Pitman Publishing.

Ignjatović, M. & Svetlik, I. 2003. European HRM clusters. *EBS Review*, autumn 2003: 25–39.

Koopman, P. L., Den Hartog, D. N. & Konrad, E. 1999. National culture and leadership profiles in Europe: some results from the GLOBE study. *European Journal of Work and Organizational Psychology*, 8(4): 503–520.

Koubek, J. & Vatchkova, E. 2004. Bulgaria and Czech Republic: countries in transition. In C. Brewster, W. Mayrhofer & M. Morley (eds.), *Human Resource Management in Europe: Evidence of Convergence*. Amsterdam et al.: Elsevier.

Leat, M. 1998. *Human Resource Issues of the European Union*. London: Financial Times Management.

Mesner-Andolšek, D. & Štebe, J. 2004. Prenos upravljanja človeških virov na vodje (The transfer of HRM on to management). In I. I. Svetlik & B. Ilic (eds.), *Razpoke v zgodbi o uspehu – primerjalna analiza upravljanja človeških virov* (*The Cleavages in the Success Story – A Comparative Analysis of HRM*). Ljubljana, Sophia.

MKW GmbH 2001. *Exploitation and development of the job potential in the cultural sector in the age of digitalization. Obstacles of mobility for workers in the digital culture in the European Union, study commissioned by the European Comission, DG Employment and Social Affairs*. Brussels.

Mlady, M. 2004. *Regional unemployment in the European Union and candidate countries in 2003*. Eurostat, Statistics in focus, 3/2004.

Narusk, A. 2004. Valismaa peibutab eestlasi ajutise tööga. *Päevaleht*, 22 March.

OECD 2003. www.oecd.org/edu/eag2003 (accessed autumn 2003).

Renwick, D. & MacNeil, M. C. 2002. Line manager involvement in careers. *Career Development International*, 7(7): 407–414.

UNCTAD 2004. http://www.unctad.org/Templates/WebFlyer.asp?intItemID=2471&lang=1 (accessed autumn 2004).

Vaughan-Whitehead, D. C. 2003. *EU Enlargement Versus Social Europe?* Cheltenham, UK; Northhampton, USA: Edward Elgar.

Deregulatlon: HRM and the flexibility-security nexus

3

KOEN DEWETTINCK
Country specific sections:
Belgium: **KOEN DEWETTINCK & DIRK BUYENS**
France: **CÉLINE AUGER & FRANÇOISE DANY**
The Netherlands: **TON WILTHAGEN**

The flexibility challenge

Flexibility is more and more associated with economic success and competitiveness (Heckman 2002; Jensen 1999; Siebert 1997). Organizations are expected to overcome rigidity so as to survive in volatile, competitive and ever-changing markets. Research on organizational flexibility has highlighted the critical role of human resource management (HRM) practices in enabling organizations to respond quickly to developments in technology, to greater uncertainty and competition in product markets, as well as increasing workforce diversity. Indeed, as Kalleberg (2001, 2003) argued, creating workforce flexibility is one of the issues that has been at the forefront of the debate in HRM in recent years. The HRM function is not only expected to develop systems that maximize employee performance, but also to facilitate the alignment between organizational and individual goals and to create an agile workforce. Such a workforce does not only have flexible skills but is also willing to move freely between tasks (Guest 1987).

The need for organizations to become more flexible also puts constraints upon the economic and social policies of national governments, including in relation to employment. At the European level, the belief that Europe's employment problems and challenged competitiveness are the result of the inflexibilities in its labour markets has gradually emerged since the 1980s. It was forcefully articulated in OECD's Jobs Report (OECD 1994) and has been reiterated in countless official publications and academic discussions (Siebert 1997; Heckman 2002). As a result, European countries embarked on deregulation in the labour market.

To support and stimulate the member states in these endeavours, the European Union (EU) delineated an employment strategy characterized by dialogue and benchmarking between the members states, rather than through regulations and directives. The idea was to leave member states with the main responsibility for tackling their unemployment and strengthening their competitive position, while the EU planned to add value through peer pressure and identification of best practices. For example, to encourage adaptability in business and employees, the 1998 EU employment guidelines proposed several benchmark indicators, such as a decrease in the collective and individual working time and the average collective and individual working time.

The security challenge

However, next to addressing the demand for flexibility expressed by firms, the demand for job security expressed by workers is an equally important concern. In an era of company restructuring and downsizing, this is one of the biggest challenges the HR-function is confronted with: How to improve employees' contribution in a climate that does not guarantee security or long-term employment prospects? This question reflects a unique set of challenges for the field of human resource management, requiring them to re-focus and challenge conventional wisdom about organization structures, job design, organization culture, employee expectations and motivation and the related HR systems and processes required to implement new ways of working (Flood et al. 1996).

At the national and European level, job security is an equally important concern, which has led the European Union to take some important steps that increased labour market regulation. Social protection, job security, health and safety regulation, etc. were presented as the benefits of the single market that must accrue for the labour. The publication of the Social Charter in 1989, the incorporation of the Social Charter into the Maastricht treaty, and the increase in the number of directives on working conditions in the 1990s were all related to this initiative.

Regulations to protect employment raise especially difficult questions in a period of rapid and pervasive economic change. Some features of the current economic environment, including rapid shifts in technology and innovative forms of business organization, flexible workplace practices and intense competitive pressures, have resulted in a heightened perception of job insecurity. Even as fears of job losses reinforce the demand for public and private measures to enhance job security, it is sometimes asserted that it may be difficult to reconcile such protection with the flexibility required for firms and national economies to prosper today.

Thus, in an attempt to reconcile the demand for flexibility in the labour market by firms with the demand for job security expressed by workers, the European Union has developed a policy in which both deregulation (to increase flexibility) and regulation (to protect employment) have been emphasized. Because of the different tendencies, we see notable differences in how different European countries have tackled this flexibility issue.

The nexus between flexibility and security also plays a role at the company level. As mentioned before, because of the highly volatile and changing environment, one of the major challenges for HR professionals is in creating flexibility in the human resources of the company (Buyens *et al.* 1999; Dietz *et al.* 2004), both in numerical terms (reducing or increasing the number of employees on a short term basis) and in terms of employability (multi-skilling of employees so that they can easily take up new jobs). On the other hand, in order to maintain a motivated and committed workforce, it is important to create some continuity and stability within the firm. Companies have to deal with this nexus within the framework that is imposed by the European and country specific legislative framework. Previous comparative research on HR-practices in Belgium, the Netherlands and France (Buyens *et al.* 2004) has indicated that the legislative context is indeed highly important for explaining differences in the actual use of, for example, flexible working patterns.

In this chapter, we will look at how France, the Netherlands and Belgium, three Western European countries, have dealt with this labour market issue and how governmental policies have influenced this process. This chapter assesses how employers, employees and government have evaluated these policy changes, how they have dealt with the flexibility-security nexus (Wilthagen & Tros 2004) and how this has impacted on actual HR-practices.

Degree of regulation in France, the Netherlands and Belgium

The degree to which employment is protected illustrates the degree of labour market regulation in a country. Employment protection regulations refer to the rules that govern hiring and firing decisions, such as the duration of work contracts, conditions of dismissal and severance. The OECD has developed an index to measure the strictness of employment protection legislation (EPL) (Bertola *et al.* 1999). The index is broken down into three components: regulations governing the terms and conditions of permanent contracts in case of individual dismissals; additional provisions in the face of mass layoffs; and regulations governing the possibility of hiring on temporary contracts. Figure 3.1 shows OECD's EPL index (Y-axis) for the three countries.

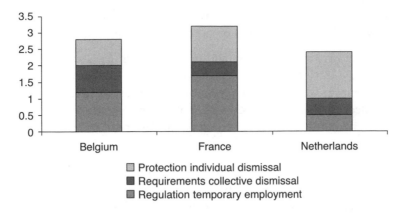

Figure 3.1 Strictness of employment protection in Belgium, France and the Netherlands

Source: OECD, Employment Outlook, 1999

Looking at the general level of employment protection regulation, Figure 3.1 indicates that the labour market in France is most regulated, followed by Belgium and finally the Netherlands.

Looking at the three distinct EPL-components, we see even stronger differences. In the Netherlands, there is very strict protection against individual dismissal, while temporary employment regulation is very loose. In contrast, France has a system in which temporary work is heavily regulated. Finally, in Belgium there are very strict requirements for collective dismissal, while temporary employment is moderately regulated.

Thus, while the three countries are neighbouring members of the European Union, even this very rough assessment of regulation indicates that there are notable differences in the way these countries have developed their labour market policy.

The Belgian case: Belgium's solution to create employment flexibility and security: short term gains, but what about the long term implications?

Economical context and labour market policy in Belgium

The Belgian economy grew slowly in 2002 and 2003. In 2002, GDP grew 0.7 per cent and the expected growth for 2003 was less than 1 per cent. Total employment rate decreased in 2002 and a further decline was expected for 2003. The total degree of labour market participation has stagnated (only 59.9 per cent in 2002) and is the lowest among all EU members for older workers. Unemployment rate was 7.3 per cent in 2002, which is a stronger increase than the EU average. The expectation was that unemployment rate would increase to 8.2 per cent in 2003. Regional labour market differences (Wallonia versus Flanders) still exist and the fiscal and non fiscal pressure on labour is still very high.

To deal with these issues, the Belgian federal government has committed itself to creating 200,000 new jobs by 2007. This would bring the total degree of labour market participation to 65 per cent. In September 2003, a labour market conference was held among the federal and regional governments and the social partners, i.e. representatives of employers and employees. Several measures were proposed and agreed to foster job creation and activate the labour market, such as fostering employability by providing more and better employee training; decreasing the indirect labour cost, stimulating active reorientation policies in case of company downsizing and creating new jobs in the social economy by introducing financial incentives.

Creating flexibility in Belgium

A 1999 study by Sels and Van Hootegem (Sels & Van Hootegem 1999) on the flexibility-security issue indicated that in Belgium flexibility is primarily internal-numerical in nature. This means that numerical flexibility, i.e. the adaptation of the number of employees to the demand, is mainly achieved through shift work, work during non-standard hours and temporary unemployment. The most recent results of the Cranet-survey that were collected in Belgium (Buyens & Soens 2004; for the Cranet project see Brewster *et al.* 2004; 2000) confirms this. The study indicates that 60 per cent of Belgian companies work on weekends and 76 per cent use shift work. Furthermore, 86 per cent use overwork as a flexible labour arrangement. Almost all companies in the survey (97.8 per cent) report that they use part-time work arrangements. However, for almost half of the companies, the percentage of part-time workers is less than 10 per cent (Buyens & Soens 2004).

The system of temporary unemployment is another way to create more flexibility. In specific cases, e.g. when production is cyclical; in times of economic decline; because of technical reasons, bad weather or a strike, it allows companies to lay-off blue-collar workers on a temporary basis in exchange for unemployment benefits. In this way, the contract between employer and worker is suspended on a temporary basis.

Temporary unemployment is thus an atypical form of a labour market measure that reconciles the need for flexibility and security. It fosters employment security as it helps companies in avoiding to impose mass lay-offs during an economic downturn. On the other hand, it provides employers with the flexibility to attune their workforce to cyclical or temporary demand changes. Through this system of temporary unemployment, companies are less dependent on temporary employment and TWA contracts to achieve flexibility.

However, Sels & Van Hootegem (1999) point out some disadvantages of this system. Though it increases the efficiency of training efforts as trained workers are kept in the company in times of economic decline, it may also have a restraining influence on employee training. The reason is that periods of overcapacity may be an ideal time for training because lower productivity while on-the-job learning may be acceptable. As it may be more attractive to temporarily lay-off workers, companies may refrain from investing in employee development during down periods.

The system of temporary unemployment explains why temporary employment is less used in Belgium in comparison with the neighbouring countries, especially the Netherlands, where flexibility is mainly achieved through contractual flexibility and temporary work.

Creating employment security in Belgium

According to the OECD-numbers presented in the introduction, Belgium has a rather strict legal framework with regard to collective dismissals. Indeed, the Ministry of Employment and Labor plays an important role in company restructuring activities. More specifically, federal government acts as a mediator in the negotiations between the social partners on the restructuring measures to be taken.

Because of several massive closings of Belgian subsidiaries of multinationals which had a huge impact on local unemployment rates, Federal government made the required consultation and communication procedure in the case of downsizing more elaborate. The aim was to build in more guarantees for successful social dialogue within the companies before a downsizing decision could be implemented.
By obliging employers to formulate their arguments to downsize and to look for alternative solutions, they are forced to take a broad perspective on the issue (Dewettinck & Buyens 2000). When the information and consultation procedure is not observed, employers may be forced to reintegrate the laid-off employees and to pay back government's financial support.

This support requires the recognition as a 'company in difficulties'. It opens up the possibility for companies to downsize their labour force through a system of early retirement. Employees older than 52 (and in some cases 50) and with a minimal 20 years of seniority may be laid-off and referred to with the status of early-retired, while the company is excused of the liability to replace the early-retired by fully unemployed. Thus, through the statute of 'company in difficulties' companies are enabled to lay-off workers in a socially acceptable way. A downside of this system is, however, that downsizing companies are in fact stimulated, despite

Table 3.1 Used measures in case of downsizing (percentages of companies that use it)

Methods to downsize	Belgium	Europe
Recruitment stop	26.4	38.8
Early retirement	43.7	33.2
Voluntary dismissal	18.6	31.8
Compelled dismissal	18.6	30.1
Internal reorientation	8.2	33.4
Outplacement	18.3	14.6
Suspension of temporary contracts	37.4	32.0
Outsourcing	19.8	20.5

Source: Cranet-survey 1995

the more strict information and consultation procedure, to refer workers to the external labour market in case of downsizing.

Table 3.1 shows different downsizing options and their use by companies in Belgium and the European Union. The table indicates that Belgian government's policy clearly influences companies' downsizing behaviour. In Belgium, early retirement is used much more than dismissal procedures. For other European companies, this is exactly the opposite. Also striking is that in Belgium, only 8.2 per cent of companies state that they use internal reorientation practices, while the European average is more than 33 per cent. Another important detriment of this system is that it fosters non-activity of older employees. Not surprisingly, the degree of activity among the elderly (55 to 64 years old) is much lower in Belgium than in other European countries. While the European average is about 40 per cent, in Belgium, only about 27 per cent of citizens between 55 and 65 actively participate in the labour market.[1]

Evaluation of flexibility and security measures for the Belgian labour market and relevance for HRM

The central aspects of the Belgian Law on flexibility and security are summarized in Table 3.2.

Though the general OECD-estimation seems to indicate that Belgium has a rather strictly regulated system concerning collective dismissal, a more fine-grained look shows that this refers mainly to the information and consultation procedure. The HR-function seems not to be hindered too much in their actual use of collective dismissal. In fact, governmental policy is encouraging it by its early-retirement system. Despite the fact that increasing the participation degree of 50-plussers is an important objective of the Belgian labour market policy and that changing the early-retirement system seems to be the most important element to achieve this, the social partners agreed to postpone the introduction of specific measures to the next

Table 3.2 Central aspects of the Belgian law on flexibility and security

Flexibility	Security
Regulation of fixed term contracts: *Without specifying an objective reason:* four successive contracts permitted for up to two years (each > 3 months), or for up to three years (each > six months) with the authorisation of the social and labour inspectorate. *With an objective reason:* no restrictions	**Notification requirements for collective dismissal:** *Notification of employee representatives:* Obligation to inform and consult with Works Council or trade union delegation *Notification of public authorities:* Notification of sub-regional employment office and report on the results of consultations giving full information of planned dismissals
Regulation of TWA (temporary work agency) employment: Limited to objective situations Replacement of absent workers: limited to 12 months Temporary increase in workload: 18 months or extended by collective agreement Exceptional work: maximum 3 months	**Delay before notice can start:** 30 days delay after notification to the sub-regional employment office, can be lengthened to 60 days by the sub-regional employment office manager **Severance pay:** Severance pay during four months equivalent to half the difference between UB and net remuneration (up to a ceiling). Reduced to 3 months when the notice period exceeds 3 months

Source: OECD Employment Outlook 2004

interprofessional negotiation round. This system of 'early retirement' is defended by both employers and employee representatives. Consequently, HR-managers are happy to use it as it creates flexibility while it also enables them to downsize without too severe consequences for the individual employees impacted by the downsizing decision.

To conclude, in this section, we looked at two systems that aim to balance between flexibility and security. We limited our scope to these two systems because they seem to be typically Belgian and common practice in Belgian HRM. Through the system of temporary unemployment, companies have some flexibility to temporarily attune the size of their workforce to economic situations, without having to lay-off workers on a permanent basis. Not surprisingly, Belgian HR managers widely use this system and defend it very much, the disadvantage being that opportunities to increase the employability of the workforce (internal flexibility) is not fully exploited yet. Through the system of 'early retirement', the Belgian government has created a vehicle for companies to lay-off workers in a socially acceptable way. The problem is, however, that this system does not stimulate, and in fact, it hinders an increase of labour market participation from workers between 55 and 64 years of age. Thus, though this system may create some security in the short run, because of its detrimental labour market implications – low participation degree of older workers and less effort to reorient employees within the company – it may jeopardize employment security in the long run.

The Dutch case: towards reflexive deregulation and re-regulation: 'flexicurity' in the Netherlands

Flexicurity is increasingly regarded as a promising way to deal with the flexibility-security nexus (Muffels *et al.* 2002; Wilthagen 2002; Wilthagen & Tros 2004) as discussed in the introduction to this chapter. In the Dutch case, the emphasis will be on regulating atypical work and temporary agency work in particular – a topic that is key to companies' HRM and staffing policies in the Netherlands.

The concept of flexicurity can be defined as:

> . . . a policy strategy that attempts, synchronically and in a deliberate way, to enhance the flexibility of labour markets, the work organization and labour relations on the one hand, and to enhance security – employment security and social security – notably for weaker groups in and outside the labour market on the other hand.
>
> (Wilthagen & Rogowski 2002: 250)

Flexicurity Dutch-style

Up until the 1980s, the Netherlands was seen as a country with a relatively inflexible labour market, characterized in particular by stringent protection against dismissal and a passive social security policy. During these same years, unemployment figures grew dramatically and the number of occupational disability benefits began to grow exponentially. The focus in those days was on numerical – in particular, external – flexibilization of labour. This focus broadened in the 1990s to include key legislation and collective agreements on flexibility and security. In 1996, the employers' and employees' organizations entered into an agreement at national level on 'Flexibility and Security', following a policy memorandum on this subject in 1995 by the Minister of Social Affairs and Employment. Both initiatives formed the basis for the Flexibility & Security Act which came into effect on 1 January 1999. This 'flexwet' led to a large number of changes in the law governing dismissal and social security law (see Table 3.3).

Table 3.3 Central aspects of the Dutch law on flexibility and security

Flexibility	*Security*
– Fixed term employment contracts: after three consecutive contracts or when the total length of consecutive contracts totals three years or more, a permanent contract exists – Maximum term for TWA-employment (formerly six months) is abolished – Withdrawal of formal permit requirement for TWAs – Dismissal notice period is in principle one month and four months at maximum (used to be six months) – Shortened and less complex dismissal notification procedure	– Introduction of two so-called presumptions of law which strengthen the position of atypical workers, the existence of an employment contract is more easily presumed – Minimum entitlement to three hours' pay for on-call workers each time they are called in to work – Regulation of non-payment risk for on-call workers – A worker's contract with a TWA is considered a regular employment contract (some freedom for agency and agency worker to start and end the employment relationship during first 26 weeks) – Special dismissal protection for employees engaged in trade-union activities – Feasibility of reinstatement emphasized in dismissal cases at the lower court (e.g. in case of employees on sick leave)

Another aspect that has affected flexibility and security in Dutch policy orientation is the stimulation of part-time work. The extremely strong growth of part-time work has been partly autonomous, but the act has provided an extra impulse. Table 3.4 shows that part-time work is much more common in the Netherlands than it is in France or Belgium. Further, it indicates that the percentage of part-time workers in the Netherlands had already been high in the 1990s and has continued to increase until now.

Table 3.4 Part-time employment in Belgium, France and the Netherlands

	Part-time employment as a proportion of total employment				
	1990	*2000*	*2001*	*2002*	*2003*
Belgium	13.5	19.0	17.0	17.2	17.7
France	12.2	14.2	13.8	13.7	12.9
Netherlands	28.2	32.1	33.0	33.9	34.5

Source: OECD Employment Outlook, 2004

Evaluation of flexicurity measures for the Dutch labour market

In general, the Flexibility & Security Act, submitted as 'good practice' in the National Plan of Action on Employment 1999, was evaluated by employers and employees as guardedly positive (Grijpstra *et al.* 1999; de Klaver *et al.* 2000; Van den Toren *et al.* 2002). There had been a shift from loose to fixed employment relationships, and the new legislation did not form an obstacle to this positive development on the labour market. Indeed, the HR-function in the Netherlands was and still is using part-time work as an important vehicle to deal with the flexibility-security nexus. Furthermore, the social security position of 'external-flexible' employees did improve somewhat. However, the many interruptions in work patterns continued to cause problems in obtaining unemployment benefits. Taking the results of these evaluations together, it seems that this Dutch example of a flexicurity policy clearly contains an explicit and well-considered trade-off between forms of flexibilization, i.e. enhanced external numerical flexibilization (slight reduction of dismissal protection in standard employment relations, far-reaching liberalization of the temporary work market), and forms of security for weak groups, i.e. more employment and employability security for temporary agency workers (and other non-standard workers such as on-call workers). In this sense, the Dutch flexicurity system has proven to be fairly sound.

The French case: the advantages and drawbacks of a highly regulated approach: introduction of the 35-hour week in France

As illustrated in the introductory section of this chapter, French labour market policy is characterized by a strong degree of regulation. A current issue in France that illustrates this high degree of regulation is the introduction of the 35-hour week, a topic which has caused a lot of ink to flow in France. It is a nice case to illustrate different models of state intervention and their accompanying advantages and drawbacks. It shows in particular the limits of so-called 'interventionist' policies in favour of more 'decentralized' practices.

Reduction of working time: introduction in France

From 1996 a first legislative action was taken by the French government to reduce the number of working hours of employees (the Robien Law). The aim of this law was to favour employment. Companies could benefit from a 40 per cent reduction of employers' social security contributions the first year (and a 30 per cent reduction the following five years) on the condition that they reduce the duration of work of all or part of their payroll by 10 per cent. In return, employers had to increase their workforce by 10 per cent (by 15 per cent for a reduction of 15 per cent or more) and maintain this level for at least two years. This law contained, in addition to this 'offensive plan' in terms of the creation of employment, a 'defensive' plan with the aim of avoiding redundancies and lay-offs (Doisneau *et al.* 2000).

Because the reduction of working time has been the subject of unremitting protest in France, (CFDT – French trade union – 2000) the French government was encouraged to reform the legislative measures to accompany these economic and social changes. The Aubry Law, passed in June 1998, imposed the progressive transition from a 39-hour to a 35-hour working-week. This new legislation falls within the tradition of right-wing laws passed throughout the twentieth century which enabled French employees to go from a 48-hour week before 1936 to the 39-hour week in 1982, and to see an increase in their paid holiday leave from two weeks in 1936 to five weeks per year in 1982.

The Aubry Law was introduced in two phases, with an interval of two years. In the first phase (June 1998), the goal was to 'prepare the ground' and to inform employees and especially employers of changes advocated by the state in terms of the legal duration of working time. Companies and social partners were incited to anticipate the changes to come by negotiating the reduction of working time (RWT) as quickly as possible and in the best possible conditions. This anticipation was rewarded by financial aid for companies who reduced the working time by at least 10 per cent of all or part of the payroll to bring it down to 35 hours (or possibly less). The Aubry Law was basically an incentive and rewarded firms which anticipated the transition to 35 hours in 2000. It can be considered as an extension of the Robien Law and constitutes a combination of incitement and constraint (Lattes 2000). As a result of this law, the number of signed agreements increased drastically, from 13,000 in 1998 to 31,000 in 1999, including 25,000 agreements on a reduction of working hours to 35 (Lattes 2000).

In January 2000, the Aubry II Law confirmed the decrease of working time to 35 hours per week or to 1,600 hours per year. In this way, in just over a century, the working time of French employees has been brought down from 3,000 hours to 1,600 hours per year (CFDT 2000). By passing this law, the French legislator gave the message that only strong regulation can conciliate the necessary adaptation of the labour market while maintaining social cohesion (Castel & Schnapper 1997). However, because this law not only aims to fight against unemployment, but also to improve the working conditions of employees, some perceive it to be a threat to the liberty and efficiency of companies.

The organization of the transition to 35 hours in the framework of the Aubry II Law is left to the initiative of the social partners. This conferred autonomy of social partners will give rise to contrasted realities at the level of negotiation conditions and work reorganization approaches, as well as at the level of decisions about pay, e.g. the effects of the reduction of working time on remunerations and future pay rises. While some companies have undertaken to 'attempt the redefinition and restructuring of HR' others content themselves with rethinking the principles of 'personnel administration' (Naud 2000).

Box 3.1 Reduction of working time (RWT) in France (Aubry II Law)[2]

The effective work duration[3] is fixed on 35 hours per week (or 1,600 hours per year) in all industrial and commercial establishments, public or private, professional people, non-trading companies, trade unions, associations, agricultural, crafts and co-operatives establishments, firms from the agricultural sector; whatever their workforce.

It's important to note that this legal work duration is neither a minimum (employees can have a part-time job) nor a maximum, but a reference duration. If their employer asks them, employees can work beyond this legal duration. These additional hours can be part of the annual quota[4] which is at the employer's disposal, or apart from it, and some compensations are given to employees:

– wage rise (at least 10 per cent)
– obligatory compensating time off

Additional hours can be considered on a monthly basis in the firms where collective work duration is higher than the legal duration, in the maximal work during limits.

All employees are covered by the 35 hours regulation in France except:

– sales representatives
– commercial firms' directors
– non salaried managers, salaried company managers
– 'concierges' in a private block of flats
– domestic employees
   child minders

Appraisal and current situation of the law on RWT

At the end of the year 2000, the Aubry Law had apparently born fruit. Practically one employee out of two had moved to a 35-hour week, i.e. 62 per cent of employees of big companies and less than 8 per cent of those with 20 or less employees (Passeron 2002). Other positive consequences of this law included a considerable increase in company negotiation and a revived social dialogue.

In 2001, most employers already applying the 35-hour week declared that the social climate of their establishment had been improved thanks to negotiations relating to RWT; even if the introduction of RWT had brought about grievances in nearly 25 per cent of companies (Bunel *et al.* 2002).

Employees appeared to be more satisfied: 59 per cent considered that RWT had led to an improvement in their daily lives. Only 13 per cent stated deterioration (Estrade *et al.* 2001). Their appreciation was, however, slightly different concerning the improvement of work conditions. It seemed that the improvement in the quality of daily life concerned as much, if not more, life outside work than the work life itself.

This apparent success must not lead us to forget that strong differences exist in individual situations, depending particularly on the sector of activity. Therefore, whereas certain employees today do not work more than 32 hours per week (to conserve the advantage that they have always had in relation to other employees), others experience a working week of over 40 hours. 'Executives' working for a flat rate, for example where the working time is not subjected to a precise control, still see no reduction in their working time.

Above all, although the debate concerning the effects of the 35-hour week on the French economy continues to be fierce[5] (Bunel *et al.* 2002), there are today several attempts to 'soften' the law.

More generally, we can remember here the parliamentary mission to evaluate the 35-hour week proposed in May 2004 to abolish all reference to the legal duration of working time.[6] Some point out the dangers of such a measure which could 'accentuate the disparities of the employment regime and the remuneration between branches, with the risk of making recruitment difficulties which already exist even worse' (Reynaud 2004). However, recent declarations of the French government leave us to think that the trend to individualize working time will be accentuated. French Prime Minister Jean-Pierre Raffarin foresees, for example, that the overtime carried out by employees and placed on their 'time-off due' account could be paid to employees rather than being 'recovered'. More globally, we will remember that the orientation of the French government is to lift the constraints which weigh down the players to leave more room for local agreements and individual negotiations. Thus, the French Prime Minister decided to change some measures of the 35-hour law which are, according to him, inappropriate in many cases.

> ### Box 3.2 The 35-hour reform of Jean-Pierre Raffarin[7]
>
> On 9 December 2004, the French Prime Minister presented his '2005 contract', containing some new measures concerning 35 hours in France.
>
> - Employees who want to work more than the legal work duration will earn more. After having put it in a 'time-off due' which was softened considerably, those who do not want to use their overtime for leisure can get additional payment.
> - The legal additional hours quota is now 220 hours per year and per employee compared to 180 hours before this reform and can be increased by collective agreements at the branch or firm level.
> - For SMEs with less than 20 employees exceptional agreement extended to the end of 2008.

The French case: conclusion

The evolution of legislation in relation to working time in France demonstrates a progressive deregulation of employment markets in the sense that the weight of the framework of collective action is decreasing.

The Aubry II Law, in particular, shows a will to restrain economic activity. Nevertheless, it gives an essential role to negotiation. Moreover, by placing the need to align the principle of the 35-hour week with the principle of calculating working hours on a yearly basis, this law recognizes flexibility as a fundamental principle of work organization.

Planned and actual current revisions of the law demonstrate the will of the French government to make the employment market 'more fluid, more open and more efficient'.[8]

General conclusion

To reconcile the demand for flexibility with the demand for job security, is not only a major challenge for the HR-function but also for national and European governmental bodies. The European Union has developed a policy in which both deregulation to increase flexibility and regulation to protect employment have been emphasized. This approach enabled European countries to attune their policies to country-specific labour market characteristics. Not surprisingly, we see rather strong differences in how Belgium, France and the Netherlands have dealt with the challenges their labour market is confronted with.

In each of these countries, we focused first on systems that attempt to increase competitiveness, while at the same time balancing between flexibility on the one hand and security on the other hand. Second, we investigated the impact of these policy regulations on actual HR-practices in companies. As the findings presented in this chapter illustrate, the HR-function and its practices to deal with the flexibility-security nexus at the company level are considerably impacted by governmental regulations. Of particular interest were the legal frameworks that accompany such efforts and the implications of it in terms of evaluations of employers, employees and government. Because we focused on specific systems that are rather typical for each of the countries, we were able to show a rich variety of country-specific measures that all aim to reach a similar objective: making the local labour market more competitive, while at the same time balancing employment flexibility and security. Though each country has its own systems, approach and its own challenges, a common theme emerges: the paradoxical effect of propelling deregulation by central institutions producing regulations about deregulation.

As this chapter makes clear, this paradox is not only emerging at a pan-European level, but also at the country, regional and even industry level. A consistent finding over the three countries involved is that the negotiation process between the social partners is not always boosting the pace of change. However, it consistently constitutes a crucial factor for successful labour market reform. In this sense, it seems that balancing flexibility and security is not only a matter of balancing between regulation and deregulation, but also, and probably even more, a matter of structurally anchoring the confrontation between the distinct parties that have a stake in labour market regulation. At the company level, this is one of the crucial roles the HR-function could embrace: being a broker between a company's management and workforce, by developing policies, systems and procedures that reconcile the flexibility and security needs of both parties.

Notes

1 Eurostat, 2003.
2 Source: French Ministry of Employment web site: www.travail.gouv.fr
3 The effective work duration is 'the time in while the employee is at employer disposal and must be in accordance with his instructions, without being free to attend to one's affairs'.
4 The annual quota is freely fixed by the employer and the social partners (conventional quota). If it's not the case, there's a 'regulation quota': 180 hours per year and per salaried.
5 In October 2003 for example, the Finance Minister, Alain Lambert, even declared that 'without the 35-hour week (. . .) France would probably have a GDP of less than 3%' of the public deficit (*Libération* 4 October 2003).
6 *Le Monde* 25 May 2004.
7 *Le Monde* 9 December 2004.
8 *Le Monde* 3 October 2003.

References

Bertola, G., Boeri, T. & Cazes, S. 1999. *Employment Protection and Labour Market Adjustment in OECD Countries: Evolving Institutions and Variable Enforcement.* Geneva. International Labour Office.

Brewster, C., Mayrhofer, W. & Morley, M. 2000. *New Challenges in European Human Resource Management.* London: Macmillan.

Brewster, C., Mayrhofer, W. & Morley, M. 2004. *Human Resource Management in Europe. Evidence of Convergence?* Oxford: Elsevier/Butterworth-Heinemann.

Bunel, M., Coutrot, T. & Zilberman, S. 2002. *Le passage à 35 heures vu par les employeurs.* Dares: Premières Synthèses.

Buyens, D. & Soens, N. 2004. *HRM at the Beginning of the 21st Century. Internal Working Paper.* Vlerick Leuven Gent Management School.

Buyens, D., Vandenbossche, T. & De Vos, A. 1999. Flexibility in profile – an empirical analysis based on the data of 394 Belgian Companies. In C. Brewster, W. Mayrhofer & M. Morley (eds.), *New Challenges for European Human Resource Management.* London: Macmillan.

Castel, R. & Schnapper, D. 1997. Non le travail ce n'est pas fini. *Libération,* le 24 juin 1997.

CFDT 2000. *Cent ans de réduction du temps de travail* http://www.cfdt.fr/actualite/emploi/rtt/archives/rtt_074.htm (accessed 5 janvier 2000).

de Klaver, P. M., Klein Hesselink, D. J. & Miedema, E. P. 2000. *Experiences With and the Effects of the Flexibility and Security Act: Second Assessment [Ervaringen met en effecten van de Wet Flexibiliteit en Zekerheid. Tweede meting].* Den Haag: Ministerie SZW.

Dewettinck, K. & Buyens, D. 2000. *Analysis of Organisational Strategies to Reorient Employees in Case of Downsizing. [Analyse van bedrijfsstrategieën ter heroriëntering van werknemers bij downsizing].* Research-report for the Flemish government.

Doisneau, L., Arnaud, S., Bartouilh de Taillac, C., Roederer, T. & Serravalle, S. septembre 2000. *La réduction du temps de travail d'un dispositif à l'autre, une comparaison des conventions Robien et Aubry.* Dares: Premières Synthèses.

Estrade, M-A., Méda, D. & Orain, R. mai 2001. *Les effets de la réduction du tps de travail sur les modes de vie: qu'en pensent les salariés un an après ?* Dares: Premières Synthèses.

Flood, P. C., Gannon, M. J. & Paauwe, J. 1996. *Managing Without Traditional Methods.* Reading, MA: Addison Wesley.

Grijpstra, D., Klein Hesselink, D., de Klaver, P. & Miedema, E. 1999. *First Experiences With the Flexibility and Security Act [Eerste ervaringen metde Wet Flexibiliteit en Zekerheid].* Den Haag: Ministerie SZW.

Guest, D. E. 1987. Human resource management and industrial relations. *Journal of Management Studies,* 24(3): 303–321.

Heckman, J. 2002. *Flexibility and Job Creation:Lessons for Germany, NBER Working Paper No. 9194.*

Jensen, R. 1999. *The Dream Society: How the Coming Shift From Information to Imagination Will Transform Your Business.* London: McGraw Hill.

Kalleberg, A. L. 2001. Organizing flexibility: the flexible firm in a new century. *British Journal of Industrial Relations,* 39(4): 479–504.

Kalleberg, A. L. 2003. Flexible firms and labour market segmentation. *Work and Occupations,* 30(2): 154–174.

Lattes, J-M. 4 décembre 2000. *La loi Aubry II, an I, bilan et perspectives, conférences dans le cadre des 'Rencontres de la Manufacture'.*

Muffels, R., Wilthagen, T. & van den Heuvel, N. 2002. *Labor Market Transitions and Employment Regimes: Evidence on the Flexibility-Security Nexus in Transitional Labor Markets.* Berlin: WZB DiscussionPaper (FS I02 204).

Naud, D. 2000. *La réduction du temps de travail : valorisation des ressources humaines ou administration du personnel, site rh-info*, 21 août 2000.

OECD 1994. *The OECD Jobs Study: Evidence and Explanations*. Paris.

Passeron, V. avril 2002. *35 heures: trois ans de mise en ?uvre du dispositif 'Aubry I'*. Dares: Premières Synthèses.

Reynaud, B. 2004. La durée du travail est l'affaire de l'Etat. *Le Monde*, 25 mai 2004.

Sels, L. & van Hootegem, G. 1999. Belgium-the Netherlands: battle for more flexiblity [België-Nederland: strijd om de meeste flexibiliteit]. In J. van Hoof & J. Mevissen (eds.), *Channeling. New Forms of Labour Market Steering in Belgium and the Netherlands [In banen geleid. Nieuwe vormen van sturing op de arbeidsmarkt in België en Nederland]*. Amsterdam: Elsevier/SISWO.

Siebert, H. 1997. Labor market rigidities: at the root of unemployment in Europe. *Journal of Economic Perspectives*, 11 (3): 37–54.

Van den Toren, J. P., Evers, G. H. M. & Commissaris, E. J. 2002. *Flexibility and Security. Effects and Effectiveness of the Flexibility and Security Act [Flexibiliteit en zekerheid]*. Den Haag: Ministry of Social Affairs and Employment.

Wilthagen, T. 2002. Effecten en doeltreffendheid van de Wet Flexibiliteit en Zekerheid. Den Haag: min. SZW. Employment and labour markets, *Paper for the British Journal of Industrial Relations 'The Politics of Employment Relations' Conference*, Cumberland Lodge, The Great Park Windsor, UK: 16–17 September 2002.

Wilthagen, T. & Rogowski, R. 2002. Legal regulation of transitional labor markets. In G. Schmid & B. Gazier (eds.), *The Dynamics of Full Employment: Social Integration through Transitional Labor Markets*. Cheltenham: Edward Elgar.

Wilthagen, T. & Tros, F. 2004. The concept of flexicurity: A new approach to regulating employment and labour markets, *European Review of Labour and Research*, 10, 2 (Summer), 166–186.

European employment relations: from collectivism to individualism?

ERLING RASMUSSEN AND TORBEN ANDERSEN

Introduction

The theme of a constant decline in union membership, union influence and collective bargaining has been a mainstay in employment relations research and in media reports over the last two decades (Ackers *et al.* 1996; Leisink *et al.* 1996; Martin & Ross 1999). Many Western OECD (Organization for Economic Co-operation and Development)countries have recorded significant declines in union membership since the 'golden' post-war period (Marglin & Schor 1990). This process of decline has often happened over several decades (Visser 1991). This chapter discusses the reasons for this decline and points to social, economic and technological changes which have all had a negative influence on the role of collectivism in employment relations (Bacon & Storey 1996; Phelps Brown 1990). While the demand side – especially multinational enterprises, labour market flexibility and new work patterns (Connell & Burgess 2004; Felstead & Jewson 1999) – has played a dominant role, the supply side has been important through changes in family patterns, career expectations and individual preferences (Hakim 2000; Rasmussen *et al.* 2004).

Many countries have experienced significant falls in collective bargaining and union membership but this has not happened to the same degree in all countries. A few countries even still record high union density levels and a considerable role for collectivism. At the same time, the locus and the content of collective bargaining have adjusted considerably. This indicates that changes in collectivism can take many forms, and that changes may be more complex than just a straightforward shift from collectivism to individualism. This raises the inevitable questions of why there have been different national and industry trends, and why collectivism plays a much greater role in some European countries. The chapter also discusses several areas – for example the recent growth in European Works Councils – where collectivism has been strengthened (Waddington 2003; Whittal 2000).

It has been argued – by Brewster, Larsen and others – that European HRM is quite different from American HRM (Brewster 1999; Brewster & Larsen 2000; Gooderham et al. 2004). This includes the theoretical distinction between 'universalist' and 'contextual' paradigms and different approaches to strategic HRM, but it also implies different configuration and weighting of HRM practices. These differences can partly be explained through the greater role of state intervention and collective action in European countries. In light of the recent decline in the role of collective action, as well as the growing importance of multinational enterprises, this raises the question of whether American and European HRM have started to converge (Brewster et al. 2004; Katz & Darbishire 2000).

More importantly, it raises the issue of how HRM has contributed to, and been influenced by, a decline in collectivism. In what areas can changes be detected and has the diminished impact of collective bargaining influenced changes in HRM? While HRM has certain tendencies towards promoting individualized employer–employee relationships, it is also argued that HRM can blossom in a collectivist environment. It is a distinct characteristic of HRM in many European countries that it often co-exists with a strong, institutionalized union presence at workplace level.

In order to make the discussion of 'European' HRM trends more manageable, we mainly focus on trends in the UK and Denmark (this also allows us to contextualize our subsequent discussion of developments in the financial sector in the two countries). Furthermore, the discussion is restricted to three areas where HRM is expected to have influenced union activity and collective bargaining: employee communication and increased flexibility in remuneration and working time. To ensure comparability across the various countries, we mainly draw on Cranet data.

Finally, the discussion of changes in the British and Danish banking industries illustrates some of the key features of the general shift towards individualism. It points to factors such as mergers and the rise in multinational firms, the impact of new technology and changed work organization, as well as the impact of new employment patterns and individual preferences. It also shows, however, that there are considerable differences between the patterns in the two countries – making national norms and institutions crucial factors – and highlights some interesting firm-specific approaches (Andersen 1997).

Decline in collectivism: trends and themes

In the period after 1945, trade unions had a golden period in many OECD countries where growing membership, increased pay and employment conditions, improved social welfare and a crucial role in public policy-making went hand-in-hand with full employment, expanding public services and strong economic growth (Marglin and Schor 1990; Ross and Martin 1999). With the tide turning in the 1970s, the last three decades have been rather different and in several countries unions have been under severe attack from hostile governments, public sector restructuring and shifts in employment patterns. Especially in some Anglo-American countries – the USA under Reagan, the UK under Thatcher and New Zealand in the 1990s – unionism and collective bargaining were opposed vigorously as obstacles to more efficient 'free' labour markets. Overall, these changes have questioned the unions' role in a more 'globalized market' and in national public policy-making. In particular, it has impacted negatively on union density rates and the ability to conduct collective bargaining effectively.

As can be seen from Table 4.1, many OECD countries have recorded large decreases in union density levels. Unions in the USA, UK, Germany, France and Italy have experienced particularly large declines. While the figures in Table 4.1 do

Table 4.1 Changing union density rates, selected OECD countries: 1980 and 2000

Country	1980	2000	Change (1)
Austria	57%	37%	−20
Belgium	54%	56%	2
Denmark	79%	74%	−5
Finland	69%	76%	7
France	18%	10%	−8
Germany	35%	25%	−10
Ireland	57%	38%	−19
Italy	50%	35%	−15
Luxembourg	52%	34%	−18
The Netherlands	35%	23%	−12
Norway	58%	54%	−4
Portugal	61%	24%	−37
Spain	7%	15%	8
Sweden	80%	79%	1
Switzerland	31%	18%	−13
United Kingdom	51%	31%	−20
United States	22%	13%	−9
OECD average (2)	32%	21%	−11

(1) Percentage point change; (2) OECD weighted average

Source: Knox 2004: 28 (based on OECD information)

signal that the anti-union governments in the USA and the UK have corresponded with significant decreases, this cannot be the whole explanation since density levels have also declined in countries where governments have avoided anti-union actions. As discussed in the next section, unions have obviously faced a range of adverse conditions which has cut across national trends.

It is important to stress that there is considerable variation across countries and the picture of constant, terminal declines exaggerate the situation for unionism and collective bargaining in many OECD countries. As Tables 4.1, 4.2 and 4.3 indicate, a number of countries still record high union density levels, union membership is growing in several countries, and union influence is still considerable within particular countries, industries and organizations.

While union density levels have often suffered over the last two decades, density figures are rather imprecise estimations based on different statistical measures and calculations, constituting 'a particular thorny issue in labour statistics' (EIRO 2004a: 13). This can be seen by comparing density figures in Tables 4.1 and 4.3. There are some considerable differences between the national union density levels in the two tables. To get a more comprehensive picture of unionism and collective bargaining,[1] it is also necessary to distinguish between density rates and membership and between density rates and bargaining coverage.

When Tables 4.1 and 4.2 are compared, the difference between union density and union membership rates become obvious. While some countries – for example Germany, the UK and Austria – have had overall declines in union membership, the membership figures in Table 4.2 look much healthier than the density figures in

Table 4.2 Changing union memberships, selected European countries: 1993 and 2003

Country	1993	2003	Change (1)
Austria	1,616,000	1,407,000	−12.9
Belgium	2,865,000	3,061,000	6.8
Denmark	2,116,000	2,151,000	1.7
Finland	2,069,000	2,122,000	2.6
Germany	11,680,000	8,894,000	−23.9
Ireland	432,000	515,000	19.2
Italy	10,594,000	11,266,000	6.3
Luxembourg	97,000	139,000	43.3
The Netherlands	1,810,000	1,936,000	7.2
Norway	1,325,000	1,498,000	13.1
Sweden	3,712,000	3,446,000	−7.2
United Kingdom	8,804,000	7,751,000	−12.0

(1) Percentage point change
Figures for both years where not available for France and Spain

Source: EIRO 2004a

Table 4.3 Union density and bargaining coverage, selected countries, 2001

Country	Union density (%)	Bargaining coverage (%)
Denmark	88	83
Finland	79	90
Sweden	79	90
Belgium	69	90
Austria	40	98
Italy	35	90
Portugal	30	87
Germany	30	67
United Kingdom	29	36
The Netherlands	27	88
Japan	21	21
United States	14	15
France	9	90–95

Source: Gooderham *et al.* 2004: 14 (based on EIRO figures)

Table 4.1. This can partly be explained through differences in statistical calculations and the periods measured but there are also other factors at play (Visser 1992). It can be argued that European unions have also faced a more benign economic environment in the last decade, where strong economic growth and expanding employment have enhanced unions' membership prospects in several countries. However, the difference between density and membership figures indicate that the unions have had difficulty in recruiting and retaining members in a changing labour market. It has been particularly difficult to recruit and retain people in service sector and atypical jobs (Dølvik 2001).

Finally, it is important to consider the locus and content of collective bargaining. Tripartite negotiations still feature strongly in several European countries – for example, Austria, Ireland and the Netherlands – and industry level bargaining is important in countries like Denmark, Germany and Sweden. However, overall there has been a shift downwards with a stronger emphasis on workplace arrangements. This has been influenced by strong employer pressure and, in an attempt to engage with employers, unions have then adjusted their thinking, strategies and language. This has influenced the content of collective bargaining with unions becoming more focused on costs, productivity and efficiencies.

> Some people have been asking why unions are so interested in productivity these days. Unions have always been interested in improved economic performance provided that the gains are shared. What has changed in recent years is that a consensus is emerging that the workplace is the right place to focus on getting such improvements.
>
> (Conway 2005: C2)

Another crucial factor has been the rise in 'globalization' where multinational enterprises, international cost differences and new technology have undermined traditional forms of collective bargaining. Multinational enterprises have shifted the locus of decision making upwards to levels less susceptible to union pressures (Bean 1994; Cooke 2003; Kochan *et al.* 1986). The threat of 'regime hopping' – where production and services are shifted to low-cost countries – have featured in academic debates for some time and has gained further currency through the current debates of outsourcing in the USA and Europe. While it was previously production facilities that were shifted overseas, new technology has opened for major relocation of services too (with call centres being a potent example). Again, unions have been forced to adjust collective bargaining strategies and the bargaining agenda.

With the above caveats in mind, it seems safe to maintain that unionism and collective bargaining have been under severe pressure over the last two to three decades, and this has prompted adjustments in collective bargaining in many European countries. In the literature, this adverse situation has been explained through a combination of demand and supply factors. It allows us to recognize that the post-war period was a rather unique period, since it produced an array of factors which facilitated union membership: low unemployment, industries with large workplaces constituted a major share of total employment, strong growth in manufacturing and public sector jobs and a prevalence of standard, full-time employment. There were also – as Phelps Brown (1990) has argued – more homogenous and stable communities supporting unionism.

Contrary to this array of facilitating factors, over the last decades there has been a number of political, economic and employment changes which have undermined unionism. As Ross and Martin (1999) stress, unions have been faced – in a more hostile political environment – with structural changes and the already mentioned 'double shift' in the locus of bargaining and decision-making.

> Simultaneously, decisions most important to unions moved away from national arenas 'upward' toward transnational arenas and 'downward' toward subnational ones, transferring matters from arenas where unions could be effective toward those where they were weaker. . . . Other trends accompanying the 'double shift' included demographic and structural changes in the labour force (such as feminization and tertiarization). Growth in part-time, temporary, and 'atypical' jobs increased the proportion of the labour force that unions had not organized well. The abandonment of full employment as an economic goal may have been most damaging, however. By the end of the 1980s, a shift in policy that put top priority on price stability had been completed.
>
> (Ross and Martin 1999: 8–9)

These changes are encapsulated in the popularity of concepts such as: competitiveness and organizational performance, labour market flexibility and lean production, atypical work and the 'end of the job'.

Although cost-cutting, organizational restructuring, labour market flexibility pressures have been driven by employers[2] there have also been considerable supply side factors. These have been driven by changes in demographics, family and work patterns, and career expectations and individual work-life preferences. The 'feminization' of the workforce, as female participation rates have climbed over several decades, has coincided with a rise in atypical employment in many countries (O'Reilly & Fagan 1998; Rubery et al. 1999).[3] Similarly, the rise in single parent families has often necessitated further labour market flexibility. This has also coincided with a major shift in employee thinking. Career expectations have shifted and while 'boundaryless career' theory clearly exaggerates the choice available (Pringle & Mallon 2003), new age cohorts bring their own and different expectations to the labour market (Hollinshead et al. 2003: 55–58). As recent career and preference theories have stressed, it is the *diversity and variation over time* in people's perceptions and choices which are often the dominant features of the current labour market (Crompton & Harris 1998; Hakim 1995 and 2000; Pringle & Mallon 2003). Together, these changes have made 'atypical' employment become nearly a form of 'typical' employment (Spoonley 2004; Visser 2002) and, in the process, it has raised major recruitment and retention issues for unions (as well as for HRM – see Parker and Inkson 1999).

The return of collectivism?

While union density levels are under pressure in most European OECD countries there are also several signs which point to growth opportunities. Table 4.2 shows that several countries have recorded significant increases in union membership in recent years. Additionally, unions still have considerable influence as indicated by the bargaining coverage levels presented in Table 4.3. However, the key arguments for keeping an open mind about the future directions of collectivism is associated with two trends: the growing importance of 'union renewal' – changing union strategies and policies – and the recent 'Europeanization' of employment relations, which have presented several new avenues for unions (Hoffman et al. 2002).

Union renewal has taken many forms, including the so-called partnership approach, targeting new employee groups and atypical employment, making the bargaining agenda more comprehensive, and building coalitions with 'grassroots movements'. The partnership approach has existed for a while, particularly amongst Scandinavian unions, but it has recently become a key strategy for British unions (Guest and Peccei 2001; Heery 2002). It is a rather broad strategy and it is contested amongst British unions. While it appears to have been only a modest success so far it is suited to enhance workplace presence, a strong point of British and Scandinavian unionism (Heery 2002: 29). Targeting new employee groups and atypical employment has often been associated with the 'organizing model', and it appears to be the only way to bolster union density in the fast-growing service sectors. Again, the focus becomes workplace presence and activities.

The coverage of new employee groups and atypical employment demands a more comprehensive bargaining agenda – including the provision of 'secondary benefits' (Olson 1965). This allows for a growing diversity amongst employees which recognizes that solidarity based on common identity and common interests is no longer obtainable. Instead it is necessary to develop, what Hyman (2001) has called, 'mutuality despite difference solidarity'. This can partly be accommodated through a more decentralized and flexible determination of employment conditions. Scheuer (2004) has suggested that employees could be allowed to choose between different types of benefits – in his case study between more holidays or more pay – equivalent to so-called 'cafeteria benefits' in HRM. These approaches do compete head on with benefits provided by employers – for example, it appears that job-related pension schemes are the new frontier (see Due & Madsen 2003; Madsen 2003) – but in terms of flexible working arrangements and productivity it aligns with key employer interests. It is also one area where the national, industry or occupational strength of unions can be an important lever. Finally, 'coalition building' with community and single-issue organizations have been suggested as an avenue forward. This also leads to a focus on 'grassroots' issues and impacts on the bargaining agenda.

The 'Europeanization' of employment relations has been fostered through a long-running process of enhancing employment regulations – as well as company statutes and social measures – in order to facilitate a reasonably smooth integration within the European Union (Knudsen 1995). These regulations have often taken the form of recommendations or statutory employment minima which have subsequently influenced national regulations. For example, a statutory minimum wage has recently been introduced in Ireland and the UK as these countries move closer to EU employment regulations (Atterbury *et al.* 2004). Overall, EU regulations have given more scope for union activity and the role of the 'social partners' has become more encompassing over the last decade. Additionally, the introduction of further information and consultation rights – the establishment of European Works Councils in all large companies operating in two or more EU countries as well as two further EU Directives about information and involvement (Knudsen 2004: 27) – could have major impacts for collectivism (Waddington 2003; Whittal 2000). Access to information and consultation provides legitimacy to union activities, and the institutionalized employee 'voice' could be a major lever in the attempts to broaden membership and collective bargaining.

Thus, this section has indicated how the decline in collectivism is a rather complex process. First, there has been a decline in some countries but it is not a pervasive trend and there are some counter-trends. Second, collectivism is influenced by an array of complex changes which prompt new forms and combinations of collectivism and individualism.

Decline in collectivism and HRM practices: their role and implications?

The previous section has overviewed the general and national trends while this section will focus on organizational changes. The organizational level is not considered enough in the employment relations debates of collectivism, since analyses of various European 'models' often focus on tripartite or bipartite national or industry agreements. For example, the Irish and Dutch 'miracles' have been sustained by national agreements and compromises but the effects on workplace level is seldom discussed (e.g. Auer 2000; Visser & Hemerijk 1997). This is the level where HRM policies and practices are located and it is also, as shown above, where most attempts to renew and enhance collectivism are pursued.

The reversal in fortunes for unionism and collective bargaining has coincided with a rise in the popularity of the HRM concept. For at least two reasons, it would be an obvious conclusion to expect some kind of causality or connection between the two trends. First, the American origin of HRM has often linked the concept with non-union workplaces or a union-substitution approach (see Beaumont 1991; Guest 1989). Second, there has been a strong focus on labour costs and efficiencies – the stress being on 'resources' in the HRM concept – in the so-called 'hard' versions of HRM (for a discussion of the 'hard' versus 'soft' versions of HRM, see Storey 1989). There are clearly HRM models, strategies and practices which are patently anti-union and where union-substitution or union-avoidance are part and parcel of the perception of HRM (Gooderham et al. 2004: 8–9).

However, it is taking the case too far to expect an outright causality as there are many different HRM models and strategies. Even proponents of unionism acknowledge that the pressure on unionism and collective bargaining stems from a complex mix of changes, of which HRM only constitutes a minor part (see Ackers et al. 1996: 32; Mayrhofer et al. 2000: 229). It is also important to acknowledge that European HRM approaches are different from the quintessential American HRM model (Brewster 1999; Brewster & Larsen 2000; Gooderham et al. 2004; Sparrow et al. 2004). These differences can partly be explained through the greater role and legitimacy of state intervention and collective action in European countries (Morley et al. 1996).

> The US theories with their implications of virtually autonomous organizations, sits uncomfortably with the European reality. In Europe organizations operate with restricted autonomy: constrained at a national level by culture and

legislation, at the organizational level by patterns of ownership, and at the HRM level by trade union involvement and consultative arrangements.

(Brewster & Larsen 2000: 25)

Talking about 'European' HRM is an artificially constructed model that only makes sense when trying to distinguish it from the, equally artificial, American model. As European countries have only recently started to construct common employment regulations, there are vast differences between the various national norms, institutions and employer-employee attitudes. Even countries normally grouped together in employment relations research – say Ireland and the UK or the Scandinavian countries – have, despite their communalities, somewhat different employment regulations and record different trends in the role of collective bargaining and HRM practices (Atterbury *et al.* 2004; Rogaczewska *et al.* 2004; Lindeberg *et al.* 2004). While the growth in EU employment regulation could facilitate a convergence towards a 'European model' over time, this has yet to happen (Mayrhofer *et al.* 2004).

European convergence and divergence

It has often been argued that stronger employer–employee communication is a core part of HRM; it is a way to facilitate greater employee commitment (Morley *et al.* 2000). However, it is this direct – no 'third party intervention' – that could potentially make union representation less necessary. As Mayrhofer *et al.* (2000: 229) have asked: 'will individual(ized) communication take over from more collectivist or union communication?' There is no doubt that many firms have increased their communication efforts over the last decade. Mayrhofer *et al.* (2000: 230) found that across all European countries surveyed, organizations had increased their 'downward' (management–employee) communication efforts. This increase had occurred consistently across a range of communication channels and across employee groups. In particular, organizational strategy and financial information were communicated more regularly to employees. There has also been an increase in 'upward' communication as part of 'open door' policies and emphasis for sharing of ideas as part of improving service and production quality.

However, it is this direct communication without any 'third party intervention' that could potentially make union representation less necessary. Mayrhofer *et al.* (2000: 229) have made a similar point: 'Will individual(ized) communication take over from more collectivist or union communication?' Cranet surveys have recorded a rise in 'more collectivist ways of communication' through unions and employee representatives: 'Overall therefore our data point to a new balance between individualized and collective communication which, when viewed against the backdrop of a partially changing, though largely stable, trade union role, might suggest the need for a modified concept of HRM' (Mayrhofer *et al.* 2000: 237–238).

Support from employee representatives is often seen as crucial to 'selling the message' efficiently (Brewster & Larsen 2000). Furthermore, the full effect of EU Directives institutionalizing information and consultation rights has yet to be seen (Knudsen 2004). The significant role of collective communication can even be detected in current British HRM practices:

> On the other hand, trade union influence on organizations overall showed less tendency to decrease than the declining trade union density might suggest. This may be because of the trend for some organizations to increase the use they make of representative bodies to communicate major issues to employees.
>
> (Cranet UK Executive Report 2003: 10)

Thus, communication strategies to raise employee commitment may be a form of union avoidance but in 'European' HRM both collective and individual forms of communication are growing and create additional organizational synergies (Morley *et al.* 2000: 162–164).

It has been suggested above, that the shift towards workplace based bargaining with a high emphasis on flexible, often individualized arrangements, could undermine collectivism. Recent trends in decision making on remuneration in Danish organizations show why unions have had to adjust their bargaining strategies, regardless of high union density levels in Denmark (Rogaczewska *et al.* 2003: 104).

In Denmark during the period 1995–2003, primary decisions on remuneration have moved away from the national level and instead decision making has moved upwards and downwards. It has moved upwards to the international head office – doubled from 7 per cent to 15 per cent of responding organizations in the nine-year period. It has moved downwards to workplace level – from 8 per cent to 38 per cent of responding organizations in the 1995–2003 period. This has corresponded with a decline in the importance of national or industry collective agreements in the determination of pay levels (see Rogaczewska *et al.* 2003: 106, Table 3). Instead there has been a rise in localized/regional level collective bargaining and, in particular, in individually agreed pay levels. These individually agreed pay levels now cover the majority of managers, technical and specialist staff and office staff. It is only amongst skilled and semi-skilled blue-collar workers, that the traditional national and industry collective agreements cover the vast majority and with individually agreed pay levels covering around a third of blue-collar workers. Still, even in this last category there has been a major rise – from 9 to 32 per cent – during the period 1995–2003. In short, the Danish figures illustrate the 'double shift' mentioned by Ross & Martin (1999), and they show significant rises in individually agreed remuneration.

Unsurprisingly, the UK trends are moving in the same direction but with a more fundamental shift towards organization-based bargaining. While public sector bargaining still happens to some degree at national or industry level, this is seldom the case in the private sector. During the 1990s, there was a sharp decline in national agreements and most large companies had instituted either organization-wide, site-level or no bargaining at all. The latter option has been growing strongly, with the latest 2003 Cranet survey finding that over a third of firms had no union representation at all. Thus, the Cranet UK Executive Report (2003: 11) states: 'The predominant level for bargaining is at company and at the individual level, showing the continuing move towards the individualization of the employment contract'. This has had a fundamental impact on pay flexibility with the majority of organizations having variable pay schemes – the creed of rewarding 'high achievers' has become firmly entrenched (Atterbury *et al.* 2004: 53).

Working time arrangements is an area which has always been high on the union agenda, and European unions have recorded significant 'wins' over the last two decades. In some countries, the reduction in standard weekly working hours during the 1980s and 1990s has been spectacular. There have been major reductions in Scandinavia, Germany and the Netherlands and the 35-hour week in France has caused it to have international notoriety. This is an area where there is a distinct difference compared to the USA, both in terms of weekly working hours and annual holidays. In fact, English-speaking OECD countries appear to have a culture of long working hours, which is distinctly different from levels in most Continental European countries (*The Economist* 2000, Brewster & Larsen 2000: 133). Again changes at EU-level will be important: the 48-hour EU Working Time Directive will probably further enhance the working time differences between EU and non-EU countries.

Unions have often overcome strong employer resistance to reduction in weekly working hours by acquiescing to more working time flexibility. This is also often in the interest of their members who appreciate more working time flexibility, whether it be part-time, flex-time or additional pay through overtime or penal rates. 'The most widely used form of flexible working in Europe is part-time work. This is an area in which northern Europe leads the world' (Brewster & Larsen 2000: 131). Visser (2002) has labelled the Netherlands 'the first part-time economy'. The rise in part-time work has continued over several decades and unions have worked hard to improve employment conditions for part-timers. There are signs, however, that the spectacular rise in part-time work may come to an end. Part-time work has declined in Denmark in the last 20 years (Rasmussen *et al.* 2004), organizations in other Scandinavian countries have also recorded decreases (Brewster & Larsen 2000) and young, well-educated women appear – often for career reasons – less keen on part-time work.

Interestingly, fixed-term or temporary employment appears to dominate more in Southern Europe. Robinson (1999) has argued that this is caused by employers' reactions to union attempts to secure job security in the face of high unemployment. This is supported by Cranet data which has also suggested another explanation.

. . . we know from other studies that the development of flexibility shows a tendency to be driven by the north. Papalexandris (2000: 134) observes as a general trend that in countries where workers are more highly paid there is more room for part-time work whereas in countries with lower wages employees have difficulties accepting part-time pay.

(Mayrhofer *et al.* 2004: 428)

Finally, Cranet data highlights that there has been less-than-expected growth in some more 'fancy' forms of working time arrangements, such as annual hours, flexiwork and term-working (Brewster & Larsen 2000: 134–135; UK Executive Report 2003: 8–9). Similarly, teleworking has grown less than predicted though there are indications that its time may yet come.

The rise in flexibility has coincided with growing concerns over sub-standard employment conditions and displaced workers (Brewster & Larsen 2000: 224). It is problematic that HRM's role in increasing organizational efficiency and flexibility has often aligned HRM with labour market segmentation (Deeks & Rasmussen 2002: 269). Concerns about employee welfare tends to be detached from debates about HRM strategy and practices and appears, therefore, to be more of an after-thought and just paying lip service. This is an area where strong union pressure within and outside organizations can be crucial, and it can also enhance the recruitment of members.

The shift in locus and content of bargaining constitutes an uncomfortable situation for unions as it complicates collective bargaining and it makes organizing less cost effective. Still, it is possible to balance collectivism and individualism. It appears that 'social pacts', neo-corporatist arrangements at national or industry and strong workplace representation can be levers to accommodate both collectivism and individualism (Auer 2000; Fajertag & Pochet 2000). This has been the case in Northern Europe where institutionalized workplace representation has a long tradition (see Croucher & Singe 2002). For example, increased working time flexibility in the Netherlands was facilitated through tripartite arrangements (see Rasmussen *et al.* 2004; Visser 1998). Similarly, the Danish examples of 'negotiated flexibility' through the use of institutionalized employee representation at workplace level offer another avenue (see Navrbjerg 2003; Navrbjerg *et al.* 1998). In light of the recent development of European Works Councils, this could become a very important trend in large European organizations. This may accommodate the tension between unionism and HRM practices. It may also accommodate the pressure for more flexibility under which both unionism and HRM find themselves. It is likely that employers and employees are bound to demand more flexibility in the future – employers in their quest to stay competitive and employees in their attempts to achieve a work-life balance.

Collectivism and individualism in the British and Danish financial sectors

The British and Danish financial sectors are good examples of the convergence-divergence tensions explored above, since they have faced similar competitive pressures. However, outcomes in terms of unionism and collective bargaining have varied. Increasing competitive pressures, including deregulation of the banking environment (Regini *et al.* 1999), have prompted major structural rationalizations, radically altered work organization and changed employment patterns and employment conditions. There has been a move towards financial 'supermarkets' with a broader array of products and 24-hour customer access facilitated by new technology. In Britain, the 'big four' banks have bought up smaller players (including players from other sectors) and merged into even larger conglomerates – Barclays Bank, RBS/NatWest, HSBC and LloydsTSB. In the Danish case, larger Nordic conglomerates have been formed. The two largest banks – Nordea and Den Danske Bank – now cover more than three-quarters of the Danish financial sector (at the same time, they have a strong presence in the Swedish, Finnish and Norwegian financial sectors).

Traditionally, large banks operated an extensive branch network which demanded a considerable amount of employment and allowed for a paternalistic employment approach (ILO 2001; Regini *et al.* 1999). There has been a major reduction in the number of branches over the last two decades. In Britain, about one third of all branches have been closed. There are now less than 10,000, compared to the 14,000 branches of the 1980s (ILO 2001: 44). It is a similar story in Danish banking where around a quarter of all branches have been closed (see Andersen & Hjalager 2005). Furthermore, both countries have witnessed a centralization of 'back office' administrative work into larger administrative centres, which have allowed the use of new services such as interactive telephone and web-based banking services. Finally, there have been more moves to outsource banking work in recent years,[4] though outsourcing appears to have been more widespread in Britain than in Denmark.

These changes have had considerable impact on employment patterns and career paths. Many banks have implemented considerable reductions in staff numbers. There has also been a move towards more specialized job roles and a greater use of atypical employment arrangements. Within these general changes, there have been, as Andersen (1997) has argued, distinct differences between British and Danish banks. Where British banks have increased part-time employment, it has been decreased amongst Danish banks. Tailby (2002) has also noted the rise in atypical and contingent employment in British banking. On the contrary, the Danish unions appear to have been relatively successful in protecting employment conditions and full-time jobs amongst administrative, tellers and call centre staff.

The new employment and career patterns have damaged and changed the 'psychological contract': the employee commitment and work satisfaction have been continuously discussed in recent literature (e.g. Holden 1996; ILO 2001). This is clearly problematic since employees and their contact with customers have become the lynchpin in banks' organizational and economic performance. Employee dissatisfaction has prompted, therefore, a stronger organizational focus on communication and staff survey in many banks. Both Den Danske Bank and Nordea have implemented annual employee satisfaction measurements which are carried out by external consultants and researchers. In addition, there is a stronger organizational focus on customer satisfaction and increasing the level of profitability per customer. This includes new and much more market-orientated types of expertise which have arrived in financial services (see Fleck 1996).

Employee dissatisfaction could facilitate more individualistic responses – high turnover, absenteeism, mistrust – or it could facilitate a more positive approach to unionism (see Gall 1997). However, British financial sector unions have faced declining union density and it is estimated that around 750,000 financial sector employees are not members of a union (UNIFI 2004a). In Denmark, there is high union density (above 80 per cent) and the financial sector unions appear to have consolidated their recruitment and retention of members. The difference between the two countries fits well with the overall difference in union density, and it is also aligned with collective bargaining trends. While separate staff associations exist at the major British banks and the unions are involved in negotiation over pay and redundancies (e.g. EIRO 1999), there is no longer industry level collective bargaining. Danish unions have maintained industry bargaining and they have also been able to influence the implementation of agreements at the workplace level (Mayer et al. 2001). Interestingly, the unions suggested further individualized flexibility in employment conditions in the 2003 bargaining round. On the basis of a collectively-agreed 'catalogue' of employment conditions, Danish banking employees would be able to make up their own combination of pay increases and overall working time (EIRO 2003). Unsurprisingly, employers have accepted this approach which is similar to the HRM practice of 'cafeteria benefits'.

As unions have faced restructuring amongst banks, they have themselves restructured through mergers and international collaboration (e.g. Morris et al. 2001). Recently, the British financial sector trade union UNIFI has been created and this organization has merged with the insurance employees' trade union, Amicus, in October 2004 (UNIFI 2004b). Interestingly, there has yet to be a merger between Danish financial sector unions. Instead the first cross-national (Nordic) trade union has been formed which is expected to improve the membership recruitment base further (EIRO 2004b). Finally, unions in both countries now have further possibilities because of the European Works Councils. The unfolding of this institutionalized employee participation in British banks will be interesting to watch. Quintana (2003) foresees that the larger, international British banking groups – like Barclays and HSBC – will show more interest as their different activities across

Europe require more co-ordination. Quintana stress that regional homogeneity is an important precondition for the use of European Works Councils, as has been the case with the Nordea Bank. It has agreed to place itself under the European Company Statute (EIRO 2004b), as a consequence of its major activities in Denmark, Finland, Sweden and Norway.

Conclusion

There is no doubt that there has been a decline in union density in many European OECD countries. At the same time, the locus and the content of collective bargaining have adjusted considerably. Unions and collective bargaining have clearly faced, and are still facing, a number of fundamental challenges. In some European countries, unions and collective bargaining have become 'ghettoized' in certain sectors, and they have limited impact on employment conditions across the labour market. However, in most European countries, this decline is unlikely to mean 'an end to employment relations' in the immediate future (Purcell 1993). The decline in collectivism has not happened in all countries and coverage of collective bargaining is still high in many European countries. The chapter has also pointed to several areas – particularly the recent growth in European Works Councils – where collectivism has been strengthened. As unions have faced a more difficult environment they have started to adjust their structures, strategies and practices. This is evident in our discussion of financial sector trends, though it is also evident that once unionism and collective bargaining have diminished then it is hard to reverse the trend.

Our discussion of unionism and collectivism indicates that the shift from collectivism to individualism is rather complex and can be analyzed in different ways. The complexity of the collectivism-individualism debate is further enhanced when the role of HRM is considered. 'European' HRM cannot simply be equated with a growth in individualism. While there are certain tendencies in that direction, there is also a growing focus on 'soft' HRM practices – teamwork, employee empowerment and participation – and well-established practices of collectivist approaches exist in many European countries. This chapter has stressed that there is a growth in both collectivist and individual types of practices and, for example, collectivist and individual forms of communication were often found to support each other.

The difference between European and American HRM practices has been underlined. The national contexts and impact on organizational decision making are different and it appears that convergence is not happening. It has also been shown that there are significant national and industry differences in HRM practices across European countries. In particular, the discussion of communication and flexibility in remuneration and working time arrangements has highlighted considerable variation across countries. It was found that certain types of flexibility prevail in certain countries, and they are often driven by specific constellations of demand and supply side factors. Similarly, our discussion of employment relations in the financial sector illustrates that, despite similar competitive pressures and organizational changes, there are considerable national differences in employment relations.

In short, this chapter indicates that there have been considerable changes surrounding unionism, collective bargaining and HRM across European countries, and these changes have created new employment relations patterns and practices which are much more complex than just a shift from collectivism to individualism.

Notes

1 As there are considerable national variations across sectors – public versus private sectors, manufacturing versus service sectors – and within sectors, it is necessary to analyze these variations to get a full picture. This has also become more important as cross-national/ international trends have become critical in many sectors (e.g. Katz & Darbishire 2000; Regini *et al.* 1999). However, such a detailed analysis is clearly beyond the scope of this chapter.
2 This is explored in the 'psychological contract' literature where employer strategies and actions can undermine or violate the psychological contract of employees (e.g. Parks & Kidder 1994; Rousseau 1995). While a violation of employees' psychological contract can facilitate union membership recruitment, employees may either opt for a collective or an individual response.
3 As shown by Rasmussen *et al.* 2004, there is nothing pre-determined about these trends: the rise in female participation rates can also lead to a decline in atypical employment under particular national circumstances.
4 Outsourcing has happened for a while though it appears to have changed in terms of job types and the number of jobs being lost. For example, LloydsTSB announced in November 2004 that it, as part of an ongoing strategy of outsourcing jobs, would offshore a further 1,000 jobs. Similarly, HSBC expects to offshore around 7,000 jobs from its UK processing and call centres (see www.unifi.org.uk).

References

Ackers, P., Smith, C. and Smith P. (eds.). 1996. *The New Workplace and Trade Unionism.* London: Routledge.

Andersen, T. 1997. Do institutions matter? Convergence and national diversity in the restructuring of employment in British and Danish banking. *European Journal of Industrial Relations*, 3(1): 107–124.

Andersen, T. & Hjalager, A. 2005. Ti år efter – rationalisering og beskæftigelse i danske pengeinstitutter. *Økonomi og Politik* (forthcoming).

Atterbury, S., Brewster, C., Communal, C., Cross, C., Gunnighle, P. & Morley, M. 2004. The UK and Ireland: traditions and transitions in HRM. In C. Brewster, W. Mayrhofer & M. Morley (eds.), *Human Resource Management in Europe*. Oxford: Elsevier.

Auer, P. 2000. *Employment Revival in Europe. Labour Market Success in Austria, Denmark, Ireland and the Netherlands*. Geneva: ILO.

Bacon, N. & Storey, J. 1996. Individualism and collectivism and the changing role of trade unions. In P. Ackers, C. Smith & P. Smith (eds.), *The New Workplace and Trade Unionism*. London: Routledge.

Bean, R. 1994. *Comparative Industrial Relations*. London: Routledge.

Beaumont, P. B. 1991. Trade unions and HRM. *Industrial Relations Journal*, 22(4): 300–308.

Brewster, C. 1999. Different paradigms in strategic HRM: questions raised by comparative research. In P. Wright, L. Dyer, J. Boudreau and G. Milkovich (eds.), *Research in Personnel and HRM*. Greenwich: JAI Press Inc.

Brewster, C. & Larsen, H. H. 2000. *HRM in Northern Europe*. London: Blackwell.

Connell, J. & Burgess, J. 2004. *International Perspectives on Temp Agencies and Workers*. London: Routledge.

Conway, P. 2005. Unions keen to get work moving. *NZ Herald*, 11 January 2005: p. C2.

Cooke, W. 2003. *Multinational Companies and Global Human Resource Strategies*. Westport: M. Greenwood Publishing.

Cranet UK Executive Report 2003. Cranfield: Cranfield School of Management.

Crompton, R. & Harris, F. 1998. Explaining women's employment patterns: 'orientation to work' revisited. *British Journal of Sociology*, 49(1): 118–136.

Croucher, R. & Singe, I. 2002. Flexible working time and interest representation in German and British Banking. In I. U. Zeytinoglu (ed.), *Flexible Working Arrangements*. The Hague, Netherlands: Kluwer Law International.

Deeks, J. & Rasmussen, E. 2002. *Employment Relations in New Zealand*. Auckland: Prentice Hall.

Dølvik, J. E. 2001. *At Your Service? Comparative Perspectives on Employment and Labour Relations in the European Private Sector Services*. Brussels: P.I.E.-Lang.

Due, J. & Madsen, J. S. 2003. *Fra magtkamp til konsensus. Arbejdsmarkedspensionerne og den danske model*. Copenhagen: DJØF Forlag.

The Economist 2000. The future of work. Career evolution. *The Economist*, 19 January: 93–96.

EIRO 1999. *Employment Security in Banking: The Case of the Co-operative Bank*. www.eiro.eurofound.eu.int/1999/10/feature/uk9910135f (accessed 12 January 2005).

EIRO 2003. *New Agreements Introduce 'Individual Options' for Employees*. www.eiro.eurofound.eu.int/print/2003/02 (accessed 15 January 2005).

EIRO 2004a. *Trade Union Membership 1993–2004*. www.eiro.eurofound.eu.int/2004/03/update/tn0403105u (accessed 14 January 2005).

EIRO 2004b. *Nordic Trade Union Formed at Nordea*. www.eiro.eurofound.eu.int/print/2004/11 (accessed 15 January 2005).

Fajertag, G. & Pochet, P. 2000. *Social Pacts in Europe – New Dynamics*. Brussels: OSE, ETUI.

Felstead, A. & Jewson, N. 1999. *Global Trends in Flexible Labour*. London: Macmillan.

Fleck, J. 1996. Informal information flow and the nature of expertise in financial services. *International Journal of Technology Management*, 11(1 + 2): 104–128.

Gall, G. 1997. Developments in trade unionism in the financial sector in Britain. *Work, Employment & Society*, 11(2): 219–235.

Gooderham, P., Morley, M., Brewster, C. & Mayrhofer, W. 2004. Human resource management: a universal concept? In C. Brewster, W. Mayrhofer & M. Morley (eds.), *Human Resource Management in Europe*. Oxford: Elsevier.

Guest, D. 1989. Human resource management: its implications for industrial relations and trade unions. In J. Storey (ed.), *New Perspectives on Human Resource Management*. London: Routledge.

Guest, D. & Peccei, R. 2001. Partnership at work: mutuality and the balance of advantage. *British Journal of Industrial Relations*, 39(2): 207–236.

Hakim, C. 1995. Five feminist myths about women's employment. *British Journal of Sociology*, 46(3): 429–455.

Hakim, C. 2000. *Work Lifestyle Choices in the 21st Century: Preference Theory*. New York: Oxford University Press

Heery, E. 2002. Partnership versus organizing: alternative futures for British trade unionism. *Industrial Relations Journal*, 33(1): 20–35.

Hoffman, J. *et al*. 2002. *The Europeanisation of Industrial Relations in a Global Perspective: A Literature Review*. Dublin: European Foundation for the Improvement of Living and Working Conditions.

Holden, L. 1996. HRM and employee involvement in Britain and Sweden: a comparative study. *International Journal of Human Resource Management*, 7(1): 59–81.

Hollinshead, G., Nicholls, P. & Tailby, S. 2003. *Employee Relations*. Harlow: Pearson Education.

Hyman, R. 2001. *Understanding European Trade Unionism*. London: Sage.

International Labour Organisation 2001. *The Employment Impact of Mergers and Acquisitions in the Banking and Financial Services Sector*. Geneva: ILO.

Katz, H. C. & Darbishire, O. 2000. *Converging Divergencies*. London: ILR Press.

Knox, N. 2004. Unions begin to struggle in Europe. *USA Today*, 11 Nov. 2004: pp. 27–28.

Knudsen, H. 1995. *Employee Participation in Europe*. London: Sage.

Knudsen, H. 2004. Representation and participation – unilateralism or bipartism. In J. Lind, H. Knudsen & H. Jørgensen (eds.), *Labour and Employment Regulation in Europe*. Brussels: P.I.E.-Peter Land.

Kochan, T., Katz, H. & McKersie, R. B. 1986. *The Transformation of American Industrial Relations*. New York: Basic Books.

Leisink, P., Van Leemput, J. & Vilrokx, J. 1996. *The Challenges to Trade Unions in Europe*. Cheltenham: Edward Elgar.

Lindeberg, T., Månson, B. & Vanhala, S. 2004. Sweden and Finland: small companies with large companies. In C. Brewster, W. Mayrhofer & M. Morley (eds.), *Human Resource Management in Europe*. Oxford: Elsevier.

Madsen, J. S. 2003. Introduction of 'labour market pensions' strengthens bargaining system. www.eiro.eurofound.eu.int/2003/10/feature/dk0310103f.html (accessed 22 November 2004): 4 pages.

Marglin, S. & Schor, J. 1990. *The Golden Age of Capitalism*. Oxford: Clarendon.

Martin, A. & Ross, G. 1999. *The Brave New World of European Labor*. New York: Berghan Books.

Mayer, G., Andersen, T. & Muller, M. 2001. Employment restructuring and flexibility in Austrian and Danish banking. *European Journal of Industrial Relations*, 7(1): 71–87.

Mayrhofer, W., Brewster, C., Morley, M. & Gunnigle, P. 2000. Communication, consultation and the HRM debate. In C. Brewster, W. Mayrhofer & M. Morley (eds.), *New Challenges for European Human Resource management*. Basingstoke: Macmillan Press.

Mayrhofer, W., Morley, M. & Brewster, C. 2004. Convergence, stasis, or divergence. In C. Brewster, W. Mayrhofer & M. Morley (eds.), *Human Resource Management in Europe*. Oxford: Elsevier.

Morley, M., Brewster, C., Gunnigle, P. & Mayrhofer, W. 1996. Evaluating change in European industrial relations: research evidence on trends at organizational level. *International Journal of Human Resource Management*, 7(3): 640–656.

Morley, M., Mayrhofer, W. & Brewster, C. 2000. Communication in organizations. In C. Brewster & H. H. Larsen (eds.), *HRM in Northern Europe*. London: Blackwell.

Morris, T., Storey, J., Wilkinson, A. & Cressey, P. 2001. Industry change and union mergers in British retail finance. *British Journal of Industrial Relations*, 39(2): 237–256.

Navrbjerg, S. E., Jensen, C. S. & Lubanski, N. 1998. *Den samarbejdende tillidsrepræsentant.* København, LO.

Navrbjerg, S. E. 2003. *HRM and the shop steward – sparring partner or opponent? HRM in an unionised environment*: Proceedings, 7th Conference on International Human Resource Management, Limerick, 4–6 June 2003.

Olson, M. 1965. *The Logic of Collective Action.* Cambridge, USA: Harvard University Press.

O'Reilly, J. & Fagan, C. 1998. *Part-time Prospects.* London: Routledge.

Papalexandris, N. 2000. Flexible working patterns: towards reconciliation of family and work. In C. Brewster, W. Mayrhofer & M. Morley (eds.), *New Challenges for European Human Resource Management.* Basingstoke: Macmillan Press.

Parker, P. & Inkson, K. 1999. New forms of career: the challenge to human resource management. *Asia Pacific Journal of Human Resource Management*, 37(1): 76–85.

Parks, J. M. & Kidder, Deborah L. 1994. 'Till death us do part . . .' changing work relationships in the 1990s. In C.L. Cooper & D.M. Rousseau (eds.), *Trends in Organizational Behavior.* Chichester: Wiley & Sons.

Phelps Brown, H. 1990. The counter-revolution of our time. *Industrial Relations*, 29(1): 1–14.

Pringle, J. K. & Mallon, M. 2003. Challenges for the boundaryless career odyssey. *International Journal of Human Resource Management*, 14(5): 839–853.

Purcell, J. 1993. The end of institutional industrial relations. *Political Quarterly*, 64(1): 6–23.

Quintana, M. 2003. *The different dimensions of 'Europeanisation' in the banking sector: implications for EWCs. Warwick Papers in Industrial Relations, No. 72. IRRU.* University of Warwick.

Rasmussen, E., Lind, J. & Visser, J. 2004. Flexibility meets national norms and regulations: part-time work in New Zealand, Denmark and the Netherlands. *British Journal of Industrial Relations*, 42(4): 637–658.

Regini, M., Kitay, J. & Baethge, M. 1999. *From Tellers to Sellers.* Cambridge, MA: MIT Press.

Robinson, P. 1999. Explaining the relationship between flexible employment and labour market regulation. In A. Felstead & N. Jewson (eds.), *Global Trends in Flexible Labour.* London: Macmillan.

Rogaczewska, A. P., Larsen, H. H., Nordhaug, O., Døving, E. & Gjelsvik, M. 2004. Denmark and Norway: siblings or cousins? In C. Brewster, W. Mayrhofer & M. Morley (eds.), *Human Resource Management in Europe.* Oxford: Elsevier.

Rogaczewska, A. P., Larsen, H. H. & Znaider, R. 2003. *HRM ved en milepæl. Cranet-undersøgelsen 2003.* Copenhagen: Center for Ledelse og CBS.

Ross, G. & Martin, A. 1999. European Unions face the Millenium. In A. Martin & G. Ross (eds.), *The Brave New World of European Labor.* New York: Berghan Books.

Rousseau, D. 1995. *Psychological Contracts in Organizations.* Newbury Park, CA: Sage.

Rubery, J., Fagan, C. & Smith, M. 1999. *Women and European Employment.* London: Routledge.

Scheuer, S. 2004. Employees 'support free choice' in collective agreements. http://www.eiro.eurofound.eu.int/2004/10/feature/dk0410105f.html (accessed 12 February 2005).

Sparrow, P., Brewster, C. & Harris, H. 2004. *Globalizing Human Resource Management.* London: Routledge.

Spoonley, P. 2004. Is non-standard work becoming standard? *New Zealand Journal of Employment Relations*, 29(3): 3–24.

Storey, J. 1989. *New Perspectives on Human Resource Management.* London: Routledge.

Tailby, S. 2002. *Contingent Employment in Banking in Spain, Sweden, The Netherlands and The UK.* Bristol; Report, Employment Studies Research Unit, University of the West of England.

UNIFI 2004a. www.unifi.org.uk/news/unifi/2004-mar-13a (accessed on 15 January 2005),

UNIFI 2004b. www.unifi.org.uk/news/unifi/2004-oct-21c (accessed on 15 January 2005).

Visser, J. 1991. Trends in trade union membership. *OECD Employment Outlook*: 97–134.

Visser, J. 1992. Union organization: why countries differ. *Trade unionism in the future, Conference Proceedings*, vol. 2, IX IIRA World Congress, 30 Aug–3 Sept 1992, Sydney: 158–176.

Visser, J. 1998. The Netherlands; the return of responsive corporatism. In A. Ferner & R. Hyman (eds.), *Changing Industrial Relations in Europe*. London: Blackwell.

Visser, J. 2002. The first part-time economy of the world: A model to be followed? *Journal of European Social Policy*, 12(1): 23–42.

Visser, J. & Hemerijck, A. C. 1997. *A Dutch Miracle: Job Growth, Welfare Reform, and Corporatism in the Netherlands*. Amsterdam: Amsterdam University Press.

Waddington, J. 2003. What do representatives think of the practices of European works councils? Views from six countries. *European Journal of Industrial Relations*, 9(3): 303–325.

Whittal, M. 2000. The BMW European work council: a cause for European industrial relations optimism? *European Journal of Industrial Relations*, 6(1): 61–83.

Looking inside: Embeddedness in the organization

HRM in multinational corporations: strategies and systems

5

PAUL GOODERHAM AND ODD NORDHAUG

Introduction

The purpose of this chapter is to shed light on human resource management (HRM) systems and practices in multinational corporations (MNCs). This requires an understanding of the MNC's strategy and the strategic role of the subsidiaries. Against this background we will employ the term strategic international HRM (SIHRM) in this chapter. We will focus on factors that contribute to determining the elements of this type of management.

By MNCs we mean firms which not only have substantial direct investments in foreign countries, but which also actively manage these in an integrated way. In other words, companies that simply export their products fall outside the parameters of this type of corporation, as do firms that license or franchise their products to foreign firms. Applying these two criteria – substantial foreign direct investments (FDI) and active, integrated management – means that MNCs represent a relatively recent development in that most of them have evolved after the Second World War.

IHRM is preoccupied with the management of people in MNCs and as such calls for an overview of the forces that underlie foreign direct investment (FDI). This is important not least to build an understanding of the differences between MNCs in terms of the strategies they employ and therefore also of their IHRM systems and practices. In line with this, we will now focus on the following issues:

- analysis of the driving forces behind FDI;
- the regional bias of FDI;

- the national bias of MNCs;
- the IHRM challenge.

Following these explanations we will outline our model of SIHRM.

The driving forces behind FDI

Until the late 1980s the received theory of FDI was Dunning's (1977; 1993) eclectic approach or 'OLI theory'. The central idea of this approach is that three conditions must hold for a firm to become an MNC: ownership, location, and internalization. Ownership advantages may be the possession of a patent or management abilities that other companies do not have and imply that owning these assets can earn supranatural profits in several markets. Localization advantages are to a large extent the same as decentralization advantages. That is, there must be reasons why geographically separated production within the same firm is preferred to centralized production. The fundamental trade-off is between economies of scale on the plant level and potential decentralization advantages, such as lower factor costs, transport costs or trade barriers. Finally, the firm needs to prefer internalizing the relationship with the producer in the local market over, say, licensing production to a local firm. This could be due, for example, to difficulties in writing a licensing contract that gives the parent firm sufficient protection.

However, as Dunning himself indicated, by the 1990s OLI needed to be supplemented because:

> increasingly, firms are investing abroad to protect or augment their core competencies. In such cases, they are 'buying into' foreign created assets (notably technological capacity, information, human creativity, and markets) some of which are proprietary to particular foreign firms [hence the pronounced trend towards acquisition of foreign firms, rather than greenfield investment] and others are more generally accessible to corporations, but immobile across geographical space.
>
> (Dunning 1997: 64) [our insertion]

In other words MNCs are no longer simply developing products at home and transferring these innovations to foreign subsidiaries, they are increasingly seeking to optimize their global innovative capabilities by incorporating subsidiary-specific advantages in different countries, sometimes engaging in major research at the subsidiary level (Davis & Meyer 2004). However, the extent to which critical resources will reside with the parent or with the subsidiary can vary considerably.

To date this combination of unequally distributed factor endowments combined with difficulties in using market-based arrangements such as licensing or franchising has yielded more than 60,000 MNCs with over 800,000 affiliates abroad. On a global basis, MNCs generate about half of the world's industrial output and account for about two-thirds of world trade. About one-third of total trade (or half of the MNC trade) is intra firm. MNCs are particularly strong in motor vehicles, computers, and soft drinks, having, on a global basis, 85 per cent, 70 per cent, and 65 per cent, respectively, of these markets. In some countries they are the dominant manufacturing presence. Affiliates of MNCs account for nearly 70 per cent of Ireland's manufacturing output, and over 50 per cent of Canada's. A substantial proportion of manufacturing in Britain, France, and Sweden is also accounted for by foreign-owned MNCs. All the indications are that the level of production undertaken by foreign-owned manufacturing will continue to rise. For example, by 1998 for the EU as a whole, a quarter of total manufacturing production was controlled by a foreign subsidiary of an MNC compared to 17 per cent in 1990.

The advantages of becoming a global player in manufacturing are more obvious than for service-based firms. In the case of the former the value chain can be divided across many locations. Parts of the manufacturing process can be located to low-cost countries, while R&D can be located in a region with specialized competencies with its costs spread across many markets. In the case of service firms much of the value chain has to be generated locally: that is, there is little in the way of opportunity to centralize activities to low-cost locations. To a greater or larger degree services have to be tailored for each client unlike for example pharmaceuticals, which can be mass-produced. Sharing advanced knowledge is also more problematic. In manufacturing companies it can be made available through patented technologies or unique products. In service companies it has to be transferred from country to country through learning processes. Nevertheless with the services trade liberalization in recent years the share of services in foreign direct investments (FDI) has risen significantly, particularly within telecommunications, utilities, investment banking, business consulting, accountancy, and legal services. Accenture, the management consultancy, for example, has a staff of 75,000 in 47 countries and the accountancy firm PricewaterhouseCooper has 160,000 employees in 150 countries. The emergence of new services, such as software, back-office services, call centres and data entry, has also contributed to the relative growth of services in FDI.

Regional boundaries

The 'triad' economies, the EU, the USA, and Japan, have long accounted for the bulk of global FDI. Rugman's (2001) analysis of the world's largest 500 MNCs indicates that a total of 434 are from the triad. This total has increased from 414 in 1990 indicating the permanency of the triad hegemony. Together the 434 triad MNCs currently account for 90 per cent of the world's stock of FDI, meaning that developed countries are the primary destinations for FDI. The 434 triad MNCs carry out half of all world trade, often in the form of intra-company sales between subsidiaries. However, it should be borne in mind that most of them first and foremost operate in a strong triad home base. In other words, much of the production, marketing and other business activities of MNCs is organized by regional boundaries rather than being truly global so that the bulk of FDI is concentrated within regions and neighbouring regions. In North America there are strong FDI links with Latin America and the Caribbean; Japan with Asia, whereas for the EU links are strong within Western Europe with some recent strengthening with Central and Eastern Europe. Furthermore, MNCs generally have large portfolios of purely domestic assets. Even the largest MNCs have on average nearly half of their total assets in domestic assets whereas for many smaller MNCs the proportion is substantially larger. Rugman (2001: 10) may be overstating his case somewhat when he concludes that:

> There is no evidence for globalization, that is, of a system of free trade with fully integrated world markets. Instead the evidence on the performance and activities of multinational enterprises demonstrates that international business is triad-based and triad-related. . . . European, North American and Asian manufacturing and service companies compete viciously for market share, lobbying their governments for shelter and subsidies.

However, Rugman's perspective is a useful antidote to naïve notions of the geographical scope of most MNCs, particularly smaller MNCs.

National identity

Despite the increase in globalization most MNCs have home bases that give them resolutely national identities. General Electric and Microsoft are clearly American just as Honda and Toyota are Japanese. Only one in five of the boards of ostensibly global US companies include a non-US national. Sixty per cent of Honda's sales are outside Japan, but only 10 per cent of its shares are held by non-Japanese. Toyota has forty-one manufacturing subsidiaries in twenty-four countries but no foreign managers among its vice-presidents in Tokyo. Mergers and acquisitions have little impact. DaimlerChrysler, hailed in 1998 as a merger of equals, soon became a German company with German executives taking control of the US operation while many of Chrysler's most senior executives either left or were forced out. Even within Europe with its single market and single currency pan-European companies, free of national demarcations, remain elusive. One typical variant is that pan-European ventures end up being dominated by one nationality. Thus Alstom, the transport and power engineering group, started out as a British-French joint venture but is now dominated by French executives, with the UK managers playing a junior role.

There are exceptions such as Royal Dutch/Shell and Unilever, two long-standing Anglo-Dutch groups with bi-national identities. But there are few companies with genuinely multinational identities. The most obvious exceptions tend to be located within professional services. The Boston Consulting Group now has more partners outside the USA and also generates two thirds of its revenues outside the USA. However, these are nationally owned partnerships that confer a degree of local independence. Outside professional services multinational identities are more elusive. However, because an increasing number of MNCs have more employees outside their home base country creating some inclusive corporate identity is increasingly important in order to enhance knowledge flow from subsidiary to corporate headquarters. ABB, the Swedish-Swiss engineering conglomerate, from its launch in 1988 has always insisted that it has no national axe to grind. It has a tiny corporate headquarters of only 100 employees in Zurich, an executive board comprising a variety of nationalities, and English as its working language. Swedish Percy Barnevik, ABB's first chief executive, famously insisted on fellow Swedes writing to him in English. And yet it took fourteen years from its inception and a substantial crisis before a non-Swede, Jürgen Dormann, became its chief executive.

The IHRM challenge

MNCs have a number of advantages over local companies. Their size provides them with the opportunity to achieve vast economies of scale in manufacturing and product development. Their global presence also exposes them to new ideas and opportunities regardless of where they occur. Moreover, their location in many countries can be used as a bargaining chip in obtaining favourable conditions from governments anxious to preserve inward investment and jobs. However, with all the advantages size confers there are also the potential liabilities of slowness and bureaucracy. MNCs are not necessarily successful. Indeed the Templeton Global Performance Index (Gestrin *et al* 2000) reveals that in 1998 while the foreign activities of the world's largest MNCs accounted on average for 36 per cent of their assets and 39 per cent of revenues, they only generated 27 per cent of their profits. Over 60 per cent of these companies achieved lower profitability abroad than at home. The report concludes that many MNCs are not particularly good at managing their foreign activities, particularly in regard to digesting acquisitions, and that strong core competencies do not guarantee international commercial success. Furthermore, the gap between the best- and worst-performing companies is growing.

Over 40 years ago Hymer (1960/1976) raised the question of why MNCs existed at all given that they are 'playing away from home'. Not only do they often have to compete head-on with domestic companies that often enjoy some degree of protection by national regulators, but they are also, at least initially, lacking in institutional and cultural insight.

When Wal-Mart moved into Germany it had little feel for German shoppers, who care more about price than having their bags packed, or German staff, who hid in the toilets to escape the morning Wal-Mart cheer. In the wake of losses of $300 million a year, John Menzer, head of Wal-Mart International, admitted, 'We screwed up in Germany'. As of 2004 Wal-Mart has yet to post a profit for its German operation. Indeed Wal-Mart epitomizes the performance difficulties faced by US MNCs when they move beyond culturally proximate countries such as Canada and the United Kingdom. Ruigrok and Warner (2003) suggest that in terms of performance-degree of internationalization US firms are usually characterized by an inverted J-curve. Initial internationalization into culturally related countries results in a performance improvement. However, as they expand into culturally non-proximate locations there is a decline in performance. For newly internationalizing European and Japanese firms the evidence suggests an upright U (Lu and Beamish 2004; Ruigrok and Warner 2003). This is because European and Japanese firms have to target culturally non-proximate markets from the outset. Performance improvement is dependent on learning.

Ruigrok and Warner (2003: 80) pose the following question: 'Given that firms learn on their way to high degrees of internationalization, a central question arises: which are the organizational capabilities most critical for successful operation in increasingly complex foreign environments?' Simply possessing some unique strategic capability, whether it is advanced technological expertise, marketing competencies or scale economies, is insufficient. MNCs must also have organizational capabilities that enable them to learn and respond effectively to new environments (Makino *et al.* 2004). Without these it is doubtful whether MNCs can leverage more from their assets via subsidiaries than they could through other entry strategies such as exporting or licensing.

In essence the challenge for MNCs is to retain their size, which gives them economies of scale and scope, and take advantage of their global reach which enables them to exploit new opportunities and ideas wherever they may occur. They also need to maintain their multiple country locations that not only grant them flexibility in deciding where they will source products, but which also enable them to bargain with local governments. However, it is these strengths that also represent their liabilities in that large, globally distributed companies can easily become bureaucratic and therefore non-entrepreneurial and insensitive to the many different environments in which they operate (Birkinshaw 2000). Indeed Lu and Beamish (2004) suggest that in the long run the association between geographic diversification and performance can be depicted as having a horizontal S-shape. As we observed above, in the early phase of internationalization there is a negative association. Given that learning takes place, the association becomes positive. However, beyond a threshold of international expansion, returns diminish due to the limits of the firm and its management. That is, at some point the transaction costs involved in co-ordinating and controlling geographically dispersed units outweigh the benefits of international diversification.

In broad terms the remit of IHRM is to address the liabilities involved in the various stages of internationalization by developing a corporate culture that stimulates commitment to the company, entrepreneurial attitudes and a non-parochial mindset. This must be supported by appropriate reward and career systems. Added to this is the need for structures that match the strategic thrust of the company by defining the basic lines of reporting and responsibility. However, unlike purely domestic companies the context within which MNCs operate involves national cultural differences, distance and regulations that vary by national setting and which may be biased against foreign companies.

In short, MNCs must have the capacity to respond to local conditions as well as the ability to benefit from their size through the integration of their activities. As we shall discuss in the next sections how much local responsiveness and how much global integration is needed may vary. IHRM systems must be consistently responsive to these two fundamental issues.

A framework for SIHRM

In a recent paper Schuler and Jackson (2005) reflected on the peculiarities and demands of HRM within the context of the MNC (which they refer to as the multinational enterprise, i.e. MNE) as opposed to a purely domestic firm:

> As is true for firms operating in a single country or region, MNEs strive to develop HRM systems that fit the contours of the present context – a context that is much more complex and multifaceted (than that of domestic firms) – yet anticipate the future concerns of its varied stakeholders. That is, effectively managing human resources in MNEs requires a framework for strategic international HRM (Evans *et al.* 2002; Briscoe and Schuler 2004). Strategic international IHRM has been defined as 'Human Resource Management issues, functions, policies and practices that result from the strategic activities of MNEs and that impact the international concerns and goals of those enterprises.
>
> (Schuler *et al.* 1993)

The practice of strategic international HRM involves the management of inter-unit linkages and internal operations (Bartlett & Ghoshal 1989). Managing inter-unit linkages is needed to integrate, control, and co-ordinate the units of a firm that are scattered throughout the globe (Ghoshal 1987; Galbraith 1992). Internal operations, on the other hand, encompass the remaining issues. For example, internal operations include the way a unit operates in concert with the laws, culture, society, politics, economy, and general environment of a particular location (Ballon 1992; Tung & Thomas 2003).

The purpose of the next section is to develop a framework for strategic international HRM (SIHRM) which encompasses both the management of inter-unit linkages and internal operations. The key points in this section are that:

- an SIHRM framework must be sensitive to the resources within the subsidiary as well as the parent;
- the overall strategy guiding the relationship between the two may vary considerably; the local environment must be taken into account.

The issue of fit and flexibility

Adler & Ghadar (1990: 245) have argued that: 'The central issue for MNCs is not to identify the best international HRM policy per se, but rather to find the best *fit* between the firm's external environment, its overall strategy, and its HRM policy and implementation'.

On the other hand there are other researchers in SIHRM (e.g. Schuler *et al.* 1993) who caution that as neither the external environment nor the overall strategy are static there is a need for flexibility as well as fit. In particular this manifests itself as an ongoing tension between the need for MNC integration (i.e. inter-unit linkages) and differentiation (i.e. the need for each subsidiary to adapt to its local environment).

Taylor *et al.* (1996) have developed a model of the determinants of the SIHRM system of an MNC which we, with modifications, will adopt because of its sensitivity to this integration-local adaptation tension (see Figure 5.1).

The principal dependent variable in the Taylor *et al.* model is the degree of similarity between parent and affiliate HRM systems. The first part of this two-fold model is at the level of the parent company and has as its focus the parent company's SIHRM orientation. By SIHRM orientation Taylor *et al.* (1996: 966) mean 'the general philosophy or approach taken by top management of the MNC in the design of its overall IHRM system, particularly the HRM systems to be used in its overseas affiliates'. This approach will, for example, determine whether the MNC will have an IHRM director at headquarters or whether HRM will be decentralized. It will also determine whether there will be mechanisms designed to enable sharing of HRM policies and practices with and between subsidiaries. The MNC's SIHRM orientation determines its overall approach to managing the tension between the need for integration and the pressure for local adaptation.

Taylor *et al.* argue that the choice of SIHRM orientation is the product of the firm's international strategy coupled to top management's beliefs concerning the

Corporate SIHRM

Subsidiarys SIHRM

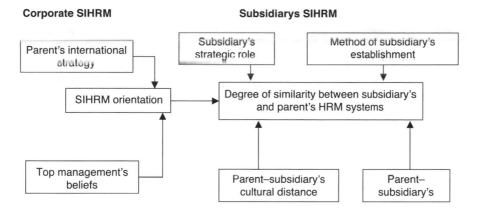

Figure 5.1 A model of SIHRM

Source: Adapted from Taylor *et al.* 1996: 965

existence and context generalizability of its HRM competence. Let us start with the role of MNC strategy.

The role of MNC strategy

It is usual to differentiate four generic variants of centrally-determined MNC strategy: the international, the multi-domestic, the global, and the transnational. Each is associated with specific structures and specific forms of SIHRM.

The international strategy

The simplest form of MNC strategy involves the establishment of a dedicated international division charged with the responsibility of overseeing and managing the international activities of the firm. These activities are not considered as integral to the parent company which remains almost exclusively focused on its home market. Initially the responsibilities of the international division may involve no more than overseeing the export of the company's products. That is, it is charged with attending to tariff and trade issues and securing and monitoring foreign agents. However, in succeeding phases sales offices are opened and manufacturing capacity established in order to better serve the company's most important markets.

Characteristic of foreign operations is that they have an adjunct or peripheral function. Despite usually being headed by parent company staff, i.e. expatriates, they are not integrated into any of the company's business units. The lack of global strategy means that decisions relating to foreign operations are made in an opportunistic or ad hoc manner.

Another trait is that they lack the resources and mandate to adapt, let alone develop, the product to any significant extent. There is a one-way transference of technology and knowledge from the parent company to its foreign subsidiaries resulting in a low degree of local responsiveness. The approach is to exploit home-country innovations in order to achieve incremental sales rather than to develop flexible or high-scale operations. In their early days this was how Colgate Palmolive and many other American companies, such as Kraft and Procter & Gamble, operated in Europe. As Vernon (1966) suggests, the international strategy is essentially a transitory strategy that is eventually superseded by one of the other three types of strategy we will now review. As such it will not figure in our discussion of SIHRM.

The multi-domestic strategy

The main driver behind Nestlé's approach to expansion outside of Switzerland was entirely different to that underlying the international. With a small domestic market expansion could only come from establishing operations abroad. In other words foreign activities were never viewed as purely incremental and this has influenced the way it has traditionally structured its operations in currently over eighty countries. Today these operations account for 98 per cent of Nestlé's $47 billion turnover. Founded in 1866, by the early 1900s it had operations in Britain, Germany, Spain, and the United States. This expansion was accompanied by a profound recognition that as tastes in human foodstuffs vary enormously from country to country, centralization was to be kept to a minimum. From its earliest days Nestlé delegated brand management authority to country managers who independently adjusted the marketing and manufacturing strategies in accordance with local tastes and preferences. In 1994 of its 8,000 brands only 750 were registered in more than one country. Even research and development was decentralized so that currently some eighteen R&D centres are located around the world. As for IT, Nestlé has 100 IT centres round the world providing separate IT support functions for most of the countries in which it operates. Currently, of its 230,000 employees only 1,600 are employed in Vevey at Nestlé's headquarters.

As such Nestlé has been labelled a multi-domestic company characterized by relatively weak global integration and pronounced local responsiveness. In more recent years though the latent tension between integration and local adaptation has come to the surface with Nestlé attempting to achieve scale efficiencies through consolidation and standardization of its global business processes. For example, for the first time in its history, Nestlé's Vevey headquarters since 2000 has a system in place that enables headquarters to know how many raw materials its subsidiaries buy, in total, from around the world. As a consequence Nestlé headquarters is increasingly able to negotiate contracts on behalf of the company as a whole and centralize its production. In other words Nestlé is moving away from an overtly multi-domestic strategy towards what we will refer to as a global strategy.

In their own ways this has been the case for many other European multi domestics such as Philips, Shell, Danone, and Unilever. It has also been the case for a number of American car manufacturers such as GM and Ford. However, any transition from a multi-domestic strategy to a global strategy is usually a slow process. Subsidiary managers used to running local fiefdoms rarely give up their prerogative to forge their own local strategies willingly. Furthermore, as Nestlé itself is well aware, the need to be responsive to different local consumer tastes can never be ignored. As Peter Brabeck, Nestlé chief executive comments: 'The emotional link to the local consumer is extremely important to our business. That is why it remains a fragmented industry and that is why we try to stay as close as possible to local consumers'.

The global strategy

By a global strategy we mean that the major line of authority lies with parent company product managers who have a global responsibility for their product line. Japanese MNCs, particularly in the electronics, computer, and automobile industries, have invariably adopted the global product division structure from the outset. Highly centralized, scale intensive manufacturing and R&D operations are leveraged through worldwide exports of standardized global products. When foreign subsidiaries are established there is no intention that they should respond actively to local market demands over and above that which is strictly necessary. In terms of strategy formulation, product development and key manufacturing subsidiaries have no more than a minor status being either off-shore (low-cost production) or server (market entry) plants.

Sony is a typical global type of MNC. It makes most of its value-added high-tech products, such as chips and personal computers in Japan, where it can monitor quality and where it has location-bound advantages not least in terms of research and development. When products become highly standardized and are no longer dependent on Sony's location-bound advantages, their production is transferred to other locations either to lower costs or to improve market entry. In relation to Europe, Sony has transferred production of audio-visual products, such as televisions and computer displays to purpose-built greenfield sites that have been managed largely according to Sony's management principles. The standardized capabilities involved are easily transferred through training programmes.

The mentality underlying the global-product division is of course far from exclusively Japanese. Ikea's history is one of having ignored local taste and bucking fragmented furniture markets by producing scale intensive globally standardized furniture. Despite serving a range of markets from Russia to North America, purchasing, distribution, and design functions remain centrally controlled and served by Swedes. Similarly General Electric functions on the basis of a distinctly uniform corporate mentality although this does not preclude non-Americans. Its ten businesses are global businesses each with its own president who co-ordinates and integrates activities worldwide.

The transnational strategy

In the early 1980s the global strategy was increasingly regarded as mandatory. With increasing competition as a consequence of decreased tariff barriers product life cycles had shortened dramatically thereby escalating research and development costs. The ability to operate under such a cost burden entailed an expanded scale of production over and above what a firm's domestic market was capable of absorbing. As such foreign markets had to be sought out just in order to 'enter the game'. A further reason to seek out foreign markets was that without a presence in every market competitors could achieve dominant positions that granted high profit margins. Dominance and strong profitability in one or more markets could then be surreptitiously used to subsidize loss-making entries into other markets.

At the end of the 1980s, however, it was argued by, for example Bartlett & Ghoshal (1989), that important as the global integration dimension is, there is also an increasing need to achieve close proximity to local markets or customers to be able to adapt products to local tastes. Customers are no longer prepared to accept a 'one-size-fits-all' product strategy. Furthermore, not only do customers have their idiosyncratic national preferences, host governments increasingly expect both local content and transference of technology. In terms of this perspective global off-shore plants based on cheap labour or global server plants making minor adjustments are no longer the critical modes of internationalization. Instead subsidiaries increasingly involve an ability to adapt and enhance products in line with local market demands.

The notion that what is increasingly driving the internationalization of firms' activities is their need to obtain and create new competencies in order to support and improve overall innovativeness, is viewed by Cantwell (1996) as representing a 'new evolutionary approach' for understanding the strategic intent of MNCs. No longer are MNCs to be exclusively viewed as agents of unidirectional international technology transfer. Instead they should be viewed as being driven by a need to develop technology and knowledge that is met by leveraging their presence in foreign locations to generate internationally co-ordinated learning processes. This is particularly the case in regard to technologically intensive industries such as pharmaceuticals and electronics, where levels of sophistication make labour costs increasingly less of an issue than skills and creativity. So, for example, while Nokia has been driven by the need to expand the market for its product it has also formalized the learning opportunities internationalization grants it by establishing learning centres outside of Finland, in China, Italy, and Singapore.

The requirements for global integration, local responsiveness and worldwide learning meant, according to Bartlett & Ghoshal, that a new MNC strategy, the transnational, was emerging:

> While some products and processes must still be developed centrally for worldwide use and others must be created locally in each environment to meet purely local demands, MNCs must increasingly use their access to multiple centres of technologies and familiarity with diverse customer preferences in different countries to create truly transnational innovations.
>
> (Bartlett & Ghoshal 1995: 127)

Bartlett and Ghoshal took ABB as their core example of this new MNC form. ABB was a heavy engineering firm that was formed in 1988 as the result of a cross-border merger between Asca AB of Sweden and BBC Brown Boveri Ltd of Switzerland. Its first chief executive officer Percy Barnevik expounded a strategic vision that, with its focus on reaping global efficiencies, while being locally responsive and ensuring worldwide learning, constituted 'almost a perfect description of the transnational' (Bartlett & Ghoshal 1995: 788). In Barnevik's words:

> We want to be global and local, big and small, radically decentralized with centralized reporting and control. . . . You want to be able to optimize a business globally – to specialize in the production of components, to drive economies of scale as far as you can, to rotate managers and technologists around the world to share expertise and solve problems. But you also want to have deep local roots everywhere you operate – building products in the countries where you sell them, recruiting the best local talent from the universities, working with the local government to increase exports. If you build such an organization, you create a business advantage that's damn difficult to copy.
>
> (Taylor 1991)

Bartlett & Ghoshal (1995) observed local responsiveness at ABB in its radical decentralization of assets and responsibilities to local operating units. Managers of the local operating units had a mandate to build their businesses as if they owned them with managers being allowed to inherit results. They also observed global integration in that the mandate of the business area manager was designed so as to facilitate horizontal integration between units with respect to knowledge, export markets, and production facilities. 'He decides which factories are going to make what products, what export markets each factory will serve, how the factories

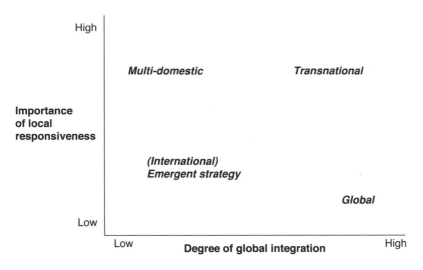

Figure 5.2 MNC strategy in terms of degree of local responsiveness and global integration

should pool their expertise and research funds for the benefit of the business worldwide' (Bartlett & Ghoshal 1995: 853). That is, any local unit may be upgraded by a business area manager to take on a central task or requested to contribute its expertise to the realization of a task at another unit.

Figure 5.2 summarizes the four generic MNC strategies we have reviewed in relation to global integration and local responsiveness.

Top management's beliefs and SIHRM orientation

Taylor *et al.* (1996: 969) define top management's perception of HRM as 'the belief, expressed in corporate as well as personal communications, that the firm's way of managing its employees gives the company an advantage over its competitors'. However, in addition to this perception of HRM competence is the issue of whether top management believes that this competence is relevant beyond its national borders. A lack of any such belief would mean that there will be no attempt to apply its HRM competence in its subsidiaries. This is often a characteristic of multi-domestic MNCs, just as a belief in the efficacy of its HRM applied beyond its borders is associated with global MNCs. In other words top management beliefs will usually precede and determine strategy formulation.

The interaction of top management's HRM beliefs and choice of strategy results in characteristic SIHRM orientations. Taylor *et al.* (1996) distinguish between three different forms of SIHRM orientation: adaptive, exportive, and integrative.

An adaptive SIHRM orientation is one in which top management of the MNC encourages the development of HRM systems that reflect subsidiary local environment (low degree of global integration and high degree of local responsiveness). In MNCs utilising this approach there would be little or no transfer of HRM philosophy, policies or practices either from the parent firm to its foreign subsidiaries, or between its subsidiaries. It is an approach that is very much in evidence in multi-domestic MNCs.

An exportive SIHRM orientation is one in which top management of the MNC prefers a comprehensive transfer of the parent firm's HRM system to its foreign subsidiaries (high degree of global integration and low degree of local responsiveness). In effect the aim is to replicate HRM policies and practices across subsidiaries with the parent determining those policies and practices. In short, unlike MNCs with an adaptive SIHRM approach, there is a high degree of control by the parent company over a subsidiary's system. In general this is the approach adopted by global MNCs, particularly in their early phase.

MNCs with an integrative SIHRM orientation attempt to take HRM 'best practices' regardless of whether they have originated in the parent firm or in the subsidiaries and apply them throughout the organization, while also allowing for some local differentiation, in the creation of a worldwide HRM system (high degree of global integration and high degree of local responsiveness). Thus, transfer of HRM policies and practices occurs, but it is just as likely to occur between foreign subsidiaries as between the parent company and its subsidiaries. In other words, transfers can go in any direction. This SIHRM orientation is associated with the transnational MNC and involves moderate control by the parent company over the subsidiary's HRM system.

MNCs do not necessarily retain their SIHRM orientation throughout their lifespan. First, the beliefs of top management concerning the value and context specificity of parent company HRM competence can change as a result of international experience. Second, the firm may change its international strategy as a response to new technological opportunities or competitive pressures. Thus, for example, ABB is today pursuing a global strategy rather than a transnational strategy. However, with this proviso, SIHRM orientations are reasonably stable not least because changes to strategy involve costs.

The subsidiary's HRM system

The second part of Taylor et al.'s SIHRM model is concerned with subsidiary-level influences. The main point to this part of the model is to point out that because of subsidiary-level influences the SIHRM orientation will not be applied uniformly to all subsidiaries. The first of these influences is the subsidiary's strategic role.

Figure 5.3 distinguishes between different types of subsidiaries according to the degree of knowledge resources they possess. The framework distinguishes the two types of subsidiary common to MNCs pursuing a global strategy: off-shores and servers. Additionally the framework includes a second type of server subsidiary. This is associated with the multi-domestic type of MNC and is different from the global server in that it has more latitude to develop resources that enable it to significantly adapt products for its local markets. Subsidiaries of the more transitory international organization type of MNC do not feature, but in principle they will fall into one of these three categories.

Figure 5.3 also includes a second dimension, the learning contribution of the subsidiary to the MNC. For all the above three subsidiary types this is low indicating that even multi-domestics have rarely systematically attempted to leverage learning from their various subsidiaries. However, MNCs have increasingly recognized that there are competitive advantages in being able to tap into and integrate critical knowledge resources wherever they may be located. MNCs are thus seeking to establish regional centres of excellence in order to tap into world-class specialist knowledge from the local scientific community, including competitors as well as universities, from where it flows back to the company's central R&D site and beyond to other sites in the firm's global network (Kuemmerle 1997). For example, nearly all of the big European pharmaceutical companies have established an R&D presence in America, particularly in high-tech clusters such as Boston and San Diego. Likewise American pharmaceutical companies, such as Pfizer, have European research facilities. Pfizer's UK research centre has been responsible for the discovery of three of its recent blockbuster drugs. The result is

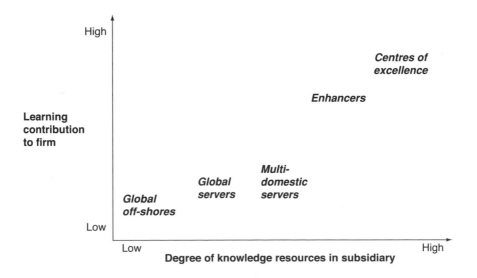

Figure 5.3 A categorization of foreign subsidiaries: degree of knowledge resources and learning contribution to the MNC as a whole

that in addition to the three subsidiary types we have distinguished one can discern subsidiaries with a developmental capacity, that is subsidiaries that not only have the capability to adapt products, but which also have the resources to enhance them or even the capability to single handedly develop new products (Kuemmerle 1997). In the latter case it is the subsidiary that is the centre of excellence within the firm for particular products and technologies (Birkinshaw 1997). Figure 5.3 illustrates the position of enhancer and centres-of-excellence subsidiaries in relation to off-shores and servers.

The resource dependence of the parent company on its subsidiaries is highest for those subsidiaries with the greatest outflow of resources to the rest of the MNC: enhancers and centres of excellence. At the same time, greater reliance by the parent company on the subsidiary will increase the power of the subsidiary over the parent company. Hence, the parent company will attempt to exercise high levels of control over these subsidiaries, but these subsidiaries will simultaneously have the power to resist these control efforts. In the case of powerful centres of excellence – powerful in the sense that there is little resource dependence on the parent company combined with resource dependence of the parent on the subsidiary – there will only be a moderate degree of similarity of subsidiary and parent's HRM systems.

In addition to the strategic role of the subsidiary, the degree of similarity between the parent company's and subsidiary HRM systems will be influenced by three other factors that constrain the exercise of the control of the parent company. The first of these is the method of establishment – it is easier to impose HR practices on a Greenfield site than on an acquisition. The second and third involve the institutional and cultural contexts of the subsidiary: the greater the institutional and cultural distance between the country of the parent company and the host country of the affiliate, the harder it is to transfer HR practices.

In relation to the issue of institutional and cultural distance Gooderham *et al* (2004) have shown that in terms of Europe, US MNCs radically modify their 'calculative' HRM practices (e.g. performance-related pay) in those countries where they experience substantial institutional distance such as Denmark, Norway, and Germany. These countries have powerful trade unions and legislation that narrow the scope for US MNCs to implement their brand of HRM in their subsidiaries. In contrast, in countries where the institutional and cultural distance is low, such as the UK and Ireland, there is no modification of HRM practices.

These differences are less of an issue for multi-domestic MNCs which have an adaptive SIHRM largely because of their sensitivity to institutional and cultural differences. Similar to the parent company's SIHRM orientation, the subsidiary's HRM system does not remain static. The strategic role of the subsidiary may change with server subsidiaries evolving into centres-of excellence, or centres-of-excellence losing their cutting-edge technological advantage and evolving into server subsidiaries. In terms of the institutional and cultural environment, perhaps particularly in regard to the former, changes may take place that makes it more viable for an MNC to seek a greater degree of integration of HRM systems.

Summary

In this chapter we have explored SIHRM on the basis of a two-fold model that distinguishes the parent company's SIHRM orientation and subsidiary-level influences. In regard to the first part of the model we emphasized the parent company strategy. This is crucial to an understanding of the degree of MNC-wide integration of HRM systems and practices. For MNCs pursuing a multi-domestic strategy there will be many locally determined variants of HRM, whereas for MNCs with a global strategy there will be considerable MNC-wide integration. In terms of the corporate HR function this will manifest itself in that the latter will be characterized by large well-resourced HR departments which are engaged in a wide range of HR activities. In the former, HR departments will be relatively small and there will be a more limited range of activities (Scullion & Starkey 2000). MNCs attempting a transnational strategy will have medium-sized departments. In addition to the strategy factor, the SIHRM orientation of the parent company is also informed by top management's beliefs in the competitive advantage and the MNC-wide relevance of its HRM systems and practices.

This chapter has emphasized that to focus purely on the SIHRM orientation of the parent company is inadequate for an understanding of MNC-wide HRM. There are a number of subsidiary-level influences which must be taken into account. The first of these involves the resource dependence of the parent company on its subsidiaries: centres-of-excellence have the power to resist integration, whereas global off-shores and servers do not. The second involves entry mode: acquisitions are generally considerably more of a challenge in terms of integration than greenfield subsidiaries. The third and fourth entail institutional and cultural distance: the greater the degree of institutional or cultural distance the more difficult it is to achieve MNC-wide integration.

Finally it is important to note that both the SIHRM orientation of the parent company and the various subsidiary-level influences are not fixed. They evolve over time. As we indicated learning enables MNCs to develop the organizational capabilities they need to improve their international performance over time (the so-called U-curve). The development of these capabilities will impinge on top management's beliefs concerning the viability of MNC-wide HRM systems and choice of strategy. The development of these capabilities is dependent on the competences of the international managers available to the MNC. It is their behaviours that set in motion the processes that facilitate the realization of the IHRM strategy.

References

Ballon, R. J. 1992. *Foreign Competition in Japan*. New York: Routledge.

Bartlett, C. A. & Ghoshal, S. 1989, *Managing Across Borders: The Transnational Solution*. Boston: Harvard Business School Press.

Bartlett, C. A. & Ghoshal, S. 1995. *Transnational Management: Text, Cases, and Readings in Cross-Border Management* (2nd ed.). Chicago, IL: Irwin.

Birkinshaw, J. 1997. Entrepreneurship in multinational corporations: the characteristics of subsidiary initiatives. *Strategic Management Journal*, 18(3): 207–229.

Birkinshaw, J. 2000. The structures behind global companies. Part 10 of Mastering Management. *Financial Times*, December 4.

Briscoe, D. R. & Schuler, R. S. 2004. *International Human Resource Management*. London: Routledge.

Cantwell, J. 1996. Transnational corporations and innovatory activities. In *Transnational Corporations and World Development*. Published by Routledge on behalf of the UNCTAD Division on Transnational Corporations and Investment. London: International Thomson Business Press.

Davis, L. N. & Meyer, K. E. 2004. Subsidiary research and development and the local environment. *International Business Review*, 13(2): 359–382.

Dunning, J. H. 1977. Trade location of economic activity and the MNE: A search for an eclectic approach. In B. Ohlin, P.-O. Hesselborn & P. M. Wijkman (eds.), *The International Allocation of Economic Activity*. London: Macmillan Press.

Dunning, J. H. 1993. *Multinational Enterprises and the Global Economy*. Reading, MA: Addison-Wesley.

Dunning, J. H. 1997. The sourcing of technological advantage by multinational enterprises. In K. Macharzina, M.-J. Oesterle & J. Wolf (eds.), *Global Business in the Information Age. Proceedings of the 23rd Annual EIBA Conference*. 63–101. Stuttgart: European International Business Academy.

Evans, P., Pucik, V. & Barsoux, J.-L. 2002. *The Global Challenge*. London: McGraw-Hill.

Galbraith, J. R. 1992. *The Value Adding Corporation*. Center for Effective Organizations, University of Southern California.

Gestrin, M. V., Knight, R. F. & Rugman, A. 2000. *Templeton Global Performance Index*. Oxford: Oxford University Press.

Ghoshal, S. 1987. Global strategy: an organizing framework. *Strategic Management Journal*, 8: 425–440.

Gooderham, P. N., Nordhaug, O. & Ringdal, K. 2004. The local context for US subsidiaries in Europe. In F. McDonald, M. Mayer & T. Buck (eds.), *The Process of Internationalisation*, pp. 135–148. Basingstoke: Palgrave Macmillan.

Hymer, S. H. 1960/1976. *The International Operations of National Firms: A Study of Direct Foreign Investment*. Cambridge, MA: MIT Press.

Kuemmerle,W. 1997. Building effective R&D capabilities abroad. *Harvard Business Review*, March–April, 75 (2): 23–24.

Lu, J. W. & Beamish, P. W. 2004. International diversification and firm performance: the S-curve hypothesis. *Academy of Management Journal*, 47(4): 598–609.

Makino, S., Isobe, T. & Chan, C. M. 2004. Does country matter? *Strategic Management Journal*, 25(10): 1027–1043.

Rugman, A. M. 2001. The illusion of the global company. Part 13 of Mastering Management. *Financial Times*, January 8.

Ruigrok, W. & Warner, H. 2003. Internationalization and performance: An organizational learning perspective. *Management International Review*, 43(1): 63–83.

Schuler, R. S. & Jackson, S.E. 2005. A quarter-century review of human resource management in the US. The growth in importance of the international perspective. *Management Revue*, 16(1): 11–35.

Schuler, R. S., Dowling, P. & De Cieri, H. 1993. An integrative framework of strategic international human resource management. *International Journal of Human Resource Management International Review*, 4(4): 717–764.

Scullion, H. & Starkey, K. 2000. The changing role of the corporate human resource function in the international firm. *International Journal of Human Resource Management International Review*, 11(6): 1–21.

Taylor, S., Beechler, S. & Napier, N. 1996. Toward an integrative model of strategic international human resource management. *Academy of Management Review*, 21(4): 959–984.

Tung, R. L. & Thomas, D. C. 2003. Human resource management in a global world: the contingency framework extended. In D. Tjosvold & K. Leung (eds.), *Cross-cultural Management: Foundations and Future*. Aldershot, UK: Ashgate.

Vernon, R. 1966. International investment and international trade in the product cycle. *Quarterly Journal of Economics*, 80: 190–207.

6

HRM in small and medium enterprises: typical, but typically ignored

ELENI STAVROU-COSTEA AND BO MÅNSON

Introduction

The implicit point of reference in most academic writing is the large organization with its functional differentiation, the relatively large number of organizational members and the relatively elaborated specialization. Yet, in terms of sheer numbers these organizations are a clear minority in Europe and most of the world. Instead, small and medium-sized enterprises (SMEs) constitute the majority of organizations. Therefore, it is surprising that this type of organization is not included in scientific research much more often.

The above is true for the human resource management (HRM) discipline as well. Outspoken or latent, much of HR writing relates to the large organization. However, HR departments, functional specialists and formal HR procedures are rarely found at the lower end of SMEs and have a different make up in the larger SMEs. Nevertheless, HRM still has to take place even among the smallest of organizations. Thus, it is interesting to analyze how HRM is done in SMEs throughout Europe.

In this chapter, we provide an overview of the various issues that SMEs face in relation to HRM. In addition, we focus on certain HRM practices that seem particularly important for SME survival and growth. These practices are staffing, training and development, and flexibility. Finally, we provide a country example for each of these practices in order to highlight the socio-cultural aspect in their application.

SMEs in Europe

Definition of SME

SMEs are vital to the world economy. They are key to employment growth as well as the development of the necessary conditions for socioeconomic prosperity. Even though no single definition of an SME exists around the globe, SMEs are considered to be non-subsidiary, independently owned firms with a specific number of employees. In Europe, an SME has to satisfy three main criteria: one is related to the number of employees, the second is related to financial status and the third is related to ownership status. Specifically, SMEs have between 10 and 250 employees, and may even include micro businesses (0–9 employees) in national statistics. Furthermore, they need to generate either a turnover total between 7 and 40 million Euros or a balance sheet total between 5 and 27 million Euros. Finally, the business must be independent, meaning less than 25 per cent owned by one enterprise or jointly by several enterprises. SMEs and micro-firms in the EU constitute 99 per cent of all businesses employing over 65 million people and providing for 53 per cent of all jobs (OECD 2002).

The European Commission has set as its purpose to make the EU the most competitive and dynamic knowledge-based economy in the world, capable of sustainable economic growth with more and better jobs and greater social cohesion. In turn, the need arises for Europe to respond as a unified body to global competition and reestablish its position in the world markets (OECD 2002). SMEs within Europe can contribute to such competitiveness; in this respect, the EU has enacted policies to support SMEs. Among these are the free movement of goods and services, easing of regulatory restrictions, and streamlining of accounting procedures (Mulhern 1995). Furthermore, the European Charter for Small Enterprises has become a key instrument for promoting the interests of small firms and a primary document of European policy.

Within Europe, the wealthier nations have greater-than-average sized SMEs, probably reflecting their ability to exploit economies of scale in their larger markets. However, in general EU businesses tend to be much smaller than those of nations like the US. Furthermore, the Mediterranean countries have the greatest prevalence of smaller firms within Europe. In fact the further north one goes in Europe, the larger average firm size tends to become. To illustrate, Denmark, Germany, France, and Britain have an average enterprise size over double that of Portugal, Spain, Italy, and Greece. The Scandinavian countries have, on average, the largest enterprises of all (Mulhern 1995).

Whether larger or smaller, SMEs usually go through common stages of development and have certain commonalities in terms of sources for assistance, prerequisites for success and HR-related competencies to address. Figure 6.1

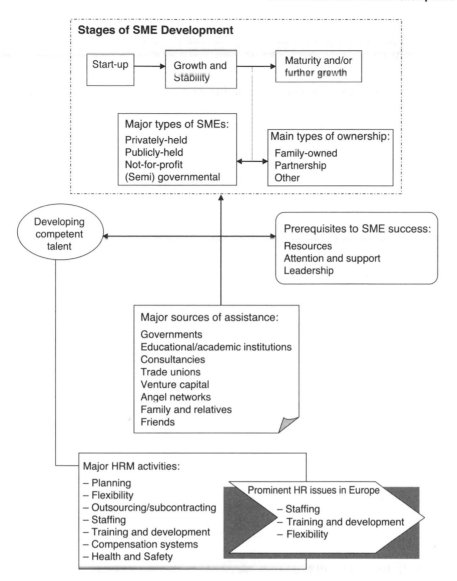

Figure 6.1 Framework of SME development

provides a basic overview of these issues and their relationship to SME success. The rest of the chapter will be organized around this figure.

Stages of SME development

Beginning with the stages of development and ownership structure, SMEs are usually founded by entrepreneurs and often become family-owned as they grow. Other times, they are partnerships or registered as limited companies or corporations and, even less frequently, they may belong to the not-for-profit sector. The more formal their status, the better their chances are for formal recognition and assistance. While the majority of SMEs are owned and run by male entrepreneurs, women constitute a sizeable number of SME founders. The highest shares of self-employed women in Europe are found in Portugal (around 38–40 per cent) and the lowest rate is found in Turkey at just 13 per cent. Women-owned businesses seem to have slower growth rates than male-owned firms, but they tend to be more stable over time and to have better dept-repayment rates. Generally female entrepreneurs tend to pay greater attention to communication, groups, and relationships than male entrepreneurs. In turn, they often use more participative management than their male counterparts (Drew *et al.* 1998). In fact, female entrepreneurship is one of the objectives promoted by the European Commission (OECD 2002).

Whether run by female or male entrepreneurs, given their size and ownership structures, SMEs are quite flexible and can play an important role in a country's innovative performance. To illustrate, entrepreneurial small firms are considered more successful than non-entrepreneurial organizations because the former are more proactive, more innovative and prepared to take greater risks. Furthermore, entrepreneurs are perceived as succeeding through their adoption of a strategy grounded in innovative behaviours which generate new positions for their organizations within a market sector. These views are quantitatively validated through studies showing that entrepreneurial firms achieve a higher sales growth rate than their non-entrepreneurial counterparts (Chaston *et al.* 2001).

Major sources of assistance

Nevertheless, SMEs often lack the resources to undertake extensive R&D projects or organizational change when warranted by market forces. In addition, SMEs face difficulties related to financing, especially during the start up phase or even to minimize late payments (Mulhern 1995). Subsidized loans to SMEs are generally fairly small throughout Europe so quite often, as shown in Figure 6.1, these firms need to look for alternative sources of financing such as trade unions, leasing companies, personal or family funds or friends. Seed capital funds have been developed in many countries to assist with high-risk projects, and local governments often support venture capital initiatives or business angel networks.

Fortunately, many SMEs seem to make the shift towards a more global orientation even if their markets are more local. For example, approximately one third of European SMEs over the past five years have reported an increasing number of international business contacts and have accounted between 24–32 per cent of turnover from cross-border activities. At the same time, such firms need assistance in meeting the challenges of a global market. Partly, such assistance needs to come from local governments through the provision of the main framework conditions that will support a vibrant SME sector. Some of these conditions include appropriate competition policies, capital and labour markets, taxation regimes, educational systems, and other mechanisms promoting the entrepreneurial spirit. Most governments apply an array of policies and programmes to promote entrepreneurship and boost development of SMEs; however these policies are not uniform throughout Europe. To illustrate, many of the restrictions that still exist in many European countries regarding flexibility, especially contingent work, have been abolished in Denmark (Hjalager 2003). Furthermore, even though a major goal within the EU is to create a pan-European harmonized tax system, today tax regimes vary substantially from country to country. The UK has a relatively favourable tax environment for small business, while France and Sweden have had high tax levels, especially raised through employers' social security contributions. However, France does have, in common with Italy, special schemes to reduce the administrative tax burden on small businesses (Mulhern 1995).

In summary, given their nature, SMEs have some unique challenges to face while at the same time they offer certain unique strengths. If these firms capitalize on their strengths, they can contribute positively and significantly to the EU economy, without ignoring national and organizational idiosyncrasies. At the same time, if these SMEs are indeed the pillars of the EU economy, then special attention should be paid to addressing the challenges they face. In turn, one of the most crucial issues underlying the above discussion involves effective management of their human resources (Chandler & McEvoy 2000).

Prerequisites for SME success

The major strength of SMEs is flexibility in the ways in which they manage human resources. At the same time, among their major challenges is in finding and utilizing human resources effectively and efficiently. As Katz *et al.* (2000: 2) explain, 'At a time of unparalleled technological development, it is the human resources that paradoxically spell success or failure for all firms, and especially entrepreneurial ones'. Competent HR skills are a prerequisite for SME success. Nevertheless, even though researchers and owner-managers recognize the importance of such skills, in practice SMEs lag behind their larger counterparts in developing them. This phenomenon may be attributed to three main interconnected factors: resources, attention, and leadership (see Figure 6.1).

Resources

SMEs have limited recourses at their discretion, especially when compared to the resources of large organizations. Due to their limited size and funds, many SMEs cannot justify full-time HRM professionals to tackle these challenges

(Klaas & Gainey 2000). As a result, HRM activities often become the responsibility of general managers, draining managerial time and resources as well as lacking the necessary expertise to carry out these activities requisitely. While it is positive for general managers to be involved in HR activities, something often missing from large organizations, these activities should not be their primary responsibility. Often, professional employer organizations, temporary employment agencies and outsourcing may offer an alternative solution to SMEs; however careful attention needs to be given in selecting the right services and service providers for them (Longenecker *et al.* 1994). Even utilizing such services is not a simple solution. Part of the issue is that HRM activities are costly and require large investments in financial and other means. If SMEs do not have these means, they cannot compete with their larger counterparts in recruiting, training, retaining, and developing their employees, through either outsourcing or in-house procedures. To illustrate, smaller firms pay lower wages and provide fewer non-wage benefits than large enterprises. As a result, they may not attract the most talented personnel. They are also less likely to have internal labour markets and so they are less able to provide career progression to skilled workers. Hence they are less likely to benefit from skilled personnel, who are more likely to prefer better paid jobs elsewhere (Storey 2002). Williamson (2000) calls this phenomenon legitimacy, explaining that because of their constraints SMEs are less legitimate and in turn less attractive employers than larger firms. Of course it is possible to attract such personnel for other reasons, such as the SME-specific experience or the flexibility.

Attention and support

The second factor is related to the limited attention and support offered to these types of firms in relation to HR. Given the importance of SMEs to the EU economy over the years, the attention they have received from local governments as well as EU administrators on HR-related issues has been delayed. In addition, the practical support they have gained from these authorities on HRM has been inadequate. Equally inadequate is the attention given in the literature to the study of HRM practices among these firms (Heneman *et al.* 2000). Furthermore, a discrepancy seems to exist between the concerns of SMEs and those explored in academic research. For example, recruitment seems to be a main concern among SMEs while only a handful of studies have been conducted on the matter (Williamson 2000; Heneman & Berkley 1999). At the same time, hundreds of studies have explored the issue of recruitment among large organizations (Heneman, Heneman *et al.* 1997). For entrepreneurs, the focus is on recruiting people who fit with the organizational culture and are able to adjust to new roles as the business grows. Compensation seems to be emphasized in the literature at about the same levels as among entrepreneurs. However, entrepreneurs view compensation in a very broad context, to include recognition, quality of life, learning, and psychological characteristics of work. Furthermore, for entrepreneurs, learning and growth include the development of employees who can perform multiple roles during growth periods for the SME (Heneman *et al.* 2000). Another important, yet neglected, issue for entrepreneurs is their ability to balance work with life requirements, especially given the large number of hours they need to spend at work. Connected to this issue is flexibility, not only for owner-managers but employees as well. Finally, training and development, while explored more than the above issues in SME research, has not yet made a strong connection with employee motivation or SME performance (Gibb 1997). From this discussion it is apparent that more emphasis and attention on the HR-related needs of SMEs is warranted, first through research in order to understand the idiosyncratic needs of SMEs in relation to HR and then through practical support in helping SMEs address these needs effectively.

Leadership

The third factor is related to the limited emphasis SME leaders themselves place on the effective and efficient utilization of their human resources. While at the beginning of the organization's life, when they are practically alone or among few employees in the enterprise, founders need to be heavily involved in the daily operations of the enterprise, as the organization grows founders should increasingly delegate responsibilities and focus on organizational strategic issues (Kirby 2003). However, it seems that SME leaders find it difficult to do that, ending up micromanaging their firms. As a result, they often overlook the importance of strategic planning, much less linking HRM to the strategic plans of the organization. Taking this issue one step further, entrepreneurs are unable to plan their exit from and replacement in the firm. Many entrepreneurs are unable to select and appoint their successors, staying in the business until their death and in many cases the tenure of these firms coincides with that of the entrepreneurs' (Stavrou 1999).

However, if an entrepreneur decides to let his/her firm grow, (s)he needs to professionalize his/her management style and plan strategically to meet the changing needs of the growing business. Therefore, unless owner-managers are heavily committed to the planning process, succession planning seems unlikely to be effective. The business-owner is ultimately responsible for the extent of formalization and implementation of a succession planning system in his or her firm. Succession planning is executive planning, the goal of which is to get the right number of properly prepared managers ready to take over when they are needed. Effective executive planning must be a function of selection and development. Selection involves knowing both current and future company needs and matching them with the right person; development deals with broadening the experience and testing the potential of the successors.

Equally important to selecting and developing executives and successors, is the recruitment and development of other personnel. In SMEs these activities center on the fit of these applicants to the existing group structures of the enterprise, as duties and responsibilities in these types of organizations are broader and less specified. Furthermore, interpersonal relationships and personal contacts, even nepotism, prevail in these situations over formal channels of communication (Heneman & Berkley 1999; Koch & Van Straten 1997; Stavrou & Swiercz 1998). These practices are not always necessarily inappropriate for SMEs, but they are certainly context specific. Given the nature of these activities, female entrepreneurs have been reported as more effective than their male counterparts. Similarly, women entrepreneurs seem more effective in their approach towards the training of their personnel, a HR activity also conducted in a more informal manner in SMEs than in larger organizations. Finally, as far as rewards and benefits are concerned, female more than male entrepreneurs tend to motivate employees through innovative techniques such as flexible work arrangements, child-care, verbal rewards, and group incentives (Drew *et al.* 1998).

However, both male and female entrepreneurs need to pay special attention to employee relations, especially when members of the owning family are actively involved in the business. For example, often family relations and loyalty to employees with seniority tend to influence the decisions of owner-managers on the employment and promotion of personnel. In some instances, family relations may be as important a factor as competence in the promotion of employees (Stavrou 2003). Furthermore, family members may experience role confusion between their role as members of the family and their role as employees in the business. Such confusion of roles may include inappropriate challenges or tolerance between family members working in the business. Research demonstrates that role confusions between the family and the business settings, along with failure to establish clear division of labour between family members in the business, can invade each other's territory and make working relationships strenuous (Stavrou & Swiercz 1998).

In turn, leaders of SMEs must place greater emphasis on the effective and efficient utilization of their human resources than they presently do. They need to apply HRM activities requisitely and carefully so that the business thrives in the long run, employees feel secure and fairly treated and family members involved, if any, feel content and able to work effectively in the business.

SMEs and theoretical frameworks

Given the above issues unique to SMEs, a number of theoretical frameworks have been utilized in the literature in order to explore and explain the use of HRM for SME success. One prominent framework is that of Wright & Snell (1998), suggesting fit and flexibility in HRM decisions. SME owners seek employees who fit with the current organizational culture but are flexible enough to adapt to organizational developments. A complementary framework is that of Agency Theory, according to which owners attempt to bring the interests of managers into alignment (Heneman *et al.* 2000). Compensation and staffing practices are two critical approaches to alignment, where business owners look for and develop/ reward managers and employees on the basis of values similar to their own. At the same time, looking at HR practices from the employee point of view may help SMEs design effective HR systems to attract, retain, and develop employees. A third framework, congruent with the other two, is that of Role Theory, where specific roles relate to multiple dimensions of performance. For the SME, flexibility, job, career, innovation, team, family, and growth seem to be important roles.

To summarize, developing competent talent could make the difference between successful and less successful SMEs. To accomplish success, an enterprise needs to pay proper attention to acquiring such talent as well as utilize requisitely the sources of assistance that are at its discretion. HR practices among SMEs do not have to be the same as those of larger organizations. In fact, some of the most successful SMEs in Europe have their own stories to tell (Hermann 1996). Below, the focus will shift onto three very important HRM activities prominent among SMEs in Europe.

Prominent HRM issues concerning SMEs in the European scene

All HRM activities are important for SME success. However, as revealed from the preceding discussions as well as extant literature, staffing, training, and developing employees as well as keeping their activities flexible are among the most important HRM challenges of European SMEs today (Heneman & Berkley 1999; Hornsby & Kuratko 1990; Carrier 1994). These activities are subject to cultural, legislative, and socio-economic considerations at national and organizational levels; and to bargaining patterns, consultative arrangements, and trade union involvement at HRM levels. Therefore, in the pages that follow each of these three practices will be discussed, highlighted by specific country examples. The countries selected, namely Cyprus, the UK, and Sweden, constitute the southeast, west, and northern borders of the EU while at the same time demonstrate three very diverse scenes of the EU environment in general and more specifically in respect to SMEs and their HR practices.

Staffing

Recruiting new employees is one of the biggest challenges facing SMEs and is a key component of organizational success (Klaas *et al.* 2000; Williamson 2000). This challenge has to do with planning for, selecting, and placing potential talent. Effective staffing efforts need to be integrated with organizational goals and are a difficult task for organizations to achieve. To illustrate, selecting the right people is not something one can know until after their placement. In turn, staffing practices for SMEs may involve a two-stage process whereby in the first stage employees are assessed in terms of their fit with the organization and in the second phase employees are assessed as to their adaptability to the future directions of the organization (Heneman *et al.* 2000).

While in the early stages of SMEs, staffing may rely mainly on founder networks, as the business grows these practices tend to include other applicants who have no connection to founders (Williamson 2000). In this respect, viewing recruitment from the perspective of the applicant, gaining important insights as to why applicants select organizations, could help SMEs design recruitment systems to best attract qualified applicants. In doing so, the most important aspect of requisite staffing practices is that they provide management with the necessary tools for selecting the right people for the right place in the organization (Jackson & Schuler 2000). Within this context, security of employment in SMEs may be useful in giving to employees the feeling of long-standing commitment of the organization and its performance. Consequently, employees generate loyalty to the organization and willingness to exert extra efforts for the organization's benefit (Pfeffer & Veiga 1999).

Staffing practices among SMEs are not uniform throughout Europe. They are contingent upon factors such as the state of unemployment, the pool of candidates available, and organizational resources at national levels (Brewster *et al.* 2004). Furthermore, staffing practices vary depending on the socio-political and cultural conditions at national levels. To illustrate, while organizations in some nations may focus on traditional recruitment and selection methods (such as application blanks and interviews), others may adopt more innovative techniques (graphology tests, psychometric inventories or assessment centres). Furthermore, countries which are going through a transition in their cultural paradigms may show a shift from traditional to more innovative techniques. One prominent example of traditional recruitment practices in transition involves Cyprus, a country that joined the EU in May 2004, becoming the EU's furthest border in the south-eastern Mediterranean EU region.

Recruitment and selection in the south-eastern Mediterranean EU corner: traditionalism at a turning point

SMEs constitute the vast majority of firms in Cyprus and their percentages are not very different from those of the EU. Among the main shortcomings of Cypriot SMEs is the lack of emphasis given by SME owners to the effective and efficient utilization of their human resources. Primary significance is attributed mostly to other functional areas of the business, such as finances, production where applicable, and operations, to the neglect of HRM. In fact, HRM as a field is quite new in the Cypriot business arena with a history of fewer than thirty years and practically no 'national' model to explain it, something not unusual for the countries of the south-eastern Mediterranean corner.

In turn, Cypriot SMEs rely on traditional methods of recruiting and selecting their employees. Recruitment relies to a large extent on family, friends, and personal referrals. The most commonly used selection methods are panel interviews, application forms, and references. Even though more advanced and reliable methods such as assessment centres and psychometric tests have been introduced, their use is not at all widespread among SMEs. In a similar fashion, managerial positions are filled internally, suggesting that some form of loyalty between organization and employees exists. It is also an indicator that many SMEs still use seniority-based systems. Nevertheless, few SMEs – mostly the larger ones in size – have implemented formal career plans, assessment centres, 'high flyer' schemes or succession plans. Furthermore, few have committed to a written policy for management development.

The traditionalism depicted above is not out of context. It represents the cultural paradigm in the region dating back to centuries BC. Much of this heritage involved common conquests, merchandizing, and customs. In turn, the business system in this region is shaped by this heritage, which over a long period of time created a related business climate. This climate is dominated by family-owned SMEs (95 per cent) where members of the workforce and staff traditionally depended on the goodwill of the owner for their well being. In those companies, decision-making centres on one person, usually the founder/owner of the firm, who refuses to delegate responsibility for fear of losing control over performance or results (Papalexandris & Stavrou-Costea 2004).

This system has worked well in the past because it fitted well with the regional culture and socio-political system. However, due to globalization and increased competition, these traditional recruitment and selection practices are slowly giving way to new, more sophisticated methods. At least new methods are being considered in Cyprus in combination with traditional ones. This shift is very positive, except for the threat for SMEs to adopt these new methods without changing their organizational cultures. If that happens, SMEs will fail not only in recruitment but also in their overall effectiveness and as a result, survival.

Given the above, the need arises for the HR function to take on a more strategic role within Cypriot SMEs as well as organizations in the greater south-eastern Mediterranean EU region, linking selection to the other organizational functions and to the organizations' long-term success (Papalexandris & Stavrou-Costea 2004). In making HR more strategic, management in these firms may have to consider outsourcing their staffing and other HR activities to professional consultants or bodies and finding innovative ways to finance them. To do so, however, top management in SMEs must be open and committed to this process.

In this respect, serious efforts are made in Cyprus to help SME owners and their management teams on ways to improve their organizations' effectiveness. Specifically, the Human Resource Development Authority (HRDA), a semi-governmental organization, has made it its priority to promote the development of SMEs in Cyprus in all aspects of HRM, putting recruitment and selection practices of these firms at the top of the list. The rationale is that if the foundations of an enterprise in terms of human resources are strong from their recruitment, then these human resources have great potential for growth and development. In addition, a new special consulting scheme has been developed by this authority with the principal aim being to improve management practices and operations of SMEs and increase their performance and competitiveness through better utilization and development of their human resources.

The idea of having such an authority is very useful, especially among European countries similar to Cyprus in which organizations are now synchronizing and professionalizing their HR activities. Such an authority would have the overall responsibility for planning and co-ordinating HR development in a country. Among its main objectives would be to subsidize research and consulting for SMEs to upgrade their management standards and restructure themselves on the basis of developments in Europe; strengthen themselves with specialized managerial personnel in order to accelerate their upgrading and modernization; and offer special skills to employees in order to improve product and service quality and to increase productivity (website of Human Resource Development Authority of Cyprus: http://www.hrdauth.org.cy).

Given the cultural paradigm in the EU south-eastern Mediterranean region (Hofstede 2001), where hierarchies, formal procedures, long-term orientation, and high uncertainty avoidance prevail, structured and co-ordinated activities offered to SMEs with the help of national institutions seems to be a good way to improve staffing and other HR practices. These practices, even if originating in the northern and central-western parts of Europe are modified to fit the local idiosyncrasies. Through such activities, SMEs in this region will maximize their chances for growth and prosperity. Other European countries with similar paradigms may also consider this approach towards helping their SMEs to develop. Nevertheless, care must be taken not to ignore their unique socio-political environment.

Training and development

Initiatives to promote training and development in SMEs are extensively promoted around Europe. This HR activity has high priority due to the well-documented training deficiencies of SMEs. While various valuable initiatives are in place, the main instrument promoting training is the European Social Fund (Mulhern 1995). One of the major challenges with regard to training in SMEs is to convince owner-managers that training is an investment and not an operational cost (Kerr & McDougall 1999). Another major challenge is to define the frameworks which describe how entrepreneurs learn from their stakeholder environment; how the stakeholders learn from them; and what both sets of partners 'need to know' and why (Gibb 1997). As mentioned earlier, resources in SMEs are by definition tighter than in larger organizations. Furthermore, the opportunity cost of workers being away for training as well as the heterogeneity of employees are high in small compared to large firms. Finally, given the opportunity cost of the training provider, the training of owners, managers, and employees in smaller firms inevitably is more generic, thus reducing the desire by owner-managers to provide for such training (Storey 2002).

However, establishing training budgets is important in ensuring the systematic institutionalization of training in these firms. Especially as SMEs grow, flexible holistic and ad hoc processes of learning become inadequate and need to be supplemented with strategies that nurture the creative solutions, personal and intuitive insights, networking and emphasis on effectiveness as necessary (Thomson & Mabey 1994). Another major challenge in terms of training among SMEs is to break the bureaucratic barriers of governmental funding available for training (Kerr & McDougall 1999). Owners often feel that the complicated application process and the long wait are often not worth the time spent. Along with that, not having the time to review all possible sources for training as well as funding for it puts SME management in a disadvantaged position. Related to the lack of time, is the lack of management experience in training within SMEs, given that general managers instead of training experts are the ones who usually take on the task of employee training (Klaas *et al.* 2000).

According to Gibb (1997), the success in learning among SMEs relates to their creative ability to learn from and adapt to the key agents with whom they interface. In this sense SMEs need to know what they should learn, how they might learn it and who from. This learning needs to be embedded not only in the owner-manager and in his or her potential management team but in all staff as well as the outside networks affecting these SMEs (i.e. suppliers) so that it becomes the shared knowledge of the business. Entrepreneurship education and training programmes are utilized in a number of countries in order to stimulate entrepreneurship. However, no one 'best practice' model exists that may be transferable across cultural borders (Ylinenpaa & Havenga 1997). Besides the need for SMEs to engage in business planning and learn how to prepare and execute a formal business plan, fundamental training and development concepts underlying the transfer of best practice centre on attitudes and motivations towards competence development. Even then, attitudes and motivators are culture specific. Below is a discussion of training and development practices in the UK, one of the initial EU member states with a history and extensive practice regarding this HR activity.

Attitudes and motivators on training and development among UK SMEs: history and practice

The contribution made by small businesses to the UK economy is widely accepted (OECD 2002; www.sbs.gov.uk/anlytical/annualsummary.pdf). The interest on SMEs in the UK began with the Bolton Committee report in 1971, which highlighted the potential contribution of SMEs to the UK economy; grew with national and local government support; and became better organized through the Business Link initiative, launched in 1992 (Oztel & Martin 1998). Over the past thirty years, it became widely recognized that training can have a very positive impact on the development of SMEs in the UK. Such training has shown enormous growth during the past decade, much of which has been funded by the government (Westhead & Storey 1996).

Looking at the issue historically, the UK Industrial Training Boards in the 1960–70s commissioned a number of initiatives to help SMEs. The problems identified over twenty years ago as leading to lack of success in training approaches, included lack of sufficient training time and unsuitable training materials. Publications and guides were considered of little use. The solutions suggested focused on training for practical problems specific to the company; support for the transfer of training into practice; and company-specific counselling (Gibb 1997). Parallel to those efforts, the notion of developing the entrepreneurial spirit in young people from schools through to graduate level was conceptualized in the UK in the early 1970s, became popular in the 1980s, fell in the early 1990s with the development of a National Curriculum and the Enterprise in Higher Education Initiative and is currently being revived with the emphasis on entrepreneurship (Gibb 2000).

A British government initiative in 1988 set up the Training and Enterprise Councils (TEC) in England and Wales and Local Enterprise Companies in Scotland. These initiatives, now substituted by Business Links (OECD 2002, www.sbs.gov.uk), promoted training in the private sector, especially among SMEs. Past national training policies in Britain have often been seen as biased against the interests and methods of smaller firms, where the norm involved informal on-the-job training rather than formal instruction away from the work site (Vickerstaff & Parker 1995). In the 1990s, further attempts were launched to improve the internal efficiency and business performance of SMEs in the United Kingdom through a number of training initiatives (Westhead & Storey 1996). Furthermore, several schemes were introduced to encourage people to enter self-employment or start their own business. The UK's Second Competitiveness White Paper placed great emphasis upon training and provided for ways to stimulate training in the smaller firm (Gibb 1997). In addition, a number of schemes to improve the quality of non-owner managers in SMEs have been introduced as well.

Parallel to the above, underpinning much of the UK training and management development effort in the 1990s has been the notion of 'competency' (Gibb 2000). This notion is inherently appealing to SMEs, placing emphasis on 'know-how' rather than 'knowing that'. Around this notion the UK has built a hierarchy of national qualifications (NVQs) and standards for management at various levels and created a system of National Training Organizations (NTOs) on a sectoral basis. However, for various reasons considerable problems have risen in stimulating small and medium enterprises to adopt this approach; a major effort is still exerted to increase SME involvement. Finally, the UK government has adopted the philosophy of organizational learning to increase SME sector survival rates during the early years of the new millennium (Chaston *et al.* 2001). Under this initiative four new policy initiatives have been implemented to support this philosophy, namely New Deal, the University for Industry, Individual Learning Accounts, and the National Grid for Learning.

Despite all the above efforts, a high degree of unplanned, reactive, and informal training activity appears in small firms, where a dedicated personnel manager or training officer is unlikely to exist. This reactive stance to training is not only a function of size and lack of management differentiation but also the effect of environmental pressures on the small firm (Vickerstaff & Parker 1995). Furthermore, little evidence is found in the UK to support the view that businesses where the founder received training perform better than those which had not. In addition, researchers have been unable to establish a clear link between SME performance or growth and the provision of training. Finally, it seems that the most-successful UK SMEs tend to train fewer workers than the less-successful group while the more-successful ones are more likely to provide formal training and less likely to undertake informal training. Nevertheless, training seems strongly related to employment and sales growth (Kitching 1998; Westhead & Storey 1996). In addition, where life-long learning is adopted by UK SMEs focused upon acquiring and incorporating new sources of knowledge into both their employee and organizational learning processes, information management capabilities within these firms are improved (Chaston *et al.* 2001).

It seems that the assumptions related to training that underlie UK SMEs are based on a short-term orientation. Furthermore, the scale, variety, and quality of management training have yet to be adequately monitored and evaluated. A related issue has to do with the seemingly limited interest among owner-managers to adhere to standards based upon National Vocational Qualifications (NVQs). Finally, on behalf of the training providers, greater effort needs to be invested in providing company specific training for SMEs. According to Gibb (2000), the most effective way of developing support for the SME might be to develop the capacity of the stakeholder network (i.e. consultants, bankers, chambers, etc.) by improving its understanding of SME relationship learning needs. As Gibb (1997: 27) noted, many of these issues relate to 'the problem of empathy and of sharing culture with the entrepreneurial small business in order to achieve effectiveness'. It is not necessary that SMEs adhere to the corporatism of larger organizations in order to be effective; SMEs will have to find their own ways of being effective even if these ways are less structured and formalistic than in their larger counterparts (Gibb 2000). But this is probably not unique to the UK situation; where SME interests collide with those of larger organizations, in countries where the latter are abundant, similar issues are bound to appear.

The important lesson to be learned from the UK situation is that training and development have been recognized as priority activities for SME success and have not only been supported by national institutions but have also been the subject of researcher investigation. If other countries follow the UK's example on research and support of training and development towards SMEs, they will begin to explore the frameworks under which training and development will contribute towards SME and by extension national economic prosperity.

Flexibility

In their efforts to attract and retain talented personnel, employers in Europe and around the globe have become increasingly flexible (Barker 1995; ILO 1997). SMEs pose no exception to this trend. Although evidence suggests that SMEs use different patterns of flexibility from their larger counterparts, these patterns have not been the subject of extensive investigation (Ruiz-Santos *et al.* 2003). Nevertheless, as mentioned earlier, SMEs are generally regarded as providing a friendlier environment where structures and processes are and must remain simpler, flexible, and adaptable (Carrier 1994). The informal setting of SMEs, affords flexibility to owner-managers necessary for their survival. Furthermore, this flexibility helps SMEs overcome low productivity and quality (Mihail 2004). For this reason, many may choose employment in SMEs as opposed to larger organizations. If flexibility is among the strongest non-financial benefits of SMEs, then this benefit should be emphasized over its often financial shortcomings, such as salaries or monetary bonuses.

The driving forces leading to the need for flexibility have their roots in economic, business, legal, technological, and sociocultural issues (Duffey 1988; Erza & Deckman 1996). To illustrate, technology has made working location in Europe less important (Brewster *et al.* 1997; Huws *et al.* 1990). Furthermore, the traditional image of the family has changed and women have become members of the active workforce (Drew *et al.* 1998; Morris & Lyon 1988; Scheibl & Dex 1998). Finally, employees in Europe are less likely to commit to a single employer during their careers while at the same time they try to balance work with life requirements (Cressey & Jones 1995).

On account of these developments in Europe, several forms of flexibility have emerged (Boyer 1988; Brewster *et al.* 1997). These vary from flexible organizational systems and flexible HR practices at one end to functional, financial, and numerical flexibility on the other. For example, to be competitive Spanish SMEs developed numerical flexibility mainly through temporary contractual work, as a result of the legal system developed during the Franco era (Ruiz-Santos *et al.* 2003) while in Greece, most SMEs use internal flexibility and tend to ignore legislation on contractual flexibility (Mihail 2004). Among the most popular uses of flexibility of SMEs in Europe are those pursuing greater organizational flexibility through numerical flexibility and more general flexible work arrangements (FWAs) of human resources in an effort to reduce labour costs. In this context, industry, strategic factors, technological systems, organizational characteristics as well as extant HRM practices seem to influence the utilization of flexibility in SMEs (Ruiz-Santos *et al.* 2003).

In addition to the above, the strategies enforced by each country form a spectrum, from environments that encourage flexibility to ones that bound it (Boyer 1988; Brewster *et al.* 1997; Valverde *et al.* 2000). To illustrate, a survey conducted by the European Federation revealed that employees in micro businesses in Greece, the UK, France, and Sweden have more unsocial working hours than other countries (Mihail 2004). Further, Italian and Spanish SMEs have the lowest rates of part-time contracts while Spanish ones have the highest rates of temporary contracts in Europe (Ruiz-Santos *et al.* 2003). At the same time, Danish legislative and collective bargaining systems seem to provide substantial opportunities for flexibility that are particularly beneficial for SMEs (Hjalager 2003). Facing the threat of a serious divergence in national policies, the EU addressed social and labour issues through several directives promoting the use of flexibility through human resources among member states (Boyer 1988). The fact that all EU countries, with the exception of the UK, have committed themselves to co-ordinating their legislative systems for implementing a supranational system affecting HRM practices is a positive indication of convergence (Brewster 1995). In addition, the trend of the European companies to be horizontally linked encourages integration of the European labour markets. Sweden and Germany are the EU member states that represent model countries for the type of flexibility practices towards which the EU leans (Cressey & Jones 1995). In addition, they have come a long way towards co-ordinating their legislative systems to EU directives. The section below focuses on flexibility practices and legislature within the Swedish context.

Flexing Swedish work arrangements: model within a conducive cultural context

The Swedish economy is a small, open economy. The industrial structure in Sweden has a high proportion of people employed in large organizations and the economic setting consists of a mix of private enterprise and national government ownership. While the public sector accounts for a large proportion of the Swedish economy and has a sizeable impact on the country's economic situation, more than 90 per cent of organizations are privately owned. In fact, if we look at the private and public sectors together, we get a picture of a country dominated by small and medium-sized organizations. According to the OECD (2002) report, 99 per cent of all private businesses in Sweden are classified as SMEs or micro-firms. The SME sector accounts for about three-fifths of total turnover and a total value added share of 57 per cent. In turn, SMEs are important contributors to Sweden's economic development (OECD 2002; Ylinenpaa & Havenga 1997). However, while the large Swedish multinational enterprises have proved highly responsive to their economic environment, small and medium-sized enterprises have proved less dynamic.

These factors are due to what has been called, the 'Swedish Model' of the 1960s and 1970s which has been characterized by large centralized institutions that dominated the Swedish society (Johansson 2004). This model imposed tax policies, labour market regulations and other market barriers that disfavoured new, small and medium, fast-growing firms. According to Johansson (2004), this model has had a damaging effect on the Swedish economy, which could have otherwise benefited from the expansion and growth of SMEs. However, during the past couple of decades, a number of institutional changes have been made and have contributed positively to the observed growth of Swedish SMEs. Nevertheless, a more consistent application of competitive pressures throughout the economy would be especially useful for the development of small and medium-sized enterprises in the private sector. Furthermore, changes in the tax system, which is one of several legal and institutional obstacles to the development of small and medium-sized enterprises, would be beneficial (OECD 1999).

Also beneficial are certain changes to the work environment in Sweden, which is defined by participation, consensus, industrial democracy, and a highly developed public sector. Union and employer federations play a central role in the negotiation process on issues like wages, working conditions and technology arrangements, whereas the state serves as an overseeing partner. This environment was slowly established after the Saltsjöbaden Agreement of 1938 (Berglund & Löwstedt 1996). Given this framework, Swedish organizations have traditionally put great emphasis on the welfare of employees. They go as far as redesigning jobs to fit the individual rather than adapting people to work. However, this framework fits more with the industrial relations approach rather than the HRM one. Nevertheless, several researchers point out a changing dynamic over the past two decades, where a transformation from a societal to a managerial corporatism is prevalent. This shift is coupled with the emergence of new forms of work organization in order to meet the demands of international markets on which the Swedish economy is heavily dependent as well as international trends (i.e. unemployment, slower economic growth) from which Sweden poses no exception (Berglund & Löwstedt 1996).

In turn, the move towards flexibility in Sweden has escalated to national-level bargaining, calling for full decentralization of wage work conditions bargaining at the plant levels (Thelen 1993). Some researchers call Sweden the poster child of alternative work schedules (Figart & Mutari 1998). This characterization is consistent with Hofstede's (2001) classification of Swedish culture as a country with a very 'feminine' work environment conducive of taking care of the needs of both genders in an egalitarian, democratic, and participative manner. That is why a number of alternative work schedules have been applied across the board in Sweden, helping achieve similar percentages between men and women in the labour force by the 1980s. According to Brewster & Tregaskis (2001), Swedish organizations are among the lowest to use fixed term contracts in the EU while they are among the highest to use temporary employment and part-time work. Overall, flexibility at work is used widely in Sweden. Nevertheless, the majority of part timers are women with children trying to balance work with life requirements (Figart & Mutari 1998).

Given the above, a number of modifications to employment security provisions entered into force during 1997. Among those, twelve-month fixed-term contracts are now available with no restrictions applying to the nature of work. SMEs and other enterprises are allowed to employ up to five persons on such contracts, and new establishments are allowed to prolong them for up to eighteen months. Regulations that give priority to part-time workers for vacant positions, on the other hand, represent a move towards greater restriction, as does the introduction of a three-year limit after which replacement contracts have to be made permanent (OECD 2003).

Indications point towards two different strategies concerning flexibility in the Swedish labour market. Some organizations use internal flexibility strategies; for instance working time flexibility or developing multi-competent staff, i.e. functional flexibility. Other organizations deploy external flexibility strategies, mainly numerical flexibility through the use of temporary contracts and providers of staffing services. These two strategies are used regardless of sector or business. (Håkansson & Isidorsson 2004). More specifically, a number of surveys show a development towards greater time flexibility in Swedish SMEs and other companies since the beginning of the 1980s. But it is difficult to determine the speed and scope of those changes. While traditional forms for the allocation of working hours like overtime and shift work are well covered in official statistics, no national statistics exist of how companies deploy flexible working time systems in accordance with organizational requirements.

Nevertheless, ample evidence shows a general drive towards time flexibility. To illustrate, a survey conducted in 1997 among 500 Swedish micro-firms and SMEs (5–200 employees) showed that 55 per cent of the companies used a flexible deployment of working hours on a daily or weekly basis and 45 per cent of the companies varied the working hours depending on seasonal or business cycle variations (SAF 1997). Other surveys give the same picture. Depending on seasonal or business cycle variations in consumer demand, companies have made agreements with unions to make it possible to increase or decrease working hours within given limits. These agreements have often included a wage system with fixed pay, regardless of hours worked, in order to ensure a steady income to employees (Lundh 2002).

In addition to time flexibility, an increase in numerical flexibility since the 1980s has been observed as well. To illustrate, by 2003 the number of people on temporary contracts reached 562,000, which equalled nearly 15 per cent of the total number employed (SCB 2004). Among those, the numbers were especially high among women and young people. In fact, the opportunities to hire temporary staff have increased since 1993. Until then the government had a monopoly of providing staff to employers through the public employment offices. In 1993 a law was passed which made it possible for private agencies to be providers of staffing services. Since then the staffing business has been expanding and now provides employment to nearly 1 per cent of the Swedish workforce (compared to 1.5 per cent in the EU). Staffing services in the segment 0–19 employees were used by 4.3 per cent during 2001–02. In the segments 20–99 and 100+, the numbers rose to 18.4 and 42.4 per cent respectively. On average, about 6.4 per cent of all Swedish establishments use staffing services. Further, these services are most widely used in the county council areas which are mainly concerned with health care (Håkansson & Isidorsson 2004).

In summary, the important lessons to be learned from the Swedish example are twofold. First, a participative culture such as the Swedish one may have positive results with the implementation of flexible work in SMEs, promoting business stability, managing gender equality, and addressing national socio-economic conditions such as unemployment and economic stagnation. Second, in order for HRM activities such as flexible work to be effective among SMEs, national laws and bargaining procedures need to be conducive to their implementation and monitoring. National systems of high social welfare, with powerful trade unions, need to prove the need for more flexible arrangements among SMEs in order to achieve a win-win situation for all stakeholders involved. Even national systems weaker on social welfare or with less powerful unions, need to explore the ways in which flexible work may help them address organizational, socio-demographic, and socio-economic issues that they face through SME development and growth.

Conclusion

SMEs are the majority of organizations in Europe and a vital part of the European economy; therefore their survival and growth are paramount. As explained earlier, while SMEs and micro-firms constitute the majority of organizations in the south-eastern EU and in turn most efforts to promote and develop HR activities centre around them, the picture changes gradually where increasingly larger organizations enter the scene as we move towards the central, western, and northern parts of Europe. In turn, the interests and needs between SME and larger organizations frequently collide within Europe, and priority or emphasis on HR activities is often given towards the latter. However, the high unemployment in Europe, forcing larger organizations to restructure, will direct the labour force towards the SME sector (Mulhern 1995). Furthermore, the EU has realized the need to provide assistance to SMEs and has institutionalized EU-wide HR-related initiatives to help SMEs compete, prosper, and develop within the European and the larger global business environment.

In addition to the EU, national and other institutions as summarized in Figure 6.1 need to provide assistance to SMEs in helping them face their unique challenges. To illustrate, consultancies, banking institutions, and venture capital networks, just to name a few, can provide practical assistance to SMEs while academic institutions can focus on enriching knowledge in relation to SME HR-related needs. Further, business-owners themselves need to pay proper attention to the HR-related activities that will help professionalize their organizations. In turn, as per Agency Theory (Heneman *et al.* 2000), with greater emphasis by SMEs, policy-makers, consultants, and researchers on the unique challenges and opportunities of small- and medium-sized enterprises in Europe, the interests of these various constituents may come into alignment for the benefit of all parties involved.

Of course we cannot talk about one best approach to the use of HRM among SMEs in Europe because, as mentioned earlier, Europe is culturally and socio-economically diverse. Borrowing from Wright & Snell's (1998) theory, fit and flexibility at both the organizational and national levels in the adoption of HR practices within Europe are a prerequisite. However, country examples like the ones discussed in this chapter may serve as food for thought for further exploration at organizational, national, and cross-cultural levels. For example, the ways in which staffing is applied in Cyprus may help other countries adopt the positive and avoid the negative applications; or the training practices and legal issues historically dealt with among UK SMEs may provide ammunition for SMEs in other countries to establish requisite training practices; and flexible practices in Swedish SMEs may provide a blueprint for SMEs and government officials (i.e. through legislation) in other parts of Europe to follow.

In doing so, the greatest challenge is how to balance resources in such a way so that Europe achieves its aim to become the most competitive and dynamic knowledge-based economy in the world. As discussed in this chapter, the effective utilization of HR among European SMEs can contribute significantly towards this aim. However to achieve that, much work is necessary in establishing the requisite structures, processes, and conditions where HR will become a competitive tool for SMEs and not a cost to overcome. In making HR a competitive tool, SMEs need not only to adapt to the stakeholder environment but also to create and bring forward the conditions to improve their position (Gibb 1997).

References

Barker, J. 1995. Family ties: Family-friendly policies are no longer a luxury, they are a competitive advantage. *Sales and Marketing Management*, 147: 18–24.
Berglund, J. & Löwstedt, J. 1996. In T. Clark (ed.), *HRM*. UK: Blackwell Publishers Inc.
Boyer, R. 1988. *The Search for Labour Market Flexibility: The European Economies in Transition*. Oxford: Clarendon Press.

Brewster, C. 1995. Towards a European model of HRM. *Journal of International Business Studies*, 26(1): 1–21.

Brewster, C., Mayne, L. & Tregaskis, O. 1997. Flexible working in Europe: A review of the evidence. *Management International Review*, 37: 85–103.

Brewster, C., Mayrhofer, W. & Morley, M. 2004. *Trends in Human Resource Management in Europe: Convergence or Divergence*. UK: Butterworth Heinemann.

Brewster, C. & Tregaskis, O. 2001. Adaptive, reactive and inclusive organisational approaches to workforce flexibility in Europe. *Comportamento Organizacional e Gestão*, 6(2): 209–232.

Carrier, C. 1994. Intrapreneurship in large firms and SMEs: A comparative study. *International Small Business Journal*, 12(3): 54–61.

Chandler, G. N. & McEvoy, G. M. 2000. Human resource management, TQM, and firm performance in small and medium-size enterprises. *Entrepreneurship: Theory and Practice* 25(1): 43–54.

Chaston, I., Badger, B. & Sadler-Smith, E. 2001. Organizational learning: An empirical assessment of process in small UK manufacturing firms. *Journal of Small Business Management*, 39(2): 139–151.

Cressey, P. & Jones, B. 1995. *Work and Employment in Europe: A New Convergence*. London: Routledge.

Dessler, G. 2000. *Human Resources Management*. New Jersey: Prentice Hall.

Drew, E., Emerek, R. & Mahon, E. 1998. *Women, Work and the Family in Europe*. London: Routledge.

Duffey, J. 1988. Competitiveness and human resources. *California Management Review*, 30(3): 92–101.

Erza, M. & Deckman, M. 1996. Balancing work and family responsibilities: Flexitime and childcare in the federal government. *Public Administration Review*, 56: 174–176.

Figart, D. M. & Mutari, E. 1998. It's about time; will Europe solve the work/family dilemma? *Dollars & Sense*, 215: 27–32.

Gibb, A. 1997. Small firms' training and competitiveness. Building upon the small business as a learning organization. *International Small Business Journal*, 15(3): 13–30.

Gibb, A. 2000. SME policy, academic research and the growth of ignorance, mythical concepts, myths, assumptions, rituals and confusions. *International Small Business Journal*, 18(3): 13–22.

Håkansson, K. & Isidorsson, T. 2004. Hyresarbetskraft. Användningen av inhyrd arbetskraft på den svenska arbetsmarknaden. *Arbetsmarknad & Arbetsliv*, 3: 187–205.

Heneman, R. L., Tansky, J. W. & Camp, S. M. 2000. HRM practices in small and medium-sized enterprises: unanswered questions and future research perspectives. *Entrepreneurship*, 25(1): 11.

Heneman III, H. G. & Berkley, R. A. 1999. Applicant attraction practices and outcomes among small business. *Journal of Small Business Management*, 37(1): 53–74.

Heneman, H. G. I., Heneman, R. L. & Judge. 1997. *Staffing Organizations* (2nd ed.). New York: McGraw-Hill.

Hermann, S. 1996. *Hidden Champions: Lessons from 500 of the World's Best Unknown Companies*. USA: Harvard Business School Press.

Hjalager, A. 2003. Virtually working: traditional and emerging institutional frameworks for the contingent workforce. *International Journal of Manpower*, 24(2): 187–206.

Hofstede, G. 2001. *Culture's Consequences*. New York: Sage Publications.

Hornsby, J. S. & Kuratko, D. F. 1990. HRM in small business: critical issues for 1990s. *Journal of Small Business Management*, 28(3): 9–18.

Human Resource Development Authority of Cyprus. http://www.hrdauth.org.cy (accessed June 17 2005).

Huws, U., Korte, W. B. & Robinson, S. 1990. *Telework: Towards the Elusive Office.* Chichester: Wiley, UK.

ILO 1997. Perspectives, part-time work: Solution or trap. *International Labour Review,* 136(4). http://www.ilo.org/public/english/support/publ/revue/persp/97-4.htm (accessed June 17 2005).

Jackson, S. E. & Schuler, R. S. 2000. *Managing Human Resources: A Partnership Perspective.* New York: South-Western College Publishing.

Johansson, D. 2004. Is small beautiful? The case of the Swedish IT industry. *Entrepreneurship & Regional Development,* 16: 271–287.

Katz, J. A., Aldrich, H. E., Welbourne, T. M. & Williams, P. M. 2000. Guest editor's comments special issue on HRM and the SME: Toward a new synthesis. *Enrepreneurship: Theory and Practice,* 25(1): 7–10.

Kerr, A. & McDougall, M. 1999. The small business of developing people. *International Small Business Journal,* 17(2): 10–20.

Kirby, D. A. 2003. *Entrepreneurship.* London: McGraw Hill.

Kitching, J. 1998. Investing in training and small firm growth and survival: an empirical analysis for the UK 1987–97. *International Small Business Journal,* 17(1): 110.

Klaas, M. & Gainey, T. W. 2000. Managing HR in the small and medium enterprise: the impact of professional employer organizations. *Entrepreneurship: Theory and Practice,* 25(1): 107–123.

Koch, C. L. Y. & Van Straten, E. 1997. *Personeelsbeleid in Enkele MKB Bedrijven.* [Personnel Management in Several SMEs]. EIM Strategic Study 9703. Zoetermeer, the Netherlands: EIM Business and Policy Research.

Longenecker, J. G., Moore, C. W. & Petty, J. W. 1994. *Small Business Management: An Entrepreneurial Emphasis.* Cincinnati: South Western.

Lundh, C. 2002. *Spelets regler. Institutioner och lönebildning på den svenska arbetsmarknaden 1850–2000.* Stockholm: SNS Förlag.

Mihail, D. 2004. Labour flexibility in Greek SMEs. *Personnel Review,* 33(5): 549–560.

Morris, L. & Lyon, S. E. 1988. *Gender Relations in Public and Private, New Research Perspectives.* Hampshire: Macmillan Press.

Morrow, C. C., Jarrett, M. Q. & Rupinski, M. T. 1997. An investigation of the effect and economic utility of corporate-wide training. *Personnel Psychology,* 50(1): 91–119.

Mulhern, A. 1995. The SME sector in Europe: a broad perspective. *Journal of Small Business Management,* 33(3): 83–89.

OECD 1999. Assessment and recommendations. *OECD Economic Surveys – Sweden,* 9.

OECD 2002. Small and medium enterprise outlook. Opinion of the economic and social committee on the proposal for a council decision on guidelines for member states' employment policies for the year 2001. www.sbs.gov.uk/anlytical/annualsummary.pdf (accessed June 17 2005).

OECD 2003. Developments in individual OECD countries: Sweden. *OECD Economic Outlook,* 73: 105–107.

Oztel, H. & Martin, S. 1998. Local partnership for economic development: business links and the restructuring of the SME support networks in the United Kingdom. *Economic Development Quarterly,* 12(3): 266–279.

Papalexandris, N. & Stavrou-Costea, E. 2004. HRM in the southeastern Mediterranean corner of Europe: the case of Italy, Greece and Cyprus. In C. Brewster, W. Mayrhofer & M. Morley (eds.), *Trends in HRM in Europe: Convergence or Divergence.* UK: Butterworth Heinemann.

Pfeffer, J. & Veiga, J. F. 1999. Putting people first for organizational success. *The Academy of Management Executive,* 13(2): 37–38.

Ruiz-Santos, C., Ruiz-Mercader, J. & McDonald, F. 2003. The use of contractual working time flexibility by Spanish SMEs. *Personnel Review*, 32(2): 164–186.

SAF-Swedish Employers Association 1997. *Undersökning bland företagsledare angående arbetstider*. Eureka Marknadsfakta.

SCB-Statistics Sweden 2004. Information från arbetskraftsundersökningarna 2004: 1. Sysselsättning och arbetslöshet 1975–2003.

Scheibl, F. & Dex, S. 1998. Should we have more family-friendly policies? *European Management Journal*, 16: 586–598.

Soidre, P. 2004. Unemployment risks and demands on labour-market flexibility: an analysis of attitudinal patterns in Sweden. *International Journal of Social Welfare*, 13: 124–133.

Stavrou, E. 1999. Succession in family businesses: Exploring the effects of demographic factors on offspring intentions. *Journal of Small Business Management*, 37(3): 43–61.

Stavrou, E. 2003. Leadership succession in owner-managed firms through the lens of extraversion. *International Small Business Journal*, 21(3): 331–347.

Stavrou, E. & Swiercz, P. 1998. Securing the future of the family enterprise: A model of offspring intentions to join the business. *Entrepreneurship Theory & Practice*, 23(2): 19–28.

Storey, D. J. 2002. Education, training and development policies and practices medium sized companies in the UK: do they really influence performance? *Omega*, 30(4): 249–264.

Thelen, K. 1993. West European labor in transition: Sweden and Germany compared. *World Politics*, 46(1): 23–49.

Thomson, R. & Mabey, Ch. 2001. *Developing Human Resources*. Oxford: Butterworth.

Valverde, M., Tregaskis, O. & Brewster, C. 2000. Labor flexibility and firm performance. *International Advances in Economic Research*, 6: 649–657.

Vickerstaff, S. & Parker, K. T. 1995. Helping small firms: the contribution of TECs and LECs. *International Small Business Journal*, 13(4): 56–72.

Westhead, P. & Storey, D. 1996. Management training and small firm performance: why is the link so weak? *International Small Business Journal*, 14(4): 13–24.

Williamson, I. O. 2000. Employer legitimacy and recruitment success in small business. *Enterpeneurship: Theory and Practice*, 25(1): 27–42.

Wright, P. M. & Snell, S. A. 1998. Toward a unifying framework for exploring fit and flexibility in strategic HRM. *Academy of Management Review*, 23: 756–772.

Ylinenpaa, H. & Havenga, K. 1997. *USASBE Annual National Conference*. San Francisco, CA.

HRM in not-for-profit international organizations: different, but also alike

7

CHRIS BREWSTER AND STEPHEN LEE

European international enterprises, but not multinational corporations

The public and private sectors in each country are not the only employers in Europe. There is also a wide range of not-for-profit (NFP) organizations in what has been dubbed the 'third sector' (Lyons 2001): churches, charities, clubs, and associations, trade unions and much of the publicly-owned services. Substantial numbers of people are employed in the NFP sector in Europe. Although employment in the (also not-for-profit) public sector has gone down dramatically in the transition economies of central and eastern Europe and marginally in some of the western European economies, there has been an extensive growth in other NFP organizations recently (Salamon *et al.* 1999). To discuss human resource management (HRM) in Europe whilst ignoring this sector would mean ignoring a large proportion of the economy.

Given the size of, and particularly the country variations in, this sector it is not possible to encompass it all in this chapter. The chapter therefore concentrates on a cross-national group of NFPs: the international organizations. These can be classified as inter-governmental organizations (IGOs) and non-governmental organizations (NGOs). The former will include 'international civil service' organizations such as the European Commission, the North Atlantic Treaty Organization (NATO), and the many United Nations (UN) agencies and programmes. What distinguishes this group of organizations is that they are legitimized, governed, and substantially funded by governments. The latter is more wide ranging, covering organizations as diverse as the Save the Children Fund, the Boy Scouts and Girl Guides, Churches and Church aid charities, the European Football Federation (EUFA) and International Football Association (FIFA). Nor are these necessarily small organizations: the International Committee of the Red Cross (ICRC), for example, has some 7,500 employees. Some of these are 'mutual-support' organizations (Hudson 1999): many of these rely heavily on volunteers as a significant part of their human resources. The Roman Catholic church might lay a strong claim to being the oldest international organization of all: preceding the multinational corporations (MNCs) by millennia. What distinguishes these organizations is that they are not-for-profit organizations independent of governments. Increasingly, the two groups have overlapped, with a lot of joint working and examples of IGOs collaborating or partnering with NGOs.

Cities like Brussels and Geneva are famously home to many of these organizations; and so are London and Vienna, Paris and Rome, Munich, Strasbourg, Luxembourg, and many other places in Europe. Some of these organizations look like MNCs in the sense that they have started in a 'home' base and spread their activities. Some of the NGOs, and all of the IGOs, are truly international organizations, with no home base and with large proportions of their employees at headquarters (HQ) being expatriates to the country in which the HQ is located. For this reason, the 'three country examples' common to other chapters will not be used here.

For nearly all these organizations human resources are, fundamentally and unequivocally, the key resource; and usually the one that absorbs the vast majority of the organizations' finances (Macpherson 2001). Yet HRM and international HRM in these bodies remain largely un-researched: hence, this chapter will be short on references. The chapter is informed by evidence from three surveys: one of HRM in UN organizations, (Brewster *et al.* 1999); one of a wider sample of international organizations, (Croucher *et al.* 2004), and one concerned with measuring the effectiveness of HRM in NGOs (Lee & Brewster 2004). This material is supplemented by knowledge gained from extensive work by the authors and colleagues on different aspects of HRM with a range of international organizations.

These organizations share with the MNCs the characteristic of being fundamentally international in all respects of their work: their aims and activities are global and their employees come from all over the world. However, unlike the MNCs, these organizations have a public character: they are either intergovernmental organizations, or publicly and visibly managed NGOs. The effect of that is that these are organizations that are, with a large or a small P, politically managed. This combination, of management that is highly international and not-for-profit with political visibility, is rare – and rarely researched in much of the academic management literature. It is certainly largely absent from the international HRM literature, nearly all of which has concentrated upon the MNC perspective.

This chapter examines in turn the background to HRM in the not-for-profit international organizations, emphasizing some of the particular issues that distinguish them from the other sectors; some of the specific HR issues exercising the international NFPs at the moment in their management of people; and current issues in the processes of managing HRM in these organizations.

Background to HRM in not-for-profit international organizations

These organizations have some unique characteristics that impact upon management in general, and specifically HRM. These can be analyzed under the following headings: objectives, nature of the organizations, governance, and management styles.

Objectives

The objectives of these organizations are not about profit maximization. For all of them, the effective husbandry of their financial resources is critical, but it is no more than a means to an end. These organizations have much larger objectives: ones which many of those involved would see as more 'moral' or 'ethical' than making profits and which impact on every element of management. They are concerned with alleviating hunger or poverty; providing medical support in times of crisis; controlling nuclear science; establishing internationally accepted rules, or a thousand other socially and ethically desirable purposes. Lyons (2001), argues that what distinguishes these organizations from profit-focused organizations are centrality of values, the complexity of revenue generation, reliance on volunteers, difficulties in judging performance, lack of clear accountability, and conflicts between the governance structures and the staff. For those managing these organizations the problem is that they, like all managers, have inevitably to make compromises in an imperfect world in order to get anything done at all; but they have to do so without the single, simple measure of the financial 'bottom line' which provides the ultimate guideline for managers in the private sector (Herzlinger 1996). The problems are inevitably exacerbated by the international nature of these organizations.
Morals and ethics are culturally bound whilst the ultimate test of worth is couched in 'right action' (Drucker 1990); the emphasis of action will vary between donors and recipients (Sargeant 1999); there will be many involved – often powerful governments – with their own 'axes to grind'. Without the simple 'bottom line' measure, even the balance of objectives within these organizations is the subject of political negotiation (Handy 1988; Hind 1995).

Nature of the organizations

Partly as a consequence of their different objectives, these organizations have more often tended to develop into different forms than is typical for private sector organizations. First, they may have no home base, or its importance may be strictly limited. Hence, for example, it may not be clear which of their staff count as the international employees: much higher proportions of the employees of these organizations tend to be based outside their home country. They may not fit standard definitions of expatriates as having been selected and sent to a foreign assignment by their organization but, in the sense that these are individuals and families who have moved to join the organization in another country and are living and working outside their own country, they share many of the concerns of expatriates: and managing them involves many of the same problems.

Second, because there is sometimes no national home base, in the IGOs in particular, much attention is paid to ensuring that the practices of one country do not come to be seen as the 'norm'. For example, the United Nations Educational, Scientific and Cultural Organization (UNESCO) in Paris has attracted a disproportionate number of employees from France and the Francophone countries (in a way that the UN organizations in French-speaking Geneva have not). A 'French style' of management is evident within the organization – and is a source of considerable concern to many staff, who want to ensure that UNESCO is not too closely associated with its HQ base. ICRC currently has a policy of internationalizing its staff away from the previous predominance of Swiss employees – a policy determined not so much by the location of its headquarters in Geneva as by an assumption that Swiss neutrality was a powerful political tool. Nowadays the organization feels well enough respected to provide that neutrality under its own label.

Third, there are political dimensions to the management of employees. Many NGOs want to be able to 'show' their recipients that they are unbiased in their selection of personnel and will employ people from a wide range of countries at headquarters. A broad geographical spread of employees is particularly important to some organizations in the United Nations and in the European Commission. Governments will demand that their country is represented in the employment structure of the organization: sometimes pinpointing specific posts or even individuals. This is a factor that would be considered differently by MNCs who are either comfortable with an ethnocentric management (Mayrhofer & Brewster 1996) or are concerned to 'get the best' irrespective of nationality.

Fourth, for reasons of historical development and political expediency many international NGOs retain a federated organizational structure, focusing power and responsibility at the national rather than international decision-making level. As a consequence, HRM policy and procedure will often remain inconsistent across national boundaries without the organization retaining the ability, at the international level (as in the MNC alternate), to resolve inconsistency and conflict in policy development and prescription.

Governance

Governance of these organizations varies with type. Fundamental to the IGOs is that their management is conducted, by agreement of the governments concerned, outside any national legislation. As a consequence, to ensure fairness and equity, most have a very strict set of rules and procedures to which they must adhere: these are not called international bureaucracies for nothing. Most are governed by executive boards composed of representatives of national governments.
The internal running of the organization is usually delegated to a CEO (variously called the Secretary General, the Director General, the President or some similar title). The CEO, and often their immediate deputies, is usually a political appointment, the result of 'horse-trading' and 'Buggin's turn' between governments. Since most of these CEOs can expect to serve more than one term, a considerable part of their energy is often devoted to ensuring that they get re-elected.
The executive board representatives, on the other hand, may be either highly placed politicians, career diplomats or specialists in relevant topics: depending on the relative importance and the nature of the organization. These governors are often rotated fairly quickly – most diplomats, for example, will change their posting every few years – and rarely see HRM as a key area for them.

At the same time, the governance of these organizations is generally more transparent than that of MNCs. It is not just their mission statements and financial results that are open to researchers and other interested parties, but their governance meeting agendas, the papers for those meetings and the minutes are also often available to any web-browser with the necessary interest and the stamina. These are in some ways very open organizations.

> A sign in the UN building in Geneva says 'Smoking Discouraged'!
>
> An official explained: 'well, we wanted to just ban it, but if Fidel Castro comes in here with a cigar, who is going to tell him to put it out?'

Governance problems in the NGOs vary considerably and depend on the type of organization that is being considered. However, a crucial distinctive element in the nature of governance in NGOs is that it remains the ultimate responsibility of part-time volunteers, usually meeting no more than four or six times a year in the form of a trustee board or committee of management.

Recruitment of trustees and board members without the motivation of financial reward remains an increasingly difficult challenge. Recruiting trustees with the right skill base to support all of the management disciplines necessary in highly complex international NGOs is increasingly difficult, as is the ability to balance gender, ethnic and geographic representation at board level in a manner increasingly required by powerful external stakeholder groups (i.e. donor and recipient governments, foundations, and institutional funders).

The presence of HRM specialist skills at board level in these organizations is often under represented or non-existent, dwarfed by the more urgent priorities associated strategically with the demands of resource attraction (fundraising and marketing) and resource allocation (service provision, campaigning, and education) (Sargeant 1999).

The direct consequence of these factors often leads to a situation where despite remaining hugely dependent upon effective HRM implementation to ensure mission accomplishment, many international NGOs consistently fail to incorporate HRM analysis and debate at the strategic level in any concerted manner (Lee & Brewster 2004).

Organizations such as the churches and their charitable off-shoots often feel subjected to a higher power than man and governance structures are often historical and opaque. Some of the charitable trusts are similarly opaque, but the majority of charities have to abide by strict rules laid down by governments, which include questions of financial transparency and propriety. Unlike the IGOs, the NGOs are subject to national laws and these vary: but there are usually clear requirements on the way these organizations are to be governed if they wish to maintain the tax advantages of charitable status. Some charities and similar organizations make a point of ensuring that their governance is as open as possible – others see that as unnecessary, distracting from their mission or even threatening.

Management styles

This combination of different objectives and different employees can create real, and different, HRM problems for these organizations and different approaches to the way that they manage people. In terms of controls, the problems become especially acute when dealing with employee performance.

In managerial approaches to staff, the not-for-profit international organizations can sometimes exhibit attitudes that would surprise even some of the more sophisticated profit-focused organizations. Thus, managers who believe strongly in the mission of their organization above all else, seeing it perhaps as God-given, or as a serious task that will lead to improvement of the lot of mankind, are sometimes unsympathetic to the needs and problems of staff. Given a choice between responding to an employee's family difficulties or the urgent fulfilment of an ethical, demanding requirement linked to the mission, some managers find it hard to accept that employees may need to 'abandon' the recipients of their work for a 'personally indulgent' reason.

Given the moral basis of these organizations and their espoused, quintessentially caring nature, it is both ironic and a source of major threat to their continued effective operation that these international organizations have been subject to criticism both internally (from field staff) and externally (from independent evaluations, government and institutional funders) regarding their HRM management practices.

Long working hours and stress are common in the NGO sector, surveys of field staff indicate that over 50 per cent of relief staff routinely work more than 60 hours a week. Complaints relating to selection, career development, appraisal procedures, poor communication between home and field environments, and conflict between expatriate and local aid workers have been documented (Pickard 1997).

In response the international NGOs have themselves launched a pan-European initiative, establishing People In Aid, a consortium of personnel and training managers tasked to promote a voluntary code of HRM 'best practice' covering the recruitment, training, welfare, security, communication, and counselling needs of front line field staff in international NGOs (People In Aid Code of Good Practice 2003). Similarly, the Association of HRM in International Organizations was established in 2002 with the objectives of improving the quality of HRM specialists in such organizations and upgrading their reputation.

Even where 'best practice' in these areas has been defined, the differing political and ethical demands mean that measuring it and dealing with it can be problematic. The employees are committed to the wider purposes, not to the organization. They may, for example, be focused on the problems of child poverty and be unprepared to bother themselves with budgetary issues. They may be committed to getting more done in the particular disadvantaged region of Africa (from which they come or to which they have devoted themselves) and are unconcerned about the problems of regions which they see as anyway privileged in comparison. Less acceptably, perhaps, they may be concerned about their personal status back home or the comfort of their future. Dealing with these issues can create peculiar problems for the organization. Attempting to discipline a Mauritanian can bring accusations of discriminating against the only north-west African on the staff; disciplining a citizen of the United States can bring a reaction from the government that (they may point out) 'is paying your bills'.

HRM issues in the foreground

Here we examine the employees themselves, culture clashes, mobility, and performance measurement.

Employees

The employees themselves tend to be different from the international employees of an MNC. In the IGOs they are usually highly educated, internationally minded, linguists, and internationally mobile. They may be very differently motivated: for some, at least, it is the possibility of 'doing good', 'making a difference', 'helping those who most need it' which directs their contribution to these organizations and their working life. Others will have joined the organization as the peak of a career: if you are one of the world's top nuclear physicists you may well have an objective of having this proven by being employed for a period in the UN's International Atomic Energy Agency in Vienna; similarly, space scientists want to work for the European Space Agency. Some may be attracted to the international environment and enjoy the idea of working with people from many different nationalities. Yet others will be seconded by their governments: the Organization for European Security and Co-operation, for example, has most of its professional staff on short-term secondments from the member states.

Much of the current work on expatriates continues to support findings from earlier research amongst MNC employees about the general lack of preparedness before assignments, the lengthy adjustment period to assignments abroad, and the difficulties and dissatisfaction of expatriates upon return from assignments (for recent summaries see the chapters in Harris *et al.* 2003; Harzing & von Ruysseveldt 2004; Tayeb 2005). However, many of these NGO and IGO employees have deliberately sought their employment outside their home country, with the express intent of starting a new career in these organizations. This group of self-initiated foreign employees (SEs) has received little coverage in the literature (for exceptions see Inkson *et al.* 1997; Suutari & Brewster 1998; Jokinen *et al.* 2005).

Box 7.1

Suutari & Brewster (2001, 2003) identified a group of 'international bureaucrats' in their sample of Finnish expatriates who had gone independently to another country – to work in these kinds of NFP organizations. Although the numbers were small and have to be treated with caution they were:

- more likely to be female (29 per cent – significantly above the 15–20 per cent usually found);
- older than other expatriates;
- more interested in the international experience and in professional development;

- rarely supported with induction or cultural training compared to most expatriates (though some organizations, such as the European Meteorological Satellite Organization [Eumetsat], do extensive work on this),
- felt more constrained by the organization; in contrast to the higher levels of independence and self-initiative reported for MNC expatriates;
- clearer than MNC expatriates about the compensation and benefits package they were signing up to and more satisfied with it.

Once again, employees of NGOs are more varied, ranging from people whose main qualifications may just be commitment and enthusiasm, to people at the very peak of their profession.

Volunteers

Significant numbers of the NGO's human resources will be unpaid (or only nominally paid) volunteers. These are people whose objectives may not match those of the organizations exactly, who may have quite different expectations of what work means and who can literally 'walk away' at any time if they feel that the work is not fulfilling enough for them. Managing such employees requires a completely different mindset on the part of managers and HRM departments (Hudson 1999).

Indeed, in many instances, the responsibility for identifying, recruiting, supporting and, where applicable, terminating the relationship with volunteers will not rest with the HRM professionals but will be distributed across marketing/fundraising, service delivery, and administrative functions. While these organizations face a very real and distinctive reputational risk in attempting to manage the activities of literally thousands of volunteers at both the national and the international level on a daily basis, it is rare that this function is managed strategically within the context of HRM.

The question of how and when organizational liability is managed within the context of volunteer management is a matter of increasing importance to international NGOs in both home and in international field markets (Martinez 2003). In home markets volunteers not only perform a wide range of administrative and management responsibilities but also engage, often completely removed from the direct control of the international NGO, in a wide variety of fundraising and campaigning activities. In emergency relief scenarios, volunteers will be recruited 'in country' to support staff effort and might comprise a mix of indigenous population, expatriate communities, and travelling communities. In each case, field-based volunteers may well be placed in situations of considerable personal stress and risk. It becomes crucial therefore that international NGOs resolve the following issues:

- Is the organization liable to third parties for the activities undertaken by its volunteers? When and where is this the case?
- Is the organization liable to its volunteers who are put at risk and/or injured in the course of their activities?
- Is the individual volunteer liable for their actions in the performance of activities linked to volunteering?

In order to minimize the risks associated with volunteer participation both at home and in the field international NGOs will need to adopt clear internal policies and procedures for the management of volunteers. At a minimum this will require clarity of volunteer job descriptions, careful selection, and screening of volunteers (particularly where they will interface directly with vulnerable beneficiary groups), clear guidelines to staff as to what constitutes minimum requirements for the supervision of volunteers, training and support programmes specifically designed for volunteers need to be institutionalized, alongside the identification and provision of adequate insurance cover. Proactive management of the interface between volunteer and paid staff activity will also be crucial in ensuring that non-discriminatory practice does not develop across these distinctive internal stakeholder groups (Forsyth 1999).

Expatriate and local staff

Amongst the employees, depending again on the type of organization, there is often a mix of international and local staff. Although some charities are run almost entirely by national staff, some actively encourage representatives from the communities they are trying to serve to work at HQ. Others take a different approach. Arguing that sending European expatriates to Africa, for example, simply reflects an old colonial mentality and fosters a dependence culture, Action Aid in the UK has made considerable strides in 'localizing' their staff: ensuring that most of their aid workers are from the communities (or at least the region) that they are serving. For the IGOs and the larger international NGOs there is usually a mixture of 'professional' staff, who are recruited internationally and expected to be international in outlook; and 'general' staff – the secretaries, cleaners, mailroom staff, drivers, etc – who are employed on local terms and conditions (even though there are usually requirements about language skills, for example). As elsewhere (Suutari & Brewster 2001, 2003) there are amongst this latter group many foreigners who have made their own way to the country and find the idea of working in international organizations attractive. This is emphasized by the fact that there is little doubt that at the lower end of the pay scales these organizations tend to pay well above the local norms.

A development that deserves more research attention is that of what have been rather unkindly called 'international brats'. The result of generations of armed and civil servants and MNC specialists moving around the world has been the creation of considerable numbers of people who feel no deep attachment to any particular country: 'My mother is English, my father is an Arab who grew up in Germany. I was born in Rome and I have lived in four different countries before moving to Geneva, where I live now. I speak four languages fluently and three or four others reasonably well. Since I work for one of the UN agencies, I pay no tax to any country and I travel on a UN pass. So "where are you from?" is not a question I find easy to answer.' There are increasing numbers of such people in Europe and they are potentially a powerful resource for any international organization.

Culture clashes

A variety of distinctive professional cultures need to be accommodated, managed, and controlled directly in relation to mission achievement in international NGOs if the organization is to remain effective. Yet it is not unusual for the strategic imperatives associated with any one of these different professional cultures to be diametrically opposed to those exhibited by other professional cultures present in the organization at the same time (Bruce 1998). Distinctive professional cultures often found in these organizations are those associated with direct service provision (medical, nursing, social welfare professionals); professionals associated with a marketing, fundraising, sales, and public relations alignment; policy prescription experts (development professionals, policy analysts, and campaigners) and those professions commonly associated with administrative and general management. It is common to find each of these distinctive professional cultures existing side by side within international organizations with individuals operationalizing the mission and the work priorities associated with their perception of it in different ways. The HRM function within these organizations must itself deliver a political solution to professional cultural diversity and the conflict that this can engender if overall organizational effectiveness is to be assured.

A different element of the culture debate reflects the astonishingly international nature of these organizations. It is very common for people from one country to be managed by and managing people from other countries. There is now enough evidence in the literature to suggest (see, as a recent edition, House *et al.* 2004) that national cultures have a significant effect on individuals' approaches to such issues as hierarchy, team-working, acceptance of personal accountability, even such aspects of work as the purpose of meetings. Intriguingly, unlike the usually ethnocentric MNCs, these much more international organizations rarely address the issue formally: it may be widely discussed in the corridors, but it is rarely raised in the main rooms. Hence there is little recognition of the issue and little training for individuals to handle it. It may be that the whole topic is simply too sensitive for these organizations.

Mobility

International HRM amongst these organizations is also distinctive. Sending people from one country to another is different when they are not originally from the first country. The places that they are sent to and the things they are doing may also be distinctive. For some of the standard-setting IGOs, where the task is to establish rules and advice for the international community and governments, much of their activities will be familiar to anyone working for an MNC. The employees will be sent to the major cities in the foreign countries, they will be dealing with senior figures in government and with senior local partners. They will be staying in the better parts of the city and living much better than most of the citizens of those places. For the aid agencies and many of the NGOs the task will look significantly different. They will often be sent 'up-country' where foreigners are rarely seen and living and working conditions are tough. They may be the only foreigners around – no 'expat community' here to shelter in. Some of them will be operating in physically dangerous places, where disease, gunshots, or landmines can have an instant and crippling or deadly effect on people a long distance from any support programmes.

Performance measurement

In a meta-analysis of empirical studies of not-for-profit organizations, Forbes (1998) found no consistent useful way of measuring performance and, indeed, argued that the effectiveness of such organizations may be unmeasurable. One result is that NFPs are often reluctant to concern themselves with the evaluation of outcomes (Poole *et al.* 2001). This applies to HRM too. By comparison with MNCs, HRM performance measurement in the international organizational context is embryonic in nature, applied inconsistently across different geographical contexts, and lacking in strategic application. Many of the reasons already identified in this chapter contribute to this lack of development. The complex nature of these organizations, the diverse cultures operating within them, the concentration of resource allocation on direct service delivery to the comparative neglect of managerial support services, all mitigate against the attainment of cohesive systems of performance measurement.

Often, the lack of adequate technology, or the lack of consistency in its distribution geographically in the field further mitigates against the consistent application of performance measurement in international NGOs as does the wide and diverse educational backgrounds of prospective respondents engaged in front line service delivery. When one considers that, in practice, the implementation of performance measurement of systems for front line emergency relief staff can create stark choices between time spent on the completion of forms and the saving of beneficiaries in immediate peril, it is not difficult to understand that HRM professionals face particular challenges in implementing performance measurement consistently across all different facets of these organizations. Geographical separation, lack of understanding of purpose or outcome by participating staff or volunteers – especially those in front line service positions – and poor staff motivation in comparison to mission critical activities all contribute toward sporadic and inconsistent performance measurement implementation and analysis.

For the IGOs the problems may be different. The rigid nature of the pay and grading systems operating in many of them, as a counter to possible favouritism or cultural bias, mean that there are few financial or promotional opportunities that can be applied to the results of performance evaluations. And many of these organizations spend little on training and development opportunities. Performance systems that have no effective outcomes quickly fall into disrepute.

Managing human resources in the international organizations

This range of background factors and issues creates a different situation for those wishing to manage or to understand HRM strategies, policies, and practices in these organizations. In order to discuss these, an even higher level of generalization will be required for this section of the chapter. The issues will be addressed under the topic headings of relevance of HRM; quality of line management; role of the HR department; innovation; and competence management.

Relevance of HRM

Whilst it has been demonstrated that international organizations are distinctive in the extent to which they rely heavily upon human resources to meet their strategic objectives and achieve their missions, it is at best ironic (and at worse, a source of considerable organizational risk), that the relevance of the strategic application of HRM remains underdeveloped in this sector (Lee & Brewster 2004; Macpherson 2001).

Lacking strategic visibility as a core strategic resource operating at the centre of these organizations, too often the HRM function itself is:

- equated exclusively with the implementation of strategic decisions that have been taken elsewhere in the organization;

- regarded by staff, management, and governing bodies alike as a tactical means to an end, rather than as a contributor to organizational strategy;
- driven by process and procedure rather than informed by policy and direction.

Numerous factors contribute to the underdevelopment of HRM as a strategic tool within international NGOs. Primary factors include:

- the perceived necessity amongst trustees and senior executives to focus resource allocation upon direct delivery of service to beneficiaries as opposed toward staff/volunteer development;
- consequent low levels of material investment in HRM strategies and in the HRM resource itself relative to both the geographic scope and size of the organization;
- a lack of specialized HRM expertise at senior management and board level relative to other management disciplines represented;
- devolved national HRM decision-making structures mitigating against cohesive policy prescription and implementation at the supra national level;
- continued priority ascribed to the HRM function to ensure the organizational capacity to respond to short term, tactical, emergencies takes precedence over longer term strategic HRM considerations.

The lack of hard empirical evidence to support HRM strategic planning that this scenario engenders only serves to further emasculate the relative significance and importance ascribed to the HRM function strategically by senior management and volunteer board members alike and the relative pecking order of the HRM contribution to the overall strategic planning process.

The administrative nature of HRM in these organizations is, for many of them, deeply engrained and self-reinforcing. For instance, job descriptions and hierarchies have been the subject of many years of debate and negotiation; they are difficult to change – due particularly to promotion being an important reward incentive. Other contractual issues such as having to deal with potential conflict between international and local conditions of service further enhance the complexities within the organizations and tend to be dealt with through additional layers of bureaucracy. These organizations may differ extensively in terms of size and therefore with respect to the amount and type of HRM support required. Overall, however, in circumstances where the objectives are complex and neither the cost implications or the effectiveness of various approaches are apparent, attempts to create and sustain cost-effective HR strategies are inevitably much more difficult than they are in MNCs.

These factors impact upon HRM in unusual ways. These organizations may, for example, have to ensure that their recruitment is seen by and open to applicants from every country in the world. This means translation costs, system costs, and processing costs. An MNC, by contrast, might feel that an advertisement put out in a particular region, in the international language used by the corporation, and requiring applicants to get themselves to certain centres for interview, might be a good way of reducing costs and ensuring relevant language capability and initiative on the part of applicants. In some IGOs and NGOs this would be seen as impossible: straightforward discrimination. Generally, the international NFPs require equal opportunity to be manifest, US-style, in quotas; rather than the European tradition of requiring that each recruitment, promotion, etc is fair in itself.

Role of the HR department

The relative lack of organization-wide commitment to and understanding of the strategic role of HRM, compared with MNCs, leads the role of the HRM function itself often to be characterized as:

- a 'supporting' rather than 'leading' function when viewed in terms of its contribution toward mission achievement;
- an administrative function that is predominately reactive to the decisions of others, not proactive in its own right;
- being emasculated by comparison with staff and budget resource allocated to other functions (i.e. service delivery, income generation etc.);
- lacking participation in the identification and selection processes associated with the appointment of the most senior staff and trustees, and;
- uninvolved in corporate strategy.

As a consequence, HRM capacity is predominately identified throughout the rest of the organization as being synonymous with the day to day management of the minutia of staff personnel and employment systems

The continued concentration and reliance by the rest of the organization on the HRM function as tactical provider and trainer of employee foot soldiers necessarily determines that with limited resources and facing global potential reach, the role of the HRM department narrows to one that can sustain little more than a reactionary response to tactical expediency. As Parmenter (1999) notes, 'the problem with most nonprofits' human resource departments is not enough humans and not enough resources'. In response, it will be interesting to see whether or not European international NGOs follow the growing trend in US-based non-profits to outsource key HRM functions to external specialist providers.

Quality of line management

A major argument in the HRM literature is that HR departments can only improve the way people are managed to a limited degree. At least, or perhaps much more significant is the role of line managers in HRM. Like organizations in many sectors, the international not-for-profit organizations are not only heavily dependent on their human resources but are heavily dependent on the quality of their line managers. And, like other sectors, individuals often get promoted into management for reasons of technical skill rather than managerial capability. The consequence is that, despite some notable exceptions, many of these managers see their role as a more senior version of their previous role: writing papers for more senior committees or dealing with more important government officials. They do not see their role as ensuring that their team is well-organized, targeted, and producing good work.

This is being addressed, with the United Nations, for example, introducing management competences for their new Senior Management Network and encouraging the various programmes and agencies to either develop their own versions of such profiles or to roll out the centrally created ones. Some of the larger charities have developed similar competency profiles. The problems that arise are familiar from other sectors: are the managers in the organizations able to use such profiles to assess their subordinates? Can the organization offer the training and development needed to fill any gaps identified?

Conclusion

This chapter has explored HRM in Europe in the not-for-profit sector and, particularly, in the international NFP sector. To understand HRM in Europe, which is the home to many such organizations and where the employees of these organizations are a significant proportion of total employment, it is important to be aware of these organizations. As with many of the chapters in books such as this, the discussion has inevitably involved a level of generalization. In practice each organization is unique: however, there are enough similarities within these organizations and enough differences between them and the private sector profit-focused organizations for this level of abstraction to be valuable. These 'normatively' based organizations have different management problems to profit-focused organizations – and different problems in and approaches to HRM. These NFPs are conscious of the learning that is possible for them from the private sector: perhaps it is time to see if there is learning that the private sector can do from these organizations. It is certainly time to ensure that future research into HRM is less neglectful of the NFP sector, so that we can all get a comprehensive understanding of the meaning and practice of HRM.

Box 7.2

In terms of standard prescriptions on HRM, an organization like *Médecin sans Frontières* is challenging. They recruit some of the most highly educated and potentially highest paid people from secure, high-status professions, who are used to working in immaculate, sterile conditions.

They offer them short-term contracts, in desperate, dirty and often life-threatening working conditions, and on low pay.

And they have queues of qualified people waiting to join them . . .

References

Anon 2003. *People In Aid. Code of Good Practice. Revised Code of Good Practice in the Management and Support of Aid Personnel.* London: People In Aid. www.peoplein aid.org.uk

Brewster, C., van Ommeren, J., Adam, J. & Farndale, E. 1999. *HRM Policies and Practices in the United Nations Family of Organizations and Related Agencies, Report for CCAQ, United Nations.* Geneva.

Bruce, I. 1998. *Successful Charity Marketing: Meeting Need.* London: ICSA.

Croucher, R., Tyson, S. & Brewster, C. 2004. *HRM Policies and Practices in International Organizations, An Analysis for AHRMIO.* Geneva.

Drucker, P. F. 1990. *Managing the Non-Profit Organization.* New York: Harper Collins.

Forbes, D. P. 1998. Measuring the unmeasurable: empirical studies of nonprofit organization effectiveness from 1977–1997. *Nonprofit and Voluntary Sector Quarterly*, 27(2): 183–202.

Forsyth, J. 1999. Volunteer management strategies: balancing risk & reward. *Nonprofit World*, 17(3): 40.

Handy, C. 1988. *Understanding Voluntary Organizations.* London: Penguin.

Harris, H., Brewster, C. & Sparrow, P. 2003. *International HRM.* Wimbledon: CIPD.

Harzing, A.-W. & Ruysseveldt, V. 2004. *International HRM.* London: Sage.

Herzlinger, R. E. 1996. Can public trust in nonprofits and governments be restored? *Harvard Business Review*, 74 (2), Mar.–Apr. 1996: 97–108.

Hind, A. 1995. *The Governance and Management of Charities.* London: Voluntary Sector Press.

House, R. J., Hanges, P. J., Javidan, M., Dorfman, P. W. & Gupta, V. 2004. *Culture, Leadership and Organizations: the GLOBE Study of 62 Societies.* Thousand Oaks: Sage.

Hudson, M. 1999. *Managing Without Profit: The Art of Managing Third Sector Organizations* (2nd ed.). London: Penguin.

Inkson, K., Arthur M.B., Pringle, J. & Barry, S. 1997. Expatriate assignment versus overseas experience: contrasting models of international human resource development. *Journal of World Business*, 32(4): 351–368.

Jokinen, T., Brewster, C. & Suutari, V. 2005. *Development of 'know how' and 'know why' career capital during internal work experiences: Contrasting self-initiated foreign work experiences and expatriation.* University of Vaasa Working paper.

Lee, S. & Brewster, C. 2004. *HRM (HRM) Performance Measurement in the Non-profit Sector: Toward a Theoretical and Practical Understanding. Proceedings of 33rd ARNOVA Conference, Los Angeles, November 2004.* Los Angeles.

Lyons, M. 2001. *Third Sector.* Sydney: Allen and Unwin.

Macpherson, M. 2001. Performance measurement in not-for-profit and public sector organizations. *Measuring Business Excellence, Bradford.* Vol. 5 (2): 13–18.

Martinez, J. M. 2003. Liability and volunteer organizations: a survey of the law. *Nonprofit Management and Leadership*, 14(2): 51.

Mayrhofer, W. & Brewster, C. 1996. In praise of ethnocentricity: expatriate policies in European multinationals. *International Executive*, 38(6): 749–778.

Parmenter, E. 1999. Play to your strengths using outsourcing to manage human resources. *Nonprofit World*, 17(1): 38.

Pickard, J. 1997. Foreign aid charities urged to clean up act. *People Management*, 3(4): 8.

Poole, D. L., Davis, J. K., Reisman, J. & Nelson, J. 2001. Improving the quality of outcome evaluation plans. *Nonprofit Management and Leadership*, 11(4): 405–421.

Salamon, L. M., Anheier, H. K., List, R., Toepler, S., Sokolowski, S. W. & Associates. 1999. *Global Civil Society: Dimensions of the NFP Sector, Institute for Policy Studies.* Baltimore: John Hopkins University.

Sargeant, A. 1999. *Marketing Management for Nonprofit Organizations.* Oxford: Oxford University Press.

Suutari, V. & Brewster, C. 1998. The adaptation of expatriates in Europe: evidence from Finnish companies. *Personnel Review*, 27(2): 89–103.

Suutari, V. & Brewster, C. 2003. Repatriation: evidence from a longitudinal study of careers and empirical expectations among Finnish repatriates. *International Journal of HRM International Review*, 14(7): 1132–1151.

Tayeb, M. 2005. *International HRM: A Multinational Company Perspective.* Oxford: Oxford University Press.

Looking at oneself:
The roles and contribution
of HRM

Measuring HRM: the acid test for managing intangible resources

ULF JOHANSON AND BO HANSSON

Introduction

Let us first consider two common comments on the issue of measuring human resource management (HRM), one coming from a researcher and another from a practitioner.

The researcher:

> The acid test for HR practices is: Is it worth it? The language of business is money. Increased cost pressure and competitiveness as well as the need to show the contribution to the overall organizational performance combined with an increasing importance of the economic logic in various segments of society lead to two major effects in HRM. HRM is increasingly viewed in economic terms. The terminological change from Personnel Management to HRM is simply an indicator for the growing importance of looking at all resources, including people from an economic perspective. Therefore, HRM has to take a very strict cost-benefit view on its activities not only in theory but also in practice. A new need of documenting activities and 'proving' contributions arises. This leads to a growing importance in HRM of the formal evaluation of HR activities and a new significance of HR costing and accounting.

The practitioner:

> Stig is working as an internal rehabilitation and health promotion consultant at a company with around 1,000 employees. Over the years, Stig has frequently used economic arguments to motivate rehabilitation and health promotion initiatives.

It is necessary and the only thing that works, and you know that we never perform any formal calculations, nor do we perform systematic follow-ups. I try to get the managers in charge to understand that it is economically infeasible not to engage in rehabilitation and preventive interventions. Imagine how much it costs to have people under-performing, or worse, having people doing nothing productive. To spend 35,000 Swedish Crowns (4,000 EUR) in rehabilitation or invest in equipment to make it possible for someone with a minor handicap to work is difficult, but making a decision to spend 180,000 Swedish Crowns (20,000 EUR) on a new machine is done easily. An employee that does not do anything productive and that has a salary of 20,000 Swedish Crowns (2,200 EUR) costs the company, with all indirect costs, close to half a million Swedish Crowns (55,000 EUR) annually. If you have an employee with a minor hand injury that needs a special tool for 30,000 Swedish Crowns (3,300 EUR), it is enough that the person improves his or her productivity by only 6 per cent of normal capacity to make it profitable to invest in the tool. We have earned considerable money since I have been able to convince managers to make these investments and because of this, many of our employees are no longer absent from work. This process takes time, however, because changing a person's attitudes is a slow process. Some people think you can change mindsets swiftly, but it takes at least 10 years.

Statements such as these are common and have been so for at least forty years. However, the proposal that HRM ought to be subject to formal evaluation as well as costing and accounting appears to be hard to achieve at the firm level. Why is this the case? Our intention in this chapter is to examine research on correlation between human resource (HR) investments and different outcomes, such as productivity and profitability, but primarily to elaborate on the different approaches to management control, specifically addressing HR. Before addressing these issues, however, we start with a brief overview of different proposals regarding management control and HR. The chapter concludes with a discussion focusing on the different approaches.

Recent management control models addressing human resources

Before treating three management control proposals addressing human resources, let us first briefly provide the definition of management control that is used in this chapter.

The management control concept

Management control is defined in various ways. The concept often refers to activities related to controlling and governing an organization (the control routines) and to the information sources/areas that the control activities are mainly based on (the control system). Anthony (1965) draws a distinction between management control systems and management control routines. He insists that the system facilitates the process and is the means on which the process occurs. The system explains *what it is*, and the process explains *how it functions*. To understand the system it becomes necessary to understand the process and vice versa. Flamholtz (1996) provides a broad definition when he defines management control as those manoeuvres that (1) motivate people to take action consistent with organizational objectives, (2) co-ordinate efforts of different parts of an organization and (3) provide information about the results of performance and operations. Consequently, Flamholtz refers to both the sources for management control (the system) and the co-ordination of activities (the process) that take place chiefly because of the measures that are taken. Environmental issues, technology, size, strategy or culture could all influence management control practices. Flamholtz proposes that control systems, which are not consistent with the value system of an organization, are likely to create a certain degree of resistance (in Emmanuel *et al.* 1990). Two other issues addressed over the years in management control definitions are whether informal systems and routines should be taken into account and who is in the position of control (i.e. manager or employee). Simon (1990) excludes informal systems and routines in proposing that management control systems are the formalized procedures and systems that use information to maintain or alter patterns in organizational activity. In contrast, Machin (1983) holds that management control systems are the formal and informal systems. He further asserts that the objective of management control systems is to help individuals control the things they do with themselves and other resources.

In this chapter we suggest a *process-oriented* definition of management control. The management control process comprises both formal and informal elements and is a process of (1) understanding, (2) communicating and (3) encouraging action in accordance with the vision and strategies of the firm. Further, the management control process is, in our view, not exclusively a top management issue. A precondition for a management control process that encourages action in accordance with the vision and the strategies is a widespread learning that includes not only the top management team but also all the employees. To facilitate learning and adapt action continuous follow-up is essential. Indicators of intangibles could be used to support understanding, communication, action and follow-up.

HR costing and accounting

In recent years, a number of models have been generated in an effort to express employees' contributions to the organization in financial terms. Although these models have often been praised as a major breakthrough, they have also been an increasing subject of criticism (Johanson 1998).

Although there are many early examples (Johanson 1992), the development did not really take off until the early 1960s, and in 1968 Brummet *et al.* proposed the concept Human Resource Accounting (HRA). Models were developed for managerial purposes and for reporting HR investments and values to capital market participants (Hermansson 1964; Brummet *et al.* 1968; Lev & Schwartz 1971). The American Accounting Association defined HRA as:

> The process of identifying and measuring data about human resources and communicating this information to interested parties. . . . It involves measuring the costs incurred by business firms and other organizations to recruit, select, hire, train and develop human assets. It also involves measuring the economic value of people to organizations.
>
> (Flamholtz 1985)

However, the idea of measuring human resources is not only derived from accountants in that psychologists and sociologists have also proposed that the financial utility of different activities in the field of HRM ought to be measured. In 1965, both Cronbach and Gleser and Naylor and Shine developed models for estimating the financial utility of personnel selection. They used the concept 'utility analysis' (UA). Nearly thirty years later, Latham & Whyte (1994: 31) defined UA as '. . . a way of forecasting the net financial benefits resulting from . . . HR interventions . . .'

To embrace both HRA and UA Gröjer & Johanson (1996) suggested the concept Human Resource Costing and Accounting (HRCA). HRCA models can be divided into the following groups: (1) the valuation of human resources (e.g. a valuation of future financial benefits of human resources discounted into present value) or human resource investments (e.g. a valuation of costs spent on recruitment or training) on the balance sheet with its corresponding depreciations in the profit and loss account, (2) a specification of human resource costs in the profit and loss account (e.g. costs for recruitment, training, sick leave and rehabilitation) and (3) UA or cost/benefit analysis of different HR investments.

Within each group, there are numerous models. Examples of HRCA applications can be found in Gröjer & Johanson (1996) and Johanson (2000).

The development of HRA was intensive during the 1960s and early 1970s, when the topic of HRA rose rapidly to the upper reaches of the research agenda. Fundamental concepts were developed in which models for the calculation of personnel costs and for the value of personnel initiatives were systematized. When the development within HRA reached its highest intensity, UA was almost entirely suspended. Similarly, when HRA lost momentum, the development within UA accelerated.

Despite severe criticism, the interest in HRCA did not vanish from the agenda (Gröjer & Johanson 1998). Following a period of quiescence during the 1980s, there has been a revived interest in HRCA from a number of international organizations (e.g. the OECD, EC, European Centre for the Development of Vocational Training and the American Society for Training and Development), national organizations and governments (e.g. Finland and Sweden), not to mention the large interest from numerous private firms. In 1991, the Swedish government proposed a legal obligation for organizations to report on HRA in the annual report in order to increase investments in the working environment. The proposal was not carried through at that time but about ten years later the government suggested a similar idea in the form of health statements (HS).

Health statement

The idea underlying HS is to visualize the connections between employee health and productivity and profitability. Unlike HRCA, there is currently no commonly proposed HS model. However, the basic idea stems from a combination of ideas from HRCA and intellectual capital (IC). Different HS development projects are presently being carried out in Sweden. For example, in one project eight local authorities work in a network to investigate if it is possible to develop a common model. So far, these eight organizations agree that a HS model should comprise the following components:

1   A statement addressing what needs to be done (or has been achieved) regarding health and the overall vision, strategies and performance of the organization. The statement includes the vision of the organization, strategies, health components, targets for each of the components, activities of each target, indicators and comments addressing the relations between all the different items.
2   A model focusing on how the work with HS should be done in order to increase attention and mobilize action.

Intellectual capital

In the middle of the 1990s, a number of OECD conferences were held to address the question on how to account for competence and other intangible resources (e.g. OECD 1997a, 1997b, 1997c & 1999). The OECD initiative was based on the notion that intangibles appear to be increasingly important as determinants of enterprise growth, productivity gains, profitability and wealth creation. However, the importance of intangibles exceeds the current ability to recognize and measure them. This gap is also evident in external reporting, which might cause mis-allocation in capital markets. To promote training and education in member countries in 1995 the EC published a White Paper called *Teaching and Learning – Towards the Learning Society* (1995). Objective 5 in the White Paper states: 'treat capital investment and investment in training on an equal basis'.

Stating it clearly and consistently the EC proposed a HRA approach when holding that training investment ought to be treated in the same way on the balance sheet as other capital investments. This was a strategy that OECD was in the process of abandoning. Instead, the OECD proposed that some kind of new reporting framework had to be constructed and then subjected to standardization. At a later conference, the concept of IC was accepted. In the conference proceedings it was stated that IC seemed to be a more promising approach than HRA (OECD 1997a).

But what is meant by the concept of IC? Lately, IC has been defined as follows: 'Value is created when the technological, human and organizational resources are aligned to enhance the processes of knowledge creation, sharing and exploitation' (E*Know-Net 2004: 5). In the report it is further proposed that IC is made up of human, structural and relational capital. However, IC is more than the sum of human, structural and relational resources of a firm. From experience with the IC concept in Danish firms, Bukh (2003) concluded that IC is about the complementary of different IC categories. If people are relevant, it is not only the employee but also the customer or user. Various people are part of a constellation and the productivity of one resource may be influenced by the investment in another. IC deals with the logic of an economy of creativity (Mouritsen 1999) by empowering individuals and structuring processes. The stories and metaphors comprising a vision of the future are as important as the measurements of intangibles (ibid.).

At the end of the 1990s, the EC encouraged a number of initiatives within the area of intangibles, and in 1998 the Commission decided to support a six-nation (Denmark, Finland, France, Norway, Spain and Sweden) research project named 'Measuring and reporting intangibles to understand and improve innovation management' (Meritum 2002). This project was mainly directed towards research in classification of intangibles, management control of intangibles and capital market deficiencies related to intangibles.

The suggestions for developing and using HRCA, HS or IC or other concepts not addressed here (e.g. The Intangible Asset Monitor, Sveiby 1997 or the balanced scorecard, Kaplan & Norton 1992) are based on many different and often conflicting agendas. Some proponents may have a management control interest (affecting internal behaviour) or a capital market interest (valuing the firm), others may have an interest in increasing the firm's competitiveness, and still others may have a quality of working life interest. The models are also based on very different ideologies. HRCA is based on the idea that because conventional accounting reports are normally discussed as the first point on the agenda of most management meetings, the potential for change is high if HR issues are illuminated in the accounting documents. The proponents of IC and other similar concepts normally have a diametrically opposing view. The new economic era with its high dependence on competence needs new non-financial tools. However, neither IC nor HS (and certainly not HRCA) completely cuts the ties to financial control. What lessons can be learned from experience with the three models? What are the similarities and what are the differences in the models?

HR measures and company performance

In the context of measuring and reporting non-financial measures a question that arises is to what extent HRM and HR measures are related to company success. Or, as the anonymous researcher stated in the introduction to this chapter, 'The acid test for HR practices is: Is it worth it?'. To what extent has the research community responded to this proposal, i.e. what kinds of studies have been performed on HR and company performance (e.g. productivity and profitability)? What are the findings? These studies will be referred to under four subheadings: employee training, health promotion, HRM practices and high performance work systems, and leadership and corporate culture.

Employee training

Several recent papers have shown that employee training generates substantial gains for firms. For HR people, these results might not be too surprising. However, because individuals can bargain their wage, or leave the firm or in other ways influence the training investment's potential pay off, most economists regard training or human capital (HC) investments as a subject tied to the individual and not to the firm. Because firms do not own these resources, labour economists have argued that firms cannot profit from training their employees. Becker (1962) attempted to resolve this issue by suggesting that some types of training are viable for investment. He divided company training into two components: general and specific training. The core idea of Becker's theory is that the party that is most likely to benefit from the investment should also be the party that pays for it. General training is useful not only to the firm providing the training but also to other firms. In a competitive labour market general training would lead to an increased wage for the employee and offset the profit for the firm that provided the training. Specific training, on the other hand, does not benefit other firms and the firm providing the training is thus more likely to benefit from this type of training investment.

However, the results from recent research suggest that companies make money on both specific and general training. A number of research papers with access to longitudinal (panel) data show that training generates large gains for firms in terms of increased productivity, profitability and market valuation (see Barrett & O'Connell 2001; Dearden *et al.* 2000; Groot 1999; Bosworth & Loundes 2002; d'Arcimoles 1997; Bassi *et al.* 2004). In the majority of these studies the direction of the relationship is established, i.e. we can, with reasonable confidence, show that training generates the performance effects and not the reverse. It is also noteworthy that these studies are from different countries (with different labour market systems) throughout the world and with several based on European datasets (for an overview of recent findings on the economic impact of training, see Hansson *et al.* 2004).

Health promotion

Much of the research on the effects of health, health promotion programmes, and absenteeism originates from the USA. In contrast to the research on training in which large-scale surveys of companies are normally used, the research on health promotion and absenteeism is generally based on studies conducted inside firms. Many of the studies use large populations of employees and an experimental research design in testing the impact of health promotion programmes and absenteeism on such company variables as medical treatment costs and health insurance costs (Pelletier 1999; Goetzel *et al.* 1999; Aldana 2001; Andersson *et al.* 2001; Golaszewski 2001; Riedel *et al.* 2001). The general conclusion from these studies is that investments in programmes for reducing absenteeism and improving the health of employees normally yield good returns. Moreover, a number of health-related issues (e.g. stress and multiple risk factors) seem to be associated with losses or costs for employers.

HRM practices

As noted previously, this area of HRM research has made some significant contributions to our understanding of the connection between HRM practices and business performance (e.g. Becker & Huselid 1997; Becker & Gerhart 1996; Huselid 1995; Ichniowski *et al.* 1995). Contrary to training research that usually has access to panel data (data over time), research on HRM practices is generally based on cross-sectional estimates, making it a bit difficult to draw firm conclusions about the direction of the relationship. In other words, the question of, 'Is it high performing firms that can afford High Performance Work Systems, or is it High Performance Work Systems that generate performance?' is difficult to disentangle. That most of the research is based on level data instead of panel data is largely because firms seldom make any large changes to their HRM policies. Measuring changes in HRM practices therefore requires extensive measurement periods.

A good deal of the inference about the impact on firm performance is thus confined to cross-sectional data (some exceptions are the studies of Ichniowski *et al.* 1995 and d'Arcimoles 1997). However, many studies use a research design that accounts for the heterogeneity among firms, resulting in statistical models that are more robust.

There has been an ongoing debate on whether bundles of HR practices are the source of value creation in firms or whether certain practices contribute more than others. There is also the question of whether HRM practices are generally applicable to most enterprises or whether they are firm- or country-specific. Concerning the latter criticism, researchers maintain that the institutional setting in Europe affects the potential to create high performance work practices because of the presence of strong labour unions and labour regulations. For instance, a Dutch study by Boselie *et al.* (2001) maintains that to apply research on high performance work practices we need to adjust the theoretical framework to suit the European situation. Nevertheless, the findings on HRM practices and company performance suggest that a number of HR-related factors contribute to company performance (see Boselie *et al.* 2001 for a more elaborate analysis of these factors). Among some of the more prominent practices are recruitment and selection procedures, reward and compensation systems, employee participation and involvement practices and training practices.

Leadership and corporate culture

The importance of leadership and corporate culture might seem to most people to be an obvious factor in contributing to company performance. Still, it is quite tricky to test these two assumptions empirically. With reference to company cases (Johanson *et al.* 2001), the study by Arvonen & Pettersson (2002) confirms a link between a personnel-oriented leadership style and cost-efficiency and efficiency in change processes. Similarly, the results of Flamholtz (2001) suggest a link between a strong corporate culture and profitability.

Apart from the above-mentioned HRM-related factors (training, health promotion, HRM practices and leadership), information about labour compensation and wages also appear to be linked to both risk and return of specific companies, suggesting that salaries are important determinants of company value (Rosett 2000; Hansson 2004). Analyses of employee wages suggest that high-wage employees (more HC) create more value for companies and that wages are important factors in understanding the pricing of companies on the stock market.

In conclusion, research on issues such as HRM, health promotion, competence and training have made some important breakthroughs in the past decade. To demonstrate the contribution of HR practices to the overall organizational performance generally gives more attention to these issues both inside and outside companies (Johanson 1992). It is important to note that these numbers, in addition to other indicators, are just rough approximations of a complex reality. Nevertheless, the research thus far suggests that following HR-related measures is important in order to appreciate what creates value in companies.

Different approaches to management control and human resources

The overall picture when it comes to what companies actually do in terms of management control with respect to human resources is difficult to assess. Some sources of information can give us a reasonable understanding of what is taking place inside firms. Among these sources are case studies (e.g. Johanson 2000; Mouritsen 1999; Johanson *et al.* 2001; Nordic Industrial Fund 2001) and the European-based Cranet survey (1999). Using the Cranet data set (1999), we have singled out three European countries (UK, Sweden and Spain) for comparisons of what firms do in terms of HR evaluation and reporting.

Figure 8.1 shows the distribution of the answers in each country to the following questions: Do you systematically analyze employee training needs (training needs)? Do you monitor the effectiveness of your training (training effects)? If yes, how often do you make a formal evaluation? Regarding the last question, we have only considered those organizations that reported using formal evaluation. Close to 80 per cent of the firms reported that they analyze training needs and close to

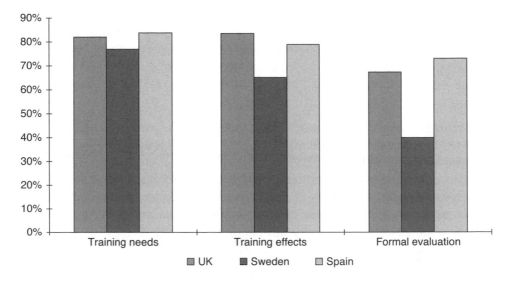

Figure 8.1 Percentage of organizations evaluating training

Source: Cranet data-set 1999

80 per cent reported that they follow up on the effectiveness of the training (with fewer organizations doing this in Sweden). Of those monitoring training, 60–70 per cent always used a formal evaluation in UK and Spain, whereas 40 per cent of the organizations performed a formal evaluation in Sweden.

Evaluations of specific HR practices thus seem to be very common in most European organizations and maybe somewhat surprisingly more common in the UK and Spain than in Sweden.

Another question concerns the practice of appraisal systems. Figure 8.2 depicts the results based on the following question: Do you have an appraisal system in operation for the following staff categories? About 90 per cent of the organizations in the UK and Sweden hold that they practice such a system for managers. The corresponding figure in Spain was 60 per cent. Nearly 80 per cent of the organizations answering the survey in Sweden have an appraisal system for workers, whereas 70 per cent and 40 per cent in the UK and Spain, respectively, reported having practiced an appraisal system even for workers.

Whereas managerial appraisal is more common in the UK as compared with Spain and Sweden, the appraisal system is more widespread in Swedish organizations because more employees are involved in each organization.

In summary, even if we do not know anything about how it works, monitoring and evaluating HR practices is, according to the Cranet survey (1999), surprisingly common in the three countries that we have selected. However, the practice of coupling monitoring and evaluating HR activities to the financial control of the organization is still not revealed. What are the experiences from the firm level

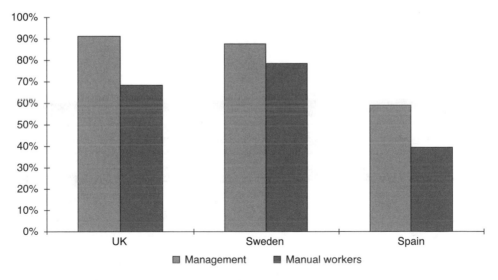

Figure 8.2 Appraisal system in operation for managers and workers

Source: Cranet data-set 1999

with models addressing the coupling between intangible resources and activities (e.g. competence or HR activities) and financial control, i.e. what is known regarding the proposal that the researcher and the practitioner implicitly raised in the introduction to the present chapter? The rest of this chapter is divided into three subsections: HRCA – the balance sheet approach, HRCA – the profit and loss account approach and HRCA – the costing or cost/benefit approach, IC and HS.

HRCA – the balance sheet approach

Company training generally involves considerable amounts of money. In a study of Swedish firms listed on the Stockholm Stock Exchange (Hansson 2005) approximately 24,000 Swedish Crowns (2,600 EUR) per employee were spent on training in 2001–02 (including all costs associated with training). For median firms answering the survey, training investments constitute about 13 per cent of the overall investments made by these firms (approximated by the relation between training investments and depreciation expenses). In some sectors (e.g. consulting) training investments constitute over 80 per cent of the overall investments. These figures show that a large part of company investments is missing in traditional accounting. In some sectors a major part of the investments is not accounted for, suggesting that the balance sheets of these companies are poor representations of their actual book value.

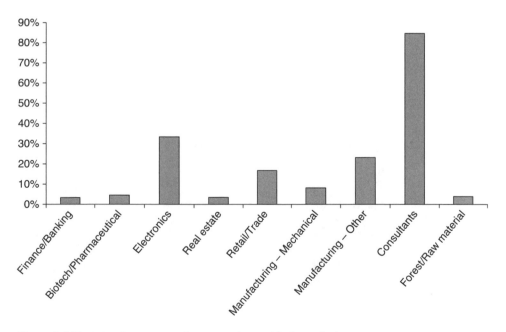

Figure 8.3 Training investments in comparison with depreciation expenses

Source: Hanson 2005

However, the balance sheet approach has encountered a number of hinders. Even if there are no mandatory norms for how an extra balance sheet should be set up, the official and audited balance sheet faces the opposite situation, i.e. there are numerous mandatory norms regulating the content of an audited balance sheet. A major obstacle is that neither employees nor investments in employees (e.g. investments in recruitment, training and rehabilitation) qualify as assets.

The advocates of a balance sheet valuation suggest that inclusion of investments in human resources ensures a more accurate value of the company investments. The opponents, on the other hand, note that the balance sheet is already an insufficient instrument to exhibit the true value of a company. It has also been proposed that a valuation of HR investments based on historical costs is not a valid measurement of the value, whereas another opportunity, a valuation based on future earnings, is consistent with present accounting conventions.

There are advantages and disadvantages concerning the controversial balance sheet issue. An exclusion of HR expenditures from the balance sheet will probably underline the general conception that HR expenditures should be regarded as costs. If they are included, the possibility of looking upon HR activities as investments will be strengthened. But how can we be sure? Is there a risk that there will be a debate about valuation principles without affecting the general view on HR expenditures? The general answer to this question is probably 'Yes!' This is the experience of an almost ten-year long debate led by the International Accounting Standards Committee that ended in a status quo situation in 1998 regarding valuing intangible resources (e.g. competence) on the balance sheet (IASC 1998). The opportunity of changing accounting norms, which largely influence our economic thinking and behaviour at the firm level, seems presently a closed matter.

HRA textbooks normally comprise different suggestions on balance sheet models (e.g. Flamholtz 1985). However, with minor exceptions, especially from the football industry, practical applications are hard to find. One exception is the Swedish telecommunication company Telia. In the 1990s, Telia published an extra balance sheet over a five-year period in which recruitment and training costs were treated as assets. The assets were written off over a three-year period in the profit and loss account. The general idea was that by treating training and recruitment as assets even in an accounting sense, managers were anticipated to increase their investments in HR. Increased HR investments were at that time viewed as a crucial issue for the survival of the company.

HRCA – the profit and loss account approach

Another means of making HR issues more transparent is to specify different HR costs in the profit and loss account. This approach has been extensively practiced in

Table 8.1 An example of different personnel cost items as percentage of total personnel costs

	Year 1	Year 2
Replacing employees	3.0	2.3
Employee redundancies	1.0	3.3
Training	6.0	4.5
Absence	2.0	1.1
Rehabilitation		0.1
Physical work environment		1.0
Trade union relations	1.0	0.6
Employee benefits	1.0	1.0
Annual leave	9.0	8.5
Miscellaneous	2.0	1.2
Wages for production	75.0	77.4

Source: Gröjer and Johanson 1996

Sweden and Finland during the past fifteen years. One of many organizations that established HR profit and loss accounts on a yearly basis was the Stockholm County Council Public Dental Care Service, cf. Table 8.1.

Using a detailed profit and loss account (this was possible because of a well functioning time-reporting system), the costs for different personnel activities are calculated both in monetary terms and as percentages of total personnel costs. This was accomplished for different departments and used in the management control process. The figures were used for comparisons between units as well as between years. 'Wages for production' is an efficiency ratio revealing how much of the personnel costs were actually used for production.

The idea of achieving attention and change by filling old instruments and routines like the profit and loss account or the balance sheet with a new content is appealing; however, what are the experiences? After several years of experience and with a number of organizations involved, the following conclusions can be drawn. The awareness of HR costs has been significantly increased and different activities have been started that otherwise would probably not have been initiated (Johanson 1992). However, one major disadvantage is that the approach is completely cost oriented. There is no alignment with the benefits of the costs and the risk of regarding HR activities as even more costly might increase in sharp contrast to the two statements provided in the introduction to this chapter (as well as the balance sheet example provided in the section above). The approach does not address the question, 'Is it worth it?'

Another hinder preventing change is the accounting routines. There are witnesses from many organizations pointing out that changes in the accounting systems have been difficult to achieve, probably because accounting is so regulated that even minor changes come into conflict with a culture that strongly appreciates stability but not change (Johanson 1999). In many organizations the HR profit and loss account has not been integrated in the general management control system. The project has ended up as a report produced by the HR department but not seriously considered by anyone else. This is not to say that the approach is a complete failure. It could perhaps be combined with other approaches which we address later in this chapter.

HRCA – the costing or cost/benefit approach

In the statements at the beginning of the chapter we found that, like UA, both the researcher and the practitioner offer a cost/benefit approach. There are numerous examples of this kind of thinking as well as many applications made during the past century within the HRM field (Johanson 1992). Before discussing shortcomings, let us provide an example in order to illustrate our point.

The calculation described here (Table 8.2) aims at clarifying which recruitment strategy to use when employing chartered accountants. The firm has compared the costs of employing a certified auditor with those of employing a newly graduated Master of Accounting who will be undergoing a five-year training programme. The current staff members are classified into three categories: a) entrance level – qualified assistant, b) after two years of internal competence development – responsible for tasks and c) after another three years, the employee typically acquires authorization as a chartered accountant. If the firm uses a headhunting strategy, the training costs will be less as compared to internal training (item 1 in Table 8.2). However, the recruitment costs (item 2) as well as the profit on each new recruitment (item 3) will be higher. In addition, it is not necessary to over-recruit to the same extent as if hiring newly graduated people among which personnel turnover is normally high. Therefore, the firm can save in terms of search costs (item 4) and training costs (item 5). Finally, the firm will not gain any profit from over-recruiting (item 6).

The calculation is based on realistic assumptions and was implemented in the 1990s, which implies that some of the figures, such as salaries, will be higher today. However, as our example, we have chosen to use the actual figures relevant at the time. Employing a Master in Accounting subject to internal training is about 300,000 SEK more expensive. Thus, which recruitment strategy should a firm choose? If the decision was made only based on this calculation, internal training would stop in favour of recruiting chartered accountants. However, other factors must be considered. What happens if all other accountancy firms close down their internal training programmes? If this occurs, it will be more difficult to recruit chartered accountants and the cost of headhunting increases. As a result, it may prove necessary to re-establish internal training programmes, resulting in higher

Table 8.2 A financial comparison between two recruitment strategies for auditors – headhunting versus internal training

1. Less training costs: 5 years × 67,000	=	335,000
2. Higher recruitment costs 20,000–200,000	=	−180,000
3. Higher profit: 2 years × (180,000 − 110,000)	=	140,000
3 years × (180,000 − 130,000)	=	150,000
4. No search costs for over-recruited: 35% × 20,000	=	7,000
5. No costs for training of over-recruited (probably the same as earlier): 35% × 335,000 : 2	=	59,000
6. No annual profit from over-recruiting (probably the same as earlier): 35% × 2 years × 110,000 + 35% × 3 years × 130,000	=	−214,000
Total approximate SEK	=	300,000

Source: Johanson 1992

costs for competence development. However, internal training has other qualitative advantages not included in the calculation. One advantage is that internal training contributes to loyalty toward the firm, which in the long-term will reduce the costs of personnel turnover. Therefore, the difference of 300,000 SEK must be weighed against other qualitative advantages.

When doing costings, some items are easier to price than others. The accounting system can be used to retrieve information about the cost of certain activities, but this is where the problem of causality arises. The relationship between effort and effect is always uncertain. For instance, can we be sure that reductions in costs because of absenteeism relate to new work methods? How can we be certain that growing sales actually are the effect of sales courses for the sales force? The answer is that we can never be sure of these kinds of relationships. But does it really matter? Although it obviously matters in scientific settings, does it matter for practitioners in action? Probably not. For the practitioner in the introduction it does not matter if he can prove his argumentation by using scientific references. He knows from experience and the people he converses with also have knowledge of what normally happens at the factory floor even if they do not translate this into monetary terms.

The idea of introducing HR costings and cost benefit analysis in a regular and systematic way i.e. to integrate with the management control of the firm causes more problems. For the past forty years, the idea of implementing HRCA has been an ambition of many people. In Sweden, numerous organizations have had that ambition and after studying some of these cases, Johanson (1999) concludes that the managers in most cases have very positive attitudes toward HRCA. Nonetheless, the usage of HRCA as a part of the management control process appears to have decreased because of three factors: 1) lack of knowledge of HR costs, values and outcomes, as well as how to calculate these, 2) missing demands from top management and 3) reward systems that fail to consider HRCA information. These findings may be interpreted in light of Cascio's (1996) postulation that UA presently suffers from three broad sets of problems. 1) theoretical and operational technical problems concerning validity, 2) inability to communicate the results from UA in a credible manner and 3) a failure to focus on critical value-adding activities within the firm.

The failure of focusing value-adding activities serves as the point of departure in the next approach.

Intellectual capital

IC aims at investigating, focusing and mobilizing the core value-adding activities in the firm. There are presently no norms to follow because the concept is new. Furthermore, it is difficult to give a precise definition of IC. Many firms prefer not to use the concept (e.g. Nokian Tyres and Swedebank which are discussed below).

The first example is Nokian Tyres in Finland (Nordic Industrial Fund 2001: 60–61). This company discloses an annual HR report with the structure described in Table 8.3.

To stress that innovation and growth requires good internal relations Nokian Tyres has implemented the 'Daily Weather', a kind of exit poll indicating the daily state of employee satisfaction of the company. It is the responsibility of management, as well as a precondition of innovation, to maintain an atmosphere of trust and creativity.

By revealing this information in conjunction with the financial information, Nokian Tyres wants to focus its management and other personnel on issues that sustain profit development. The public HR supplement is used to inform both shareholders and investors about the intangible assets of the company and as an internal tool for strategic management. The report indicates what is considered important for sustainable success, and what the management finds most essential – the welfare of committed and innovative personnel.

The second example refers to Swedebank (Johanson et al. 2001), a bank employing about 12,000 people. The aim of their IC system is to reflect on the present, past and future with the belief that good management and empowered workers affect the entire HC value. This, in turn, generates high customer satisfaction resulting in higher profitability. The bank continuously measures Human Capital (HC), Market Capital (MC), productivity and profitability. HC measures the notion of empowerment, i.e. what employees want to do, what they can do and what they actually do in relation to business. However, it does not measure how well employees get on in the organization. How well people enjoy their work is no

Table 8.3 Nokian Tyres' Human Resource Report

Section	Items/indicators
Introduction	* Business and personnel strategy
Human Resource Income Statement	* Personnel cost structure, including training and development, sickness and accidents, turnover and vacation * Sustainable development overview
Personnel structure	* Number of employees * Permanent/temporary employed * Employee turnover * Demography * Seniority
Knowledge and work ability	* Life-long learning * Teams * Education level * The management * Occupational health and safety
Internal relations	* Employee satisfaction * Internal customership * Compensation and reward system * Employee participation * Process and product initiatives * Development projects and experiments
External relations	* Customer satisfaction * University and institutional co-operation

guarantee of success in business. The bank addresses four core HR areas, namely meeting with customers, competence, organization and leadership. MC is a concept comprising for instance the way customers gauge a company's appreciation of them, how satisfied customers are with the company and how loyal the customers feel toward the company. The results of the comprehensive and systematic measurements are co-ordinated into a single large database. Of particular urgency in the database are the interrelationships between HC, MC and profitability.

The correlations have, among other things, demonstrated that leadership affects all aspects of the organization, i.e. if leadership fails, everything else fails. A high HC index propels profitability in that qualified leadership leads to increased HC. A higher HC, in turn, results in a higher MC, which subsequently affects profitability positively. On the other hand, local banks without solid leadership find it difficult to show a profit margin.

Large variation in the use of the results has been noted, from individuals who use the results extensively to those that barely use them. However, persons who are negative and never use the results have become fewer in number. Furthermore, the question is advocated from the highest management levels and is the bank's model in its follow-up business activities. When planning its activities, every local unit engages in measuring. The work with the tool and the results from the measurements have had consequences for leadership development programmes as well as for recruitment policies.

The management control process itself is also subject to continuous adjustment in an effort to improve the understanding of the specific value–creation chain of the bank. It is also subject to a follow-up routine: 1) response rates on attitude surveys are followed and analyzed, 2) statistical analysis concerning the consequences of using the measurement results is done and 3) statistical analysis on the effects of providing feedback on measurement results is performed.

The second item is strongly correlated to improvements on the HC index, MC index and financial performance at the local bank level. The third item reveals that work satisfaction and performance are significantly higher in organizational units where employees were given feedback on earlier measurements.

To ensure the survival of the HR management control system a number of routines (Nelson & Winter 1982) are followed (Johanson *et al.* 2001):

1   *Recognition and measurement routines*
    ● HC surveys
    ● MC surveys
2   *Reporting routines*
    ● continuous internal reports
    ● informal information to analysts
3   *Evaluation routines*
    ● evaluation of single indicators by each manager
    ● statistical analysis
4   *Attention routines*
    ● meetings
5   *Motivation routines*
    ● benchmarking
    ● dialogues
    ● salary bonus
6   *Commitment routines*
    ● ownership, contract
7   *Follow-up routines*
    ● analyses of response rates

The routines listed above could be related to the action model of Weick & Swieringa (1987) in the sense that meetings and dialogues direct the attention of managers and employees to the results of the measurements. These results, in combination with statistical analysis, affect *knowledge*. *Motivation* is further addressed by a clear top management demand, benchmarking and salary bonuses.

Finally, *commitment* to change is made possible by means of a contract between managers at different levels. The empirical data reveal that organizational learning processes have been affected in the way that dominating cognitive schemes and co-ordinated action have been obtained.

The health statement approach

In Sweden, the government has proposed that HS should be developed in order to mobilize attention and action in decreasing costly (both at the firm level and at the societal level) sick leave among the workforce. By directing attention to the healthy or unhealthy situations in an organization, preferably with a connection to profitability, it becomes more likely to get health issues on the management's agenda and thus decrease sick leave. One of many activities that have been performed is a three-year R&D project addressing HS and involving seven Swedish municipalities. The general idea of the project is to let these organizations, all of which claim to have serious problems with absenteeism, develop their own HS model. The focus is not only directed on substance but also on usefulness. What will the municipalities do with the HS concept? How will they manage it so that it can be used to improve the health situation amongst their co-workers? Below are some of our experiences from this project.

The experiences are very different between the seven local authorities and even between different departments within a particular local authority. Many state that the HS project has meant that issues on health, well being or personnel politics have received increased attention followed by successful processes of change. The general opinion exists that HS is important – in some cases crucial – for the municipality's future. The upcoming need for recruitment of new personnel is one of the main challenges to which the HS project can contribute. If the need for more manpower can't be solved through decreased sick leave and increased status as an attractive employer, the organizations will face serious problems in a couple of years.

The concept of HS could be understood as implying a final report of something that has already been, rather than an ambition of improving something. The most positive aspect of the concept is that it signals gravity. The concept as such is interpreted as being able to put health issues on the agenda and give health as a resource a place in the regular management control system. However, even with this argument, there are many people who are doubtful whether the HS will secure the understanding of health improvements as an investment for the future.

What should a HS contain? What should a HS report contain? One of the organizations has concluded that HS should include the following elements:

- complement traditional accounting;
- be based on HR statistics and HR costing;

- contain measurable facts as well as experienced states;
- visualize the attitudes and values in an organization;
- show the co-workers' health in a broad perspective;
- visualize the strengths and weaknesses of the work environment and organization.

Another organization is of the opinion that HS is merely an elaboration of HRCA. The organization stresses the following:

> The basis for HS is the HRCA that provides an understanding to the HR structure. An example of key ratios is number of employees, distribution according to gender, age distribution, level of education, and so on. In the HS we develop the accounting with ratios concerning the employee's work effort from a health and economic perspective . . . the statistics is then completed with some sort of measurement on perceived working situation.

By visualizing the connection between heath issues and financial control, a foundation for action is accomplished. HS should therefore be a plan for action. Although the project was not completed at the time this chapter was written, the model brought forth from the participants will likely have the following structure:

- vision;
- strategies;
- health components (e.g. elements of success);
- goals for each health component;
- activities for each health component;
- follow-up and measuring methods for each health component;
- indicators (could be ratios and statements/testimonies but it could also be illustrative HR calculations) for each health component.

The proposition of model will be accompanied by reflections on the means of implementation.

The magic of numbers has clearly made work difficult. Indicators and key ratios based on executed surveys are seen as a necessity: 'The numbers and the key ratios have become a holy grail', as a project leader in one of the municipalities stated. The term key ratio is one of the most frequently used expressions in the project. Some of the organizations became pinned down with issues regarding what can be measured. These organizations sought scientific truth on how to measure health. The project groups debated the definition of health and the components that describe and measure it without reaching any firm conclusion. The absence of scientific 'solutions' on how health and its prerequisites should be measured and managed has created frustration and an inability to act effectively. One might speculate whether it is so that the norm concerning measurements and exactness associated with science is so strong that it hinders the development of a HS based on practical experiences. None of the project groups will relinquish the chance of making measurements, but the real question is whether it is important to perform surveys if you do not know what to measure or even dare to experiment?

Conclusion: is there any way to develop management control models linking HR to management control?

The present chapter started with two proposals, one in which the practitioner proposed the use of informal HR costings when necessary and one in which the researcher offered a formal evaluation of HR activities and thereby suggesting a new significance of HRCA. The reason for practising the proposals was underlined in the second section of this chapter. However, the researcher's suggestion is by far more complicated than the practitioner's. In the text we have addressed a number of reasons for this and we will continue trying to answer the researcher's proposition.

The accounting and management control models of today are deeply rooted in traditional accounting. This implies a focus on worth and costs derived from tangible resources. That is to say, health, leadership and competence are not visible anywhere in accounting. Even if a single manager has knowledge of, for example, the profitability of investments in competence development, it would not mean that the management of the organization is run in accordance with having this knowledge. Management control and models for accounting have an inordinate advantage over other factors in controlling the agenda. Therefore, the models and control systems may require change. These changes, however, are not any 'quick fixes' if you do not settle for rough estimates. An altered use of management control systems will take time because it deals with the behaviour of human beings and organizations mainly characterized by habits and routine actions.

The lost relevance of accounting (Johnson 1998) has promoted the idea of introducing a number of new accounting and management control models (e.g. HRCA, balanced scorecard, IC, intangible assets monitor and, most recently, HS). Yet, the application of these models has faced a number of serious problems. The problems and the future applicability vary between the models. The models can be classified into monetary (e.g. but not exclusively HRCA) and non-monetary (e.g. but not exclusively IC and HS) models. Regardless of whether they are monetary or non-monetary, all the models suggest that the employee and his or her intangible resources play a highly significant role in a firm's value creation. HRCA focuses solely on the person, whereas IC and HS emphasize other intangible resources in addition to the individual. The general idea underlying HRCA is that if the accounting *content* is changed (i.e. by including HR), issues change will occur.

IC, on the other hand, proposes a completely new and non-financial framework. Whereas HRCA has a strong focus on measurement and representation, mobilization is the key word connected to IC and HS.

In the IC literature it is suggested that some intangible resources such as organizational culture and the beneficial connectivity between different intangibles can never be justifiably subject to measurement. The way of reporting on and demonstrating the importance of IC is preferably performed by means of using narratives (Mouritsen & Johanson 2005).

It might be the case that hidden behind the two kinds of models is an ontological agenda. Whereas HRCA suggests a view that there is an objective world that could be discovered, measured and represented by using correlated indicators, IC and HS suggest no such world exists. When it comes to intangible resources critical for the success of the firm, everything is in the eye of the beholder. There is no great pattern to be discovered, and in the case where we can see such a pattern, it is constructed by each individual or through the lenses of a collective culture.

Holding the former opinion represents an optimistic position. It is just to continue the efforts, where eventually the objective correlations and the objective importance of each intangible will be discovered and the puzzle will be solved.

The second opinion is much less optimistic. Is there any point in continuing to develop management control systems and processes addressing intangibles? We believe it is possible. Why? If we believe that individual action is governed by, among other things, the culture in an organization, then there is a need to affect this culture and when considering the relevance and usefulness of IC and HS even culture has to be taken into account. The acceptance of these kind of models may differ between firms as well as between countries. In a comparison between opinions from Spanish and Swedish managers and policy makers who have come into contact with IC, Chaminade & Johanson (2003) conclude that culture might affect the assumptions of looking upon the organization as a knowledge creating system and the adoption of new knowledge. Thereby culture may determine the emergence of IC management and reporting. Affecting culture is an important role for management control as we define the concept. This means that stories about the firm have to be told, including stories about both success and failure. Stories can have the format of a narrative but they can sometimes also be reduced to indicators. These indicators have to be based on measures. Even subjective constructions can be measured. That is what Swedebank and the practitioner Stig are doing. Neither Swedebank nor Stig hold that they can detect the complete objective reality that solves everything. Nevertheless, they do what they can to change in a direction they believe is correct. Consequently, using one model or the other is not *the* main issue here. Rather, the issue is about doing something to mobilize productive resources while being well aware that there is no complete new world to discover. The final response to the researcher's question at the beginning of the chapter would be that *doers* like Stig and the Swedebank show us a way to demonstrate if HR practices are worth it or not!

References

Aldana, S. 2001. Financial impact of health promotion programs: a comprehensive review of the literature. *American Journal of Health Promotion*, 15(5): 296–320.

Anderson, D., Serxner, S. & Gold, D. 2001. Conceptual framework, critical questions, and practical challenges in conducting research on the financial impact of worksite health promotion. *American Journal of Health Promotion*, 15(5): 281–288.

Anthony, R. N. 1965. Planning and control systems – a framework for analysis. *Harvard Business School Press*. Cambridge, MA: HBS.

Arvonen, J. & Pettersson, P. 2002. Leadership behaviours as predictors of cost and change effectiveness. *Scandinavian Journal of Management*, 18: 101–112.

Barrett, A. & O'Connell, P. 2001. Does training generally work? The returns to in-company training. *Industrial and Labor Relations Review*, 54: 647–662.

Bassi, L., Harrison, P., Ludwig, J. & McMurrer, D. 2004. *The impact of US firms' investments in HC on stock prices*. Washington: Federal Reserve Working Paper.

Becker, B. E. & Gerhart, B. 1996. The impact of human resource management on organizational performance: progress and prospects. *Academy of Management Journal*, 39: 779–801.

Becker, B. E. & Huselid, M. A. 1997. High performance work systems and firm performance: a synthesis of research and managerial implications. *Research in Personnel and Human Resources*, 16: 53–101.

Becker, G. S. 1962. Investment in human capital: A theoretical analysis. *Journal of Political Economy*, 70: 9–49.

Boselie, P., Paauwe, J. & Jansen, P. 2001. Human resource management and performance: lessons from the Netherlands. *The International Journal of Human Resource Management*, 12: 1107–1125.

Bosworth, D. & Loundes, J. 2002. *The dynamic performance of Australian enterprises. Working paper No. 3/02*. Melbourne Institute of Applied Economics and Social Research, Australia.

Brummet, R. L., Flamholtz, E. G. & Pyle, W. C. 1968. Human resource measurement: a challenge for accountants. *The Accounting Review*, 43: 271–224.

Bukh, P. N. 2003. The relevance of intellectual capital: a paradox? *Accounting, Auditing and Accountability Journal*, 16(1): 49–56.

Cascio, W. F. 1996. The role of utility analysis in the strategic management of organizations. *Journal of Human Resource Costing and Accounting*, 1(2): 85–95.

Chaminade, C. & Johanson U. 2003. Does culture matter in the management of intangibles? A comparative analysis between Sweden and Spain. *Journal of Intellectual Capital*, 4: 4.

The Cranet data-set 1999. *Cranfield Network on Comparative Human Resource Management Survey*. http://www.cranet.org/

Cronbach, L. J. & Gleser, G. C. 1965. *Psychological Tests and Personnel Decisions* (2nd ed.). Urbana, IL: University of Illinois Press.

d'Arcimoles, C.-H. 1997. Human resource policies and company performance: A quantitative approach using longitudinal data. *Organization Studies*, 18: 857–874.

Dearden, L., Reed, H. & van Reenen, J. 2000. *Who gains when workers train? Training and corporate productivity in a panel of British industries. Working paper 00/04*. UK: The Institute for Fiscal Studies.

E*Know-Net. 2004. *Towards a European research agenda on intangibles. Report to the European Commission.* Autonomous University, Madrid.

Emmanuel, C., Otley, D. & Merchant, K. 1990. *Accounting for Management Control.* London: Chapman and Hall.

European Commission 1995. *Teaching and Learning – Towards the Learning Society,* Luxembourg: Office for Official Publications of the European Communities.

Flamholtz, E. 1985. *Human Resource Accounting.* Los Angeles: Jossey-Bass Publishers.

Flamholtz, E. 1996. *Effective Management Control: Theory and Practice.* Boston: Kluwer Academic Publishers.

Flamholtz, E. 2001. Corporate culture and the bottom line. *European Management Journal,* 19: 268–275.

Goetzel, R., Juday, T. & Ozminkowski, R. 1999. What's the ROI? A systematic review of return-on-investment studies of corporate health and productivity management initiatives. *AWHP's Worksite Health,* 6: 12–21.

Golaszewski, T. 2001. Shining lights: studies that have most influenced the understanding of health promotion's financial impact. *American Journal of Health Promotion,* 15(5): 332–340.

Gröjer J.E. & Johanson U. 1996. *Personalekonomisk redovisning och kalkylering.* Stockholm: Arbetarskyddsnämnden.

Gröjer, J. E. & Johanson, U. 1998. Current development in human resource costing and accounting: reality present – researchers absent? *Accounting, Auditing & Accountability Journal,* 11(4): 495–505.

Groot, W. 1999. Productivity effects of enterprise-related training. *Applied Economic Letters,* 6: 369–371.

Hansson, B. 2004. Human capital and stock returns: Is the value premium an approximation for return on human capital? *Journal of Business Finance and Accounting,* 31(3–4): 333–357.

Hansson, B. 2005. *Is it time to disclose information about human capital investments? Working paper.* IPF, Uppsala University.

Hansson, B., Johanson, U. & Leitner, K.-H. 2004. The impact of human capital and human capital investments on firm performance: Evidence from the literature and European survey results. In P. Descy & M. Tessaring (eds.), *Impact of Education and Training, Third report on vocational training research in Europe: Background report,* Luxembourg: EUR-OP.

Hermansson, R. 1964. Accounting for human assets. *Occasional paper No. 14,* Michigan State University.

Huselid, M. A. 1995. The impact of human resource management practices on turnover, productivity, and corporate financial performance. *Academy of Management Journal,* 38: 635–672.

Ichinowski, C., Shaw, K. & Prennushi, G. 1995. *The effects of human resource management practices on productivity. NBER Working paper 5333.* Cambridge, MA.

IASC/International Accounting Standards Committee 1998. *International accounting standard IAS 38; intangible assets.* London

Johanson, U. 1992. *Personalekonomiska beräkningar – påverkar de? (The influence of Human Resource Costing and Accounting). Personnel Economics Institute report no 92:1B.* School of Business, Stockholm University.

Johanson, U. 1998. The answer is blowing in the wind. Training investments from a Human Resource Accounting perspective. *European Journal for Vocational Training.* European Centre for the Development of Vocational Training.

Johanson, U. 1999. Why the concept of human resource costing and accounting does not work. *Personnel Review,* 28(1/2).

Johanson, U. 2000. Human resource costing and accounting. In C. Brewster & H. H. Larsen (eds.), *Human Resource Management in Europe*: Chapter 8. Oxford: Blackwells.

Johanson, U., Mårtensson, M. & Skoog, M. 2001. Mobilising change by means of the management control of intangibles. *Accounting, Organization and Society*, 26(7–8): 715–733.

Kaplan, R. & Norton, D. 1992. The balanced scorecard – measures that drive performance. *Harvard Business Review*, 70(1): 71–79.

Latham, G. & Whyte, G. 1994. The futility of utility analysis. *Personnel Psychology*, 47: 31–46.

Lev, B. & Scwartz, A. 1971. On the use of the economic concept of human capital in financial statements. *The Accounting Review*, 46(1): 103–112.

Machin, J. L. J. 1983. Management control systems: whence and whither. In E. A. Lowe & J. L. J. Machin (eds.), *New Perspectives in Management Control*. London: Macmillan.

Meritum. 2002. Guidelines for managing and reporting on intangibles. In L. Cañibano, P. Sanchez, M. Garcia-Ayuso & C. Chaminade (eds.), *Fundación Airtel Móvil*.

Mouritsen, J. 1999. *Intellectual capital: the logic of an 'economy of creativity'.* Work in progress presented at the EIASM workshop on intangibles in Brussels.

Mouritsen, J. & Johanson, U. 2005. Managing the person: human resource costing and accounting, intellectual capital and health statements. Kapitel i Northern Lights in accounting. In S. Jönsson & J. Mouritsen (eds.), *Kommande bok.*

Naylor, J. C. & Shine, L. C. 1965. A table for determining the increase in mean criterion score obtained by using a selection device. *Journal of Industrial Psychology*, 3: 33–42.

Nelson, R. R. & Winter, S. G. 1982. *An Evolutionary Theory of Economic Change*. Cambridge, MA: Harvard University Press.

Nordic Industrial Fund 2001. *Intellectual Capital. Managing and Reporting.* Oslo: Nordic Industrial Fund.

OECD 1996. *Measuring What People Know: Human Capital Accounting for the Knowledge Economy.* Paris: OECD.

OECD 1997a. *Measuring performance in the age of intangibles. Enterprise value in the knowledge economy. Conference in Helsinki in 1996.* Boston: OECD and Ernst & Young.

OECD 1997b. *Changing workplace strategies: achieving better outcomes for enterprises, workers and society. Report on the International Conference in 1996 organised by the OECD and the Government of Canada.* Paris: OECD.

OECD 1997c. *Industrial competitiveness in the knowledge-based economy. The new role of governments. Conference in Stockholm, February, 1997.* OECD Proceeding. Paris: OECD.

OECD 1999. *Measuring and Reporting Intellectual Capital: Experience, Issues and Prospects.* Amsterdam: OECD.

Pelletier, K. 1999. A review and analysis of the clinical and cost-effectiveness studies of comprehensive health promotion and disease management programs at worksites: 1995–98 update. *American Journal of Health Promotion*, 13: 333–345.

Riedel, J. E., Lynch, W., Baase, C., Hymel, P. & Peterson, K. W. 2001. The effect of disease prevention and health promotion on workplace productivity: a literature review. *American Journal of Health Promotion*, 15(3): 167–191.

Rosett, J. G. 2000. Equity risk and the labour stock: The case of union contracts. *Journal of Accounting Research*, 39: 337–364.

Simon, R. 1990. The role of management control systems in creating competitive advantage: new perspectives. *Accounting, Organizations and Society*, 15(1/2): 127–143.

Sveiby, K. E. 1997. *The New Organizational Wealth. Managing and Measuring Knowledge-based Assets.* San Francisco: Berret-Koehler Publishers, Inc.

Weick, K. E. & Swieringa, R. J. 1987. Management accounting and action. *Accounting, Organizations and Society*, 12(3): 293–308.

HRM and organizational performance: universal and contextual evidence

IRENE NIKANDROU, RITA CAMPOS E CUNHA AND
NANCY PAPALEXANDRIS

Introduction

In the last decade, Europe has experienced some major changes, related to the process of economic and political integration. The single currency and the recent enlargement of the European Union have several implications for EU countries, their economies and the management of their organizations. Moreover, the globalization of the world economy leads to great challenges for organizations: for organizational performance, to deal with global competitors; for employees, to increase productivity as well as innovation rate and speed and for management, towards the adoption of 'best practice' models, which tend to coincide with the American model. The argument here is that competitive pressures will push nations to correct the flaws in their system by adopting global 'best practices' (Groenewegen 1997). The counter-argument holds that globalization makes the differences in national cultures and institutions even more visible as it brings, often diverse, contexts closer together (Geppart *et al.* 2003: 3). Thus, we need to understand how within an overall trend towards globalization, national cultures and institutions shape organizational form and behaviour (Child 2000).

These changes and challenges raise the need to re-evaluate human resource management (HRM) in a broader context since intense competition, changing demands, technological advances, speed, flexibility, adaptability and low cost are forces that demand a deep understanding from HR, in order to define and implement adequate HR strategies and practices.

Indeed, HR faces the threat of being viewed as a cost function to be minimized but also the opportunity to prove that it can contribute to organizational success through the development of a more strategic role, the delivery of efficient services and the facilitation of organizational change. Thus, there is a growing demand and concern for HRM to prove its utility in improving organizational effectiveness and profitability.

This demand, however, raises the issue of how to demonstrate this link. Can we defend a 'universalist paradigm' whereby strategic HRM aims at improving organizational performance through the implementation of 'best practices' that have a positive impact on organizational performance, or, on the contrary, should we stress the 'contextualist approach' and, therefore, the search for an understanding of what 'typical' rather than 'best practice' organizations are doing? (Sparrow *et al.* 2004). Alternatively, is it wise to claim a European HRM model to oppose, or at least, compare to an American HRM model? Several researchers argue that HRM in Europe has some distinctive characteristics that contribute to its unique character (Brewster & Bournois 1991; Claus 2003; Paauwe 2004; Sparrow & Hiltrop 1997). Within the European Union some characteristics of HRM that are common in the EU, but different from US patterns, include a stronger emphasis on the consultative approach requiring collaboration between different stakeholders as social partners, as well as the growth of flexible and temporary working arrangements, the role of work and leisure in people's lives and the use of the Euro, to provide greater transparency for employees on compensation and benefits. The differences in HRM within European countries stem from national factors, namely cultural values and norms, societal structure and language, from company factors, including size ownership and geographical scope of companies and also from regional factors, such as the north/south or east/west divide. The major impact of the EU being increased competition, the pressure for competitive HR practices that keep costs controlled while promoting innovation, change and human capital development, is a unifying umbrella for HRM in the EU, as well as a challenge to keep the European social model of employment. Thus, understanding similarities and differences in the link of HRM and firm performance within the EU is important to understand HRM in Europe. In this chapter, we will start by examining the impact of HRM on firm performance in Europe, considering the major HRM practices. Subsequently, we will look at some regional differences within Europe that can be detected from a comparative or contextual perspective.

Linking HRM and firm performance

There is abundant literature on the studies exploring the contribution of HRM to organizational performance. The majority of these studies report a positive link between HR systems and organizational performance. However, the theoretical rationale in these studies varies, particularly over time.

Delery & Doty (1996) identify three different modes of theorizing the study of HR impact on organizational performance: the universalistic, the contingency and the configurational perspectives.

The universalistic approach identifies HR practices that are universally applicable and successful. The underlying assumption is that 'best practices' and their adoption contribute to superior organizational performance. These studies correspond to an early stage, where specific HR practices were the object of analysis, such as compensation (Gerhart & Trevor 1996; Gómez-Mejía 1992), training (Bartel 1994), or performance management systems (McDonald & Smith 1995). One problem with this approach is that it takes a narrow view, focusing primarily on the internal characteristics of HR and on individual HR practices (Pfeffer 1994; Huselid 1995).

Contingency theorists, on the other hand, examine the interactions between HR practices, contingency factors and firm performance. Industry, sector of activity, size, ownership, organizational strategy and structure are some of the factors that influence HR activities and performance (Delery & Doty 1996; Fombrum et al. 1984; Schuler & Jackson 1987). The implicit assumption in these models, anchored in the strategy literature, is that the fit between corporate strategy and HR practices allows organizations to achieve superior performance (Schuler & Jackson 1987; Youndt et al. 1996). According to this perspective, organizations must achieve horizontal fit, that is internal consistency of HR practices, and vertical fit, that is congruence of the HR system with other organizational characteristics. Different sets of HR practices are suited for different firm strategies (Arthur 1994; Miles & Snow 1984).

The configurational approach is more complex, emphasizing how 'patterns' of HR practices are related to performance. These studies stress the impact of HR bundles on both employee and organizational performance due to the reinforcing and complementary relationships that exist between these practices, by contributing to the development of employee skills and abilities, motivation and work organization (Delaney & Huselid 1996), increasing the level of employee productivity (Ichniowski et al. 1997) and having an impact on the bottom line (Huselid 1995; Cunha et al. 2003). These configurations, or HR bundles, guarantee the link between strategy and skills (such as the bundle that includes selectivity, training and development, career development and functional flexibility), as well as the link between strategy and behaviours (the bundle that includes performance management practices – appraisal and compensation).

Measuring organizational performance

To study the impact of HRM on organizational performance we need to look to indicators used to measure performance. The majority of studies focus on only one type of indicator, while the literature emphasizes the need to use multiple criteria of performance. Following Locke & Latham (1990), there are three types of performance data available:

1   Measures of operational or bottom-line results, measuring the output of goods and services in quantitative terms (units produced, customers served) and in qualitative terms (number of errors, customer complaints). Organizational productivity tends to be used frequently as a quantitative indicator (Arthur 1994; Huselid 1995; Ichniowski *et al.* 1997; MacDuffie 1995), while product or service quality has been used as a qualitative indicator (Arthur 1994; Ichniowski *et al.* 1997; MacDuffie 1995).
2   Measures of time, including lateness, absence, lost working time, failure to meet deadlines.
3   Financial performance measures, which include indicators such as profit or total sales (Bire & Beechler 1995; Terpstra & Rozell 1993), profitability rates (Delery & Doty 1996; Huselid 1995).

A fourth category using subjective measures of performance can be added into the discussion (Delaney & Huselid 1996). The choice of subjective measures of organizational performance in international surveys is preferable to objective measures, since biases due to cultural differences in long and short-term orientations, different tax and fiscal regimes may render comparisons useless (Lahteenmaki *et al.* 1998). Evidence suggests that managers are likely to act on the basis of their subjective perceptions of performance, often in relation to that of comparable organizations, rather than on the basis of objective indicators (Day & Nedungadi 1994; Guest *et al.* 2003). Moreover, a substantial correlation between subjective and objective measures of performance has been found to exist (Pearce *et al.* 1987), and, on the other hand, objective and subjective measures of performance converge, and their relationships with dependent variables are equivalent (Wall *et al.* 2004).

Based on research developed by members of the Cranet Network (for more details, see Brewster *et al.* 2004), we will now elaborate on the link between HRM and Firm Performance in Europe, starting with a general model, which may be integrated in the universalistic approach, and then moving into the contextual approach, which identifies HRM differences between countries or regions in Europe.

HRM–performance link in Europe – a general model

Several conceptual models have been developed to study the relationship between HRM and performance. These models distinguish the context into which business strategy, HR strategy and practices are formulated; the content of strategy and HRM; and the process through which outcomes are achieved.

The Hendry & Pettigrew model (1990) (Warwick Business School) focuses on both the outer environmental context (socio-economic, technological, political, legal and competitive) and the inner organizational context (culture, structure, leadership, task, technology and business output). These linkages contribute directly to forming the content of an organization's HRM.

The Fombrun *et al.* (1984) model (Michigan Business School) emphasizes a 'tight fit' between organizational strategy, organizational structure and HRM system. Both structure and HRM are dependent on organizational strategy. This model focuses on the HRM function and develops the so-called HR cycle, in which performance is dependent on four crucial HRM practices: selection, training, appraisal and rewards. This is one of the first content models. The Michigan approach refers to context in terms of economic, political and cultural forces.

A mixture of both process and content is the Beer *et al.* (1984) model (Harvard model), which offers a descriptive, systemic approach capturing the interrelationships among various stakeholders, situational factors and HR policies and outcomes.

The general model that will be presented next is based on two previous empirical studies (Cunha *et al.* 2003 and 2004), each one of them testing models to establish the link between strategic HRM and organizational performance. An integration of the two studies will be reported, to create a general model which distinguishes antecedent characteristics, HRM content and process as well as organizational outcomes.

The two studies used European samples, based on the 1995 and 1999/2000 Cranet-E surveys. The Cranfield Network on European HRM (Cranet-E) is a comparative research network that analyzes strategic HRM in public and private organizations with more than 200 employees, cross-nationally, through surveys that provide comprehensive information on the strategic HRM of companies in a number of European countries. The same survey instrument is used in all countries, after translation and back-translation in the participating countries by a local team. The survey is organized around six sections, covering the personnel/human resource function, staffing, employee development, compensation and benefits, employee relations and communication and organizational details.

The 1995 survey is composed of a total sample of 6,289 questionnaires, with a response rate of 21 per cent (for further details see Brewster *et al.* 2000). The 1999/2000 survey covers a sample of 8,216 questionnaires, with an average response rate of 15 per cent (for further information, see Brewster *et al.* 2004).The two studies that are reported in this section used sub-samples, which only include private companies, in the services and manufacturing sectors, with 1,301 and 1,822 firms respectively for the study based on the 1995 sample and the 1999/2000 one.

Figure 9.1 below is a representation of the model that combines these two studies and shows the antecedent characteristics, the HRM content variables, the HRM process variable and the organizational outcomes.

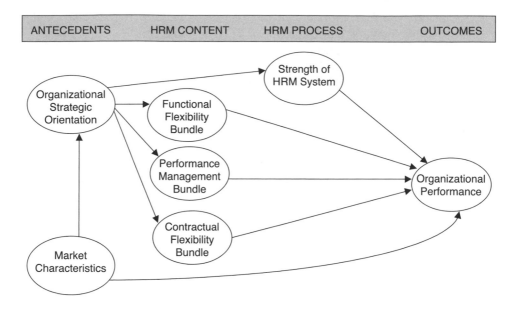

Figure 9.1 A general model of the HRM–performance link for Europe

Antecedents

According to this model, two types of antecedent characteristics can be identified – the market characteristics and the corporate strategic orientation.

Market characteristics are associated with the direct organizational environment and include not only the degree of competition an organization faces but also industry attractiveness. These forces influence organizational focus and attention to competitors (Grewal & Tansuhaj 2001) and lead top managers into a stronger effort and resource investment on environmental scanning and forecasting (Milliken 1987). Enlarging or even introducing the level of product market competition has been one of the major purposes of privatization programmes, especially in European countries such as Portugal and Greece, because it forces organizations to develop better competitive strategies and pay closer attention to costs. It has been shown (Cunha *et al.* 2003) that these market characteristics increase corporate strategic orientation by forcing organizations to perform more effective environmental scanning, to define appropriate corporate strategies and develop better internal fit among functional policies.

In addition to this effect, market characteristics, particularly industry growth, can also be expected to directly influence organizational performance, due to higher environmental munificence, notwithstanding the role played by organizational competences (Luo 1998). A munificent environment can provide the organization with plenty of resources, thus facilitating its growth.

A second variable that may be considered an antecedent in this HRM performance link model is the organizational strategic orientation. Positive correlations have been found between the degree of formal planning and firm performance (Lyles *et al.* 1993; Pearce, *et al.* 1987) because greater emphasis will be placed on improving the quality of the strategic decision-making process, such as goal formulation, developing distinctive competencies, determining authority relationships, deploying resources and monitoring implementation. Tregaskis (1997) also found that organizations with a formalized HR strategy had a higher probability of adopting practices in line with high performance work systems than those with informal or no HR strategy. The two studies based on a European sample by Cunha *et al.* (2003; Cunha & Cunha 2004) have shown that organizational strategic orientation does lead to stronger HR bundles implemented by organizations.

HR content

Studies in the last decade have shown that HRM practices contribute to organizational performance. While the early studies emphasized specific HR practices such as compensation (Gerhart & Trevor 1996), training (Bartel 1994) or performance management (McDonald & Smith 1995), later studies focused on bundles of HR practices and their impact on organizational performance, due to the reinforcing and complementary relationships between them and between practices and strategy. The link between strategy and employee skills is guaranteed by the HR bundle, which relates not only to selectivity but also to training and development, as well as career management practices – what we have called the Functional Flexibility Bundle. This set of HR practices has been found to lead to superior organizational performance (Cunha & Cunha 2004).

The link between strategy and employee behaviors is stressed by the Performance Management Bundle, which includes performance appraisal activities and variable compensation. This bundle has also been demonstrated to support organizational performance (Cunha *et al.* 2003; Cunha & Cunha 2004).

Another set of HR practices – here called the 'contractual flexibility bundle' – deals with the capacity to face changing market opportunities and increasing international competition through cost reduction. The need to have a more efficient deployment of human resources and to cope with fluctuations in workload or demand encouraged organizations to have a more extensive use of the so-called contingent labour contracts, which include part-time, fixed-term or temporary contracts, outsourcing and other types of flexibility. Although Cunha *et al.* (2003) have only used part-time contracts, which have supported organizational performance, other studies have shown that contractual flexibility, in general, has a positive impact on organizational outcomes (Lewin 2003).

HRM process

HRM bundles create the conditions to achieve strategic goals by influencing employee attributes (competencies and behaviours) as well as by creating contractual flexibility that helps organizations cope with environmental uncertainty.

However, the issue of how the HRM system as a whole can encourage employees to adopt the desired behaviours and attitudes is not addressed by the HRM content variables that have been discussed in the previous section. Bowen & Ostroff (2004) differentiate HRM content and process and stress that while content refers to specific practices intended to achieve particular goals, process deals with how the HRM system is designed and administered to send signals to employees that allow them to create a shared meaning about what is expected from them. The extent to which uniform, unambiguous expectancies regarding appropriate response patterns are induced corresponds to the 'strength of the HRM system'. Strong HRM systems should be visible, should be consistent with strategic goals and should arouse employees' agreement as to their perceptions of the event–effect relationships. The relationship of strength of the HRM system with organizational performance was supported in Cunha & Cunha (2004) and was the only variable that had an impact on organizational innovation performance.

Organizational performance

Organizational performance may be considered from a large number of perspectives: productivity, profitability, earnings per share, economic value added, innovation rate, service quality and customer satisfaction. While the financial measures tend to be short-term and lagging results, other measures such as innovation rate, customer satisfaction, productivity or service quality are leading results that stress the sustainability of the organization over time. In the above model, subjective indicators of performance were used in terms of perceived gross revenue over the past three years and profitability as compared to competitors (Cunha & Cunha 2004). Indicators for innovation performance were also used, but we were not able to support the link between HRM content and innovation; the strength of the HRM system, however, was found to significantly and positively affect this type of performance.

In this part, we have taken the 'universalistic' approach by presenting a general model of the HRM–Performance link. This model integrates several levels of analysis: market characteristics, organizational strategy, HRM content and process and organizational performance.

This model was tested and confirmed in two research studies based on a European sample, but we cannot dismiss the argument that HRM may take different formats in different countries due to the cultural and institutional contexts. In fact, a number of contextual characteristics may determine the use of different models of HRM, such as legal frameworks, educational systems, cultural characteristics or even economic structure.

In the next section we approach the HRM–performance link taking into account contextual factors that allow us to supplement resource-based approaches with a more institutional perspective, to detect hidden success factors for organizations (Boselie *et al.* 2001).

The contextual approach

A consistent body of work deals with differences in the value systems. Hofstede's work is one of the most significant in demonstrating cultural groupings around five dimensions: hierarchical distance, collectivism, masculinity, uncertainty avoidance and long-term orientation. While Portugal, for example, is a country with high power distance, mildly collectivist, feminine and strongly uncertainty avoidant, Austria is described as having a low power distance, being individualist, masculine and with tolerance of ambiguity. Both countries are relatively short term oriented. Greece is much closer to the Portuguese value systems than to the Austrian ones (Hofstede 2001). It is therefore to be expected that these cultural styles will be reflected in day-to-day management practices and that Portuguese or Greek organizations will rely on taller hierarchies with wide salary ranges, with references as an important screening method, more women in management positions and lower wage gaps between genders, more resistance to change and higher average seniority in jobs.

Institutional factors also shape the HRM systems, since organizations are not isolated from the institutional context in which they are embedded. According to the institutional perspective (Powell & DiMaggio 1991) uniform pressures from the government, labour unions, the law, industry associations or other public bodies will lead to isomorphism, through various mechanisms of coercion, normative regulations and imitation, and inversely, cross-national institutional differences should generate significant cross-national differences in managerial systems. In fact, Gooderham *et al.* (1999) have shown that national institutional embeddedness plays quite a relevant role in shaping HRM practices. In some European countries, such as Portugal, small and medium-sized enterprises are dominant, while in other countries, such as the UK, the economy is dominated by large firms. In Greece, despite the great number of small enterprises, the dominant role in the economy is increasingly played by a small number of large multinationals and in some sectors by state-owned companies. State-owned companies are also more common in some European countries and privatization programmes have been launched to infuse market competition and reduce the state influence in the economy. That has been the case of Portugal and Greece in the last fifteen years, as well as the UK.

Educational systems vary in European countries, for example in the UK we may find an educational structure more similar to the American model, while the Portuguese educational system resembles the French one, with a greater emphasis on professionalization at the first degree level of higher education. Some of these differences may fade somehow, as the EU countries tend to converge towards the model proclaimed by the Bologna treaty. A convergence in European higher education degrees, particularly at the first and second levels, may be expected to have in the medium-run an extraordinary impact on management practices, which will be reinforced by international student mobility, an increasingly important characteristic of higher education schools. We expect this convergence to start with the work expectations of young graduates, with a high willingness to have an international career. HRM in Europe has to prepare to deal with this higher mobility pattern. Important differences may also be encountered in the legislative system, particularly in industrial relations issues, being virtually impossible, in some countries, for organizations to let an employee go (the Portuguese case) while in other countries, a good cause is easily raised by management to let go of an employee. Greece is characterized by an 'immature' system of industrial relations. It is only after 1990 that company level negotiation is legally permitted and a shift to company and sectoral agreements is noticed. Greek unions are exceptional in Europe for the continued role of class politics as their dominant point of reference (Kritsantonis 1998).

For the reasons above, it makes sense to discuss some of the research studies that uncover differences in HRM practices by country or across clusters of countries in Europe. In fact, little research linking HRM and performance has been carried out in Europe, even though there is a growing interest in the area. Boselie (2002) presents an overview of studies on the subject carried outside the USA and UK. Studies from Finland, France, Germany, Greece, Ireland, the Netherlands and Spain explore the relationship giving emphasis to contingency variables such as size, technology, trade union pressure and environmental characteristics (d'Arcimoles 1997; Backes-Gellner *et al.* 1997; Boselie *et al.* 2001; Gmür 2003; Lahteenmaki *et al.* 1998; Laroche 2001; Panayotopoulou *et al.* 2003). The majority of studies are interested in the factors influencing the shape and formation of HRM policies and practices. Thus, they support that a number of exogenous influences restrict HR's room to manoeuvre and shape HR orientation and its impact on firm performance.

Within the European Union context, a central issue concerns understanding the forces that shape HRM both at a national level, allowing for intra-country comparisons, as well as at an international level, allowing for comparisons of HRM in various contexts. The next section of this chapter discusses some of the research studies that uncover differences in HRM and firm performance across clusters of countries in Europe.

HRM–performance link – a contextual model

The interest in the impact of context on HRM practices is not new. Both the classical HRM models of Beer *et al.* (1984) and Fombrun *et al.* (1984) recognize contextual factors in terms of economic, political and cultural forces. However, research in the field of HRM and performance is focused on identifying how many boxes there should be between strategic HRM and performance. It seems that there is less explicit attention to context. Brewster & Bournois (1991) propose a conceptual framework for the analysis and understanding of HRM in Europe. Ignjatovic & Svetlik (2003) and Sparrow & Hiltrop (1997) suggest that cultural factors, institutional factors such as trade unions, labour legislation, etc, business structure and the degree of state ownership and HR role and competence have an impact on HRM and its distinctive forms in Europe. Thus, to understand HRM in Europe one has to analyze HRM endogenous and exogenous factors as shaping HR practices and their impact on firm performance.

Different research studies have identified different patterns of HRM practices within Europe, revealing different economic, political, legal and cultural characteristics. Both converging and diverging tendencies of management practices contribute to the emergence of a synthesis – a European hybrid model, whereby some convergence trends between European countries coexist with signs of divergence (Mayrhofer *et al.* 2002).

In this section we discuss some of the research studies that uncover differences in HRM and firm performance across clusters of countries in Europe using the Brewster & Bournois (1991) model. The model suggests that we can evaluate HRM at various levels. Each level contributes to our understanding of HRM activities, the factors that influence and shape them and their impact, directly or indirectly, on firm performance. It is then possible to consider the interactions between business strategy, HR strategy and HR practices within the external environment embedded in national culture, power systems, legal frameworks, educational systems and employee representation provisions (in Brewster & Hegewisch 1994). Unfortunately, research on the HRM–Performance relationship in Europe is limited and unsystematic (Sparrow & Hiltrop 1997).

At the level of national context, the model brings HRM practices closer to the broader environment. At this level research does not focus on examining the relationship between HRM as the independent and performance as the dependent variable, but on understanding the influence of national context on the formulation of HR practices. Thus, a number of studies explore European patterns of HRM from an inter-country comparative perspective. Ignjatovic & Svetlik (2003) emphasize the link of HRM practices to national contexts. Using fifty-two HR indicators uncovered four clusters of European countries with distinctive forms of HRM. The Nordic cluster (Denmark, Finland, Norway and Sweden) with employee-focused HRM model, the Western cluster (UK, Switzerland, Belgium,

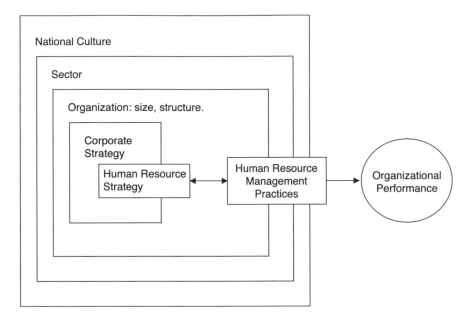

Figure 9.2 Conceptual framework for the analysis of HRM and organizational performance in the European context

Source: Brewster and Bournois (1991): 6

the Netherlands and France) with emphasis on flexibility and professionalism (professional HRM model), the Central Southern cluster (Germany, Austria, Spain, Czech Republic, Slovenia, Italy and Portugal) with management supportive HRM model, and the Peripheral cluster (Bulgaria, Estonia, Greece, Cyprus, Ireland, Northern Ireland and Turkey) with management focused HRM model.

Two recent studies, Apospori *et al.* (2004) and Stavrou *et al.* (2004) go one step further in examining the HRM–Performance link within the EU context.

Apospori *et al.* (2004) used a comparative approach to explore the direct and indirect impact of exogenous environmental factors, business and HR strategy and strategic HR practices on organizational performance in northern and southern European countries. An exploratory cluster analysis using nineteen HR indicators, resulted in two major clusters of countries. The Northern European cluster consisted of Germany, Austria, Spain, Belgium, Switzerland, Czech Republic, the Netherlands, France, Sweden, Finland, UK, Denmark and Norway. The Southern European cluster consisted of Portugal, Cyprus, Greece, Italy, Northern Ireland and Bulgaria. The study supports that clustering European countries with regard to HRM reveals differences both in the importance of HR among countries and in HR practices and a differential impact of HR practices on firm performance. Stavrou *et al.* (2004) identified three diverse yet overlapping HRM models, each of which involved a different set of EU member states. Cluster A includes superior organizations in Sweden and Finland; Cluster B includes superior organizations in the UK and the former West Germany; and Cluster C includes superior organizations in Greece, Portugal, Spain, Italy, France, Ireland, and Belgium. The study supports that as we move from northern to southern EU, the HRM–Performance relationship weakens.

As we move from the 'outer' context to the 'inner' context, we examine more closely the interactions between HR and Performance.

At the next level of analysis, that is, the direct external environment into which an organization operates, we examine the influence of *sector and market characteristics* on HRM practices and organizational performance. There are a number of studies showing that there is a link of external environmental factors, such as the strength of the economy, market growth, market turbulence, competitive intensity to organizational performance (Diamantopoulos & Hart 1993; Slater & Narver 1994). Growing markets attract new companies thus increasing competitive intensity which in turn forces organizations to give greater emphasis on creating sustained competitive advantage (Lado & Wilson 1994). Market growth has been used as an indicator of industry attractiveness which is related to the degree to which organizations define appropriate strategies with a better internal fit among functional policies (Porter 1996). Moreover, companies operating in growing markets have to systematically analyze the market and competition to respond to market needs. Thus, market growth has been linked to higher levels of formalization and systematization of corporate strategies (Cunha *et al.* 2003). In examining the link of market growth, corporate strategy, HR strategy and organizational performance, Apospori *et al.* (2004) support that there is a positive effect of market growth on strategic management and external recruitment for both northern and southern European clusters. Thus, growing markets make companies define and clarify their strategic goals and turn to the external environment to attract and recruit the human capabilities needed. Organizational performance is positively affected only indirectly through the effect of external recruitment to performance management.

The impact of sector, private and public, as a significant factor in the formulation of different HRM practices has been supported by several researchers (Boyne 2002; Sparrow & Hiltrop 1997). The issue is especially important to the European comparative scene, due to differences in the relative impact and strength of public and private sectors across Europe. Moreover, the link of HR practices to organizational performance is more clear and widespread in the private than in the public sector. The findings of Stavrou *et al.* (2004) support that superior organizations in Europe operating in both the private and public sector do not differ significantly in their use of HR practices.

At the core of the analysis is the link between corporate strategy, HR strategy and practices and organizational performance. At this level of analysis, the literature focuses on strategic HRM, providing a rich body of research describing and empirically testing corporate strategy and HRM models and the internal and external fit (Baird & Meshoulam 1988; Lengnick-Hall & Lengnick-Hall 1988; Miles & Snow 1984; Schuler & Jackson 1987).

Clearly defined mission statements and corporate strategies are part of strategic planning which contribute to the development of specific functional strategies and tactics needed to ensure the achievement of business goals. Strategy formulation affects the development of clearly defined HR strategies needed to have the human capital for competitive advantage (Poole & Jenkins 1996). Thus, companies with strategic orientation are more likely to emphasize the strategic role of HR (Apospori *et al.* 2004). However, within the European context it seems that the impact of organizational strategic orientation on organizational performance is differentiated between northern and southern European countries, with organizational strategic orientation having a direct and indirect positive impact in northern countries. In southern countries, the relationship holds only through the central role of HR in strategy formulation (Apospori *et al.* 2004).

The centrality of HR in strategy formulation underlines the organization's choice to build competitive advantage through human capabilities and the adoption of HR practices needed to attract, obtain, develop, retain and motivate a firm's human capital (Becker & Gerhart 1996). HR centrality has been found to play an important role in the adoption of HR practices across Europe. However, it has a differential impact in northern and southern EU countries (Apospori *et al.* 2004).

HR centrality is associated with more emphasis on external recruitment in the north and with internal recruitment and training in the south. A socio-political explanation could be helpful in interpreting this finding. Thus, according to Esping-Andersen (1990) and Hollinshead & Leat (1995), organizations in several northern European countries could be influenced by their liberal socio-political environment which has a strong orientation towards external labour markets, while the corporatist environment in many southern countries influences organizations towards internal labour markets. The impact of HR on organizational performance is reflected in the link of HR centrality and the adoption of performance management and communication practices. However, in northern countries communication to all employees is an issue of strategic importance to the extent that it is directly affected by organizational strategic orientation, while in southern countries, communication is a responsibility of the HR function. This may be explained by the high power distance Hofstede's cultural dimension found in southern countries. This means that top management in the south keeps a greater distance when communicating directly to all employee levels than in the north and uses HR management as a communication link with employees.

The literature on the link of HRM practices and organizational performance within the contextual approach is limited. The HRM practices used in the research reflect the extent to which companies acquire, develop, retain and motivate their employees. Thus, planning, recruiting (internally or externally) and staffing, training and development, compensation, performance management and communication and participation are the HRM practices included in the research efforts reported here (Apospori *et al.* 2004; Stavrou *et al.* 2004). Stavrou *et al.* (2004) support that there is a combination of certain key HRM practices that differentiate superior organizations from lower-performing ones. This argument is in line with the 'universalist' approach. Enriching the analysis, the argument holds that geographic context moderates the relationship between HR practices and organizational performance. Thus, training and development is the area emphasized by all superior organizations in all three clusters. However, it is the only set of practices contributing to differentiating superior from lower-performing organizations in Cluster C (Greece, Portugal, Spain, Italy, France, Ireland and Belgium). Apospori *et al.* (2004) also support that organizations in southern European countries which invest in training report high organizational performance, while this relationship is not significant in the northern cluster. Communication and participation practices differentiate superior organizations in Clusters A (Sweden and Finland) and B (UK and former West Germany), while the link of planning, compensation and staffing to superior organizational performance in the EU is weak. According to Apospori *et al.* (2004), performance management and communicating with employees are the HR practices that have a significant impact on organizational performance in both northern and southern European clusters.

Apospori *et al.* (2004) also examined the internal fit of HRM practices in the European context and uncovered some important differences in the relationships among HR practices between the two clusters. Thus, companies in the northern cluster that evaluate and compensate high performance, also emphasize training to ensure that the acquired human capital has the needed skills. On the other hand, in southern countries companies investing in performance are less likely to invest in training at the same time.

Conclusion

The European Union has promoted the integration among European countries. Toward this objective common policies and procedures have been determined, affecting all member states. The convergence thesis, supported by the universalistic perspective, has been emphasized by the proliferation of multinationals and the emergence of certain transnational practices. At the same time, cultural and institutional factors in each country, constrain the unification and transferability of HR practices, thus contributing to the adoption and adaptation of different practices within a common framework. Understanding similarities and differences within the EU is important in order to understand the unique character of the 'European' model of HRM. Thus, studies using European samples, reported in this chapter, have used both the universal and the contextual approaches in an effort to better understand the HR–organizational performance link and the factors that apply to Europe as a whole, on one hand, and those that reveal differences across countries or regions on the other. We contend that the two approaches can be used complementarily, to understand and support both convergent and divergent tendencies of HR practices in Europe.

The empirical work we summarize demonstrates that market characteristics and more specifically, market growth, influence organizational strategic orientation which strengthens the role of HR. This is in line with empirical studies which also contend that superior performance is associated with a strategic focus, particularly when it leads to the definition of a HR strategy. Moreover, the only set of HR practices that positively affect organizational performance is the performance management bundle. These impacts are felt cross-nationally, thus supporting the universalistic perspective. However, given Europe's cultural, linguistic and institutional diversity, we expect and find differences across countries or regions, that reflect this diversity (Powell & DiMaggio 1991). In a similar way, empirical work has revealed that, independently of the criteria used to differentiate regions, the northern European countries show a stronger emphasis on communication with employees and participation practices, while southern European countries emphasize training and present a more mechanistic approach to HRM.

Moreover, the empirical research we reported in this chapter opens other lines of investigation. In particular, the extent to which European HRM is importing the American model, because of the challenges raised by globalization of the economy and communication technology remains an open question. A greater focus on employee consultation with different stakeholders, in particular unions, employers' associations and government, as well as the importance of the social model of employment, with greater employment security and social benefits, differentiate European from American HRM (Claus 2003).

However, because higher education is greatly influenced by the American literature, and because of the pressures raised by globalization, HR in Europe will increasingly need to demonstrate its value and impact on the bottom-line, and therefore, define and implement practices that promote labour competitiveness and develop human capital. This means that we can identify those 'best practices' that lead to superior performance in European organizations, while at the same time examining those HR practices that positively contribute to performance in specific contexts. In the US 'universalistic' approach, the emphasis is on identifying those HR practices that seem to work in the direction of better performance and outperforming others. In the European scene, we are also interested in the factors that bring about these practices, since different routes may lead us to the same destination. Along these lines, we may benefit from the inclusion of a more balanced approach to understand the mechanisms in the European setting that link HR and organizational performance.

Future research is needed to analyze whether and how convergence is going to occur in European HRM and, if it does, whether this convergence will keep idiosyncratic European patterns or move into a more universal 'best-practices' model. The impact of the Bologna treaty, at the European academic level, should be evaluated and the increasing international mobility, in Europe and outside European borders, may be quite large in this putative convergence.

References

Apospori, E., Nikandrou, I. & Papalexandris, N. 2004. *Comparing northern and southern European countries: The differential impact of strategic HR practices on organizational performance. Working paper.* Athens: Athens University of Economics and Business.

Arthur, J. B. 1994. Effects of human resource systems on manufacturing performance and turnover. *Academy of Management Journal*, 37(3): 670–687.

Backes-Gellner, C., Frick, B. & Sadowski, D. 1997. Codetermination and personnel policies of German firms: the influence of works councils on turnover and further training. *International Journal of HRM*, 8(3): 328–374.

Baird, L. & Meshoulam, I. 1988. Managing two fits of strategic HRM. *Academy of Management Review*, 13(1): 116–128.

Bartel, A. 1994. Productivity gains from the implementation of employee training programs. *Industrial Relations*, 33(3): 411–425.

Becker, B. & Gerhart, B. 1996. The impact of HRM on organizational performance: progress and prospects. *Academy of Management Journal*, 39(4): 779–801.

Beer, M., Spector, B., Lawrence, P. R., Mills, D. Q. & Walton, R. E. 1984. *Managing Human Assets*. New York: Free Press.

Bire, A. & Beechler, S. 1995. Links between business strategy and HRM strategy in US-based Japanese subsidiaries: an empirical investigation. *Journal of International Business Studies*, 26(1): 23–46.

Boselie, J. P. 2002. HRM, work systems and performance: a theoretical-empirical approach. *Tinbergen Institute Research Series*, n.274. Amsterdam: Thela Thesis.

Boselie, J. P., Paauwe, J. & Jansen, P. J. 2001. HRM and performance: lessons from the Netherlands. *International Journal of HRM*, 12(7): 1107–1125.

Bowen, D. & Ostroff, C. 2004a. Understanding HRM-firm performance linkages: the role of the strength of HRM system. *Academy of Management Review*, 29(2): 203–221.

Boyne, G. A. 2002. Public and private management: what's the difference? *Journal of Management Studies*, 39(1): 97–122.

Brewster, C. & Bournois, F. 1991. A European perspective on HRM. *Personnel Review* 20(6): 4–13.

Brewster C. & Hegewisch, A. 1994. *Policy and Practice in European Human Resource Management: the Price Waterhouse Cranfield Survey*. London: Routledge.

Brewster, C., Mayrhofer, W. & Morley, M. 2004. *HRM in Europe, Evidence of Convergence?* Oxford: Elsevier Butterworth-Heinemann.

Brewster, C., Tregaskis, O., Hegewisch, A. & Mayne, L. 2000. Comparative research in HRM: a review and an example. In C. Brewster, W. Mayrhofer & M. Morley (eds.), *New Challenges for European HRM*. London: Macmillan.

Child, J. 2000. Theorizing about organizations cross-nationally. In J. L. Cheng & R. B. Peterson (eds.), *Advances in International Comparative Management*. Stamford: JAI Press.

Claus, L. 2003. Similarities and differences in HRM in the European Union. *Thunderbird International Business Review*, 45(6): 729–755.

Cunha, R., Cunha, M., Morgado, A. & Brewster, C. 2003. Market forces, strategic management, HRM practices and organizational performance, a model based on a European sample. *Management Research*, 1(1): 79–91.

Cunha, R. C. & Cunha, M. P. 2004. *Impact of strategy, HRM Strength and HRM bundles on innovation performance and organizational performance. Manuscript.*

d'Arcimoles, C. H. 1997. Human resource policies and company performance: a quantitative approach using longitudinal data. *Organization Studies*, 18: 857–874.

Day, G. S. & Nedungadi, P. 1994. Managerial representations of competitive advantage. *Journal of Marketing*, 58(2): 31–45.

Delaney, J. T. & Huselid, M. A. 1996. The impact of HRM practices on perceptions of organizational performance. *Academy of Management Journal*, 39(4): 949–969.

Delery, J. E. & Doty, H. D. 1996. Modes of theorizing in strategic HRM: types of universalistic, contingency, and configurational performance predictions. *Academy of Management Journal*, 39(4): 802–835.

Diamantopoulos, A. & Hart, S. 1993. Linking market orientation and company performance: preliminary evidence on Kohli and Jaworski's framework. *Journal of Strategic Marketing*, 1(2): 93–121.

Esping-Andersen, G. 1990. *The Three Worlds of Welfare Capitalism*. Princeton: Princeton University Press.

Fombrun, C., Tichy, N. M. & Devanna, M. A. 1984. *Strategic HRM*. New York: John Wiley & Sons Ltd.

Geppart, M., Matten, D. & Williams, K. 2003. *Challenges for European Management in a Global Context*. New York: Palgrave Macmillan.

Gerhart, B. & Trevor, C. 1996. Employment variability under different managerial compensation systems. *Academy of Management Journal*, 39(6): 1692–1712.

Gmür, M. 2003. Die ressource personal und ihr beitrag zum unternehmenserfolg: die personalwirtschaftliche erfolgsfaktorenforschung 1985–2002. In A. Martin (ed.), *Personal als Ressource*. München, Mering: Hampp.

Gómez-Mejía, L. 1992. Structure and process of diversification, compensation strategy, and firm performance. *Strategic Management Journal*, 13(5): 381–397.

Gooderham, P. N., Norrhaug, O. & Ringdal, K. 1999. Institutional and rational determinants of organizational practices: HRM in European firms. *Administrative Science Quarterly*, 44(3): 507–531.

Grewal, R. & Tansuhaj, P. 2001. Building organizational capabilities for managing economic crisis: The role of market orientation and strategic flexibility. *Journal of Marketing*, 65(1): 67–80.

Groenewegen, J. 1997. Institutions of capitalism: American, European and Japanese systems compared. *Journal of Economic Issues*, 31(June): 333–348.

Guest, D., Michie, J., Conway, N. & Sheehan, M. 2003. HRM and corporate performance in the UK. *British Journal of Industrial Relations*, 41(2): 291–314.

Hendry, C. & Pettigrew, A. 1990. HRM: an agenda for the 1990s. *International Journal of HRM*, 1(1): 17–43.

Hofstede, G. 2001. *Culture's Consequences. Comparing Values, Behaviours, Institutions and Organizations Across Nations*. London: Sage Publications.

Hollinshead, G. & Leat, M. 1995. *HRM: An International and Comparative Perspective on the Employment Relationship*. London: Pitman.

Huselid, M. 1995. The impact of HRM practices on turnover, productivity and corporate financial performance. *Academy of Management Journal*, 38(3): 635–670.

Ichniowski, C., Shaw, K. & Prennushi, G. 1997. The effects of HRM practices on productivity: a study of steel finishing lines. *The American Economic Review*, 87(3): 291–313.

Ignjatovic, M. & Svetlik, I. 2003. European HRM clusters. *EBS Review*, 17(Fall): 25–39.

Ibitsanonis, N. D. 1998. Greece: the maturing of the system. In A. Ferner & R. Hyman (eds.), *Changing Industrial Relations in Europe*. Oxford: Blackwell Publishers.

Lado, A. A. & Wilson, M. C. 1994. *The Mutual Gains Enterprise: Forging a Winning Partnership Among Labor, Management, and Government*. Boston: Harvard Business School Press.

Lahteenmaki, S., Storey, J. & S., V. 1998. HRM and company performance: the use of measurement and the influence of economic cycles. *HRM Journal*, 8(2): 51–66.

Lengnick-Hall, C. & Lengnick-Hall, M. 1988. Strategic HRM: a review of the literature and a proposed typology. *Academy of Management Review*, 13(3): 454–470.

Lewin, D. 2003. HRM and business performance, lessons for the 21st century. In M. Effron, R. Gandossy & M. Goldsmith (eds.), *Human Resources in the 21st Century*. Hoboken, NJ: John Wiley & Sons Ltd.

Locke, E. A. & Latham, G. P. 1990. Work motivation: The high performance cycle. In U. Kleinbeck, H.-H. Quast, H. Tierry & H. Hacker (eds.), *Work Motivation*. Hillsdale, NJ: Lawrence Erlbaum.

Luo, Y. 1998. Industry attractiveness, firm competence, and international investment performance in a transitional economy. *Bulletin of Economic Research*, 50(1): 73–82.

Lyles, M., Baird, I., Orris, B. & Kuratko, D. 1993. Formalized planning in small business: increasing strategic choices. *Journal of Small Business Management*, 31(1): 38–48.

MacDuffie, J. P. 1995. Human resource bundles and manufacturing performance: organizational logic and flexible production systems in the world auto industry. *Industrial and Labor Relations Review*, 48(2): 197–221.

Mayrhofer, W., Muller, M., Ledolter, J., Strunk, G. & Erten, C. 2002. *Converging for success? European human resource practices and organizational performance in the 1990s – an empirical analysis*. Athens: Paper presented at the 2nd International Conference, HRM in Europe: Trends and Challenges.

McDonald, D. & Smith, A. 1995. A proven connection: performance management and business results. *Compensation and Benefits Review*, Jan–Feb: 595–564.

Miles, R. E. & Snow, C. C. 1984. Designing strategic human resource systems. *Organizational Dynamics*, 13(1): 36–52.

Milliken, F. 1987. Three types of perceived uncertainty about the environment: state, effect, and response uncertainty. *Academy of Management Review*, 12(1): 133–143.

Paauwe, J. 2004. *HRM and Performance: Achieving Long Term Viability*. Oxford: Oxford University Press.

Panayotopoulou, L., Bourantas, D. & Papalexandris, N. 2003. Strategic HRM and its effect on firm performance: an implementation of the competing values framework. *International Journal of HRM*, 14(4): 680–699.

Pearce, J., Robbins, D. K. & Robinson, R. B. 1987. The impact of grand strategy and planning formality on financial performance. *Strategic Management Journal*, 8(2): 125–135.

Pfeffer, J. 1994. *Competitive Advantage Through People*. Boston: Harvard Business School Press.

Poole, M. & Jenkins, G. 1996. Competitiveness and HRM policies. *Journal of General Management*, 22(2): 1–19.

Porter, M. 1996. What is strategy? *Harvard Business Review*, 74(6): 61–75.

Powell, W. & DiMaggio, P. 1991. *The New Institutionalism in Organizational Analysis*. Chicago: University of Chicago Press.

Schuler, R. & Jackson, S. 1987. Linking competitive strategies with HRM practices. *Academy of Management Executive*, 1(3): 207–219.

Slater, S. F. & Narver, J. C. 1994. Market orientation and the learning organization. *Journal of Marketing*, 59(July): 63.

Sparrow, P., Brewster, C. & Harris, H. 2004. *Globalizing HRM*. London: Routledge.

Sparrow, P. & Hiltrop, J. M. 1997. Redefining the field of European human resource management: a battle between national mindsets and forces of business transition? *Human Resource Management*, 36(2): 201–219.

Stavrou, E., Brewster, C. & Charalambous, C. 2004. *HRM as a competitive tool in Europe*. Internal working paper, University of Cyprus, Cyprus.

Terpstra, D. E. & Rozell, E. J. 1993. The relationship of staffing practices to organizational level measures of performance. *Personnel Psychology*, 46(1): 27–48.

Tregaskis, O. 1997. The role of national context and HR strategy in shaping training and development practice in French and UK organizations. *Organization Studies*, 18(5): 839–856.

Wall, T. D., Michie, J., Patterson, M., Wood, S. J., Sheehan, M., Clegg, C. W. & West, M. 2004. On the validity of subjective measures of company performance. *Personnel Psychology*, 57(1): 95–119.

Youndt, M. A., Scott, S. A. & Lepak, D. P. 1996. HRM, manufacturing strategy and firm performance. *Academy of Management Journal*, 39(4): 836–867.

Role of HR professionals: OD consultants, strategic brokers or individual therapists?

10

CHRISTOPHER MABEY, ANNE-METTE HJALAGER AND BIRTHE KÅFJORDLANGE

Introduction

It has been argued that a key indicator of the shift towards more strategic (human resource management) HRM is the extent to which line managers take the initiative for HRM strategies (Storey 1992). Reasons for this include increasing pressure to manage through cost-centres, the need to link HRM to other aspects of day-to-day management, the growing influence of knowledge and service industries and the identification with 'customers', and the increasing 'real-time' pressure on decision-making (Larsen & Brewster 2003). There are differing views as to the distribution of power pertaining to HRM between specialists and line management. For example, in a study of the UK National Health Service, effective HRM was attributed to those instances where senior managers were involved in the formalization of HRM policy and where the quality and efficiency of the personnel support was regarded positively; whether the personnel department was staffed by professional specialists had no impact on perceived effectiveness (Guest & Peccei 1994).

In the late 1980s, Legge predicted that '. . . personnel management will lose the position of power it achieved in the 1970s and lapse into a largely administrative and welfare service' (1987: 51). This is due, she said, to the ambiguous legitimacy the function derived (in the 1970s) from being mediators, or 'shock absorbers' of trade union pressure on the one hand and policemen of line managers' propensity to ad hoc decision-making on the other. This status was badly eroded by two major recessions, persistently high levels of residual unemployment, falling union membership and restrictive labour legislation in the 1980s. More recently she has modified her view, noting that more far-sighted personnel managers are gaining credibility by operating in a new specialist role while locating themselves firmly within the management team (Legge 1996). However, Caldwell (2003) has noted that personnel professionals remain a relatively weak occupational group and face a number of challenges inherent in their role ambiguity. These include marginality in management decision making, inability to defend the boundaries of their specialist expertise from encroachment by managerial intervention, lack of clarity in specifying their business contribution and tensions in maintaining an ethos of mutuality in the face of opposing interests between management and employees.

So, is the social agenda for HRM changing, and if so, in what direction?

The HR professional: retreat or re-invention?

Managerial psychology is a discipline that has existed for many decades. Assumptions and scientific findings about learning, personalities, motivation etc have informed personnel management and HRM practices for a very long time (Statt 2000). However, the theoretical legitimacy under-girding HRM and the robustness of the insights and tools offered are not always apparent to those who are the target groups of their recruitment or management activities. As a result, HR professionals find themselves in a vulnerable position with their credibility under threat. A number of contemporary issues are pertinent here.

First, is there evidence that people management activities, traditionally the domain of the HR function, are passing to line managers? In their study of twenty-two European countries Larsen & Brewster (2003) find that, with a small number of exceptions, in each country there are significantly more organizations increasing line management responsibility than decreasing it. Earlier findings from the UK concluded that HRM was becoming increasingly vested in senior and middle line management, not just as a delivery mechanism for new approaches in employee relations, but as 'designers and drivers of the new ways': in a number of core companies the prime movers in both initiating and managing such changes were manufacturing managers rather than the 'noticeably reticent, foot-dragging personnel specialists' (Storey 1992: 194, quoted in Legge 1996). However, there is contrary evidence. An in-depth study of eight UK companies found line managers unwilling and/or unable to be involved in human resource activities due to: the lack of incentives to do so, changes in management practices being blocked by trade unions and professional associations, the pressure to achieve short-term results and time pressures resulting from downsizing and delayering (Gratton *et al.* 1999).

Second, are HR professionals equipped to operate as strategic partners, as advocated by Ulrich (1997)? Based on their study of HR in the Australian Health Care sector and a UK NHS Hospital Trust, Barnett *et al.* (1996), highlight a number of factors which assist this evolution of HR. Amongst these are, various 'credibility building measures', including how various HR practices have been put into effect; 'agenda management' – the ability to keep people issues at the centre of business decision making, the 'continuous delivery of results', and the importance of 'a range of influencing techniques' as supporting the move to a more strategic HR function. And while such power playing is attractive, the cost may be that human resource activity comes under the harsh, short-term, financial scrutiny of other strategic functions; an expectation that is at odds with the more emancipatory and developmental goals of HR activity. Hope-Hailey (1997) questions the assumptions that HR is becoming more strategic and that HR is contributing to bottom-line business performance. She finds the role of HR to be one of setting and monitoring of standards of personnel practice while the operational decision making is carried out by line managers.

Third, how willing are other organizational players to endorse a more strategic role for HRM? Truss *et al.* (2002) investigated what being strategic actually meant at Hewlett Packard and whether it was possible for HR to play a more strategic role. They argue that it is dependent on how others perceive HR and whether other functions will 'allow' HR to become more strategic. One of the key enablers that allow HR to change its role is achieving 'reputational effectiveness', defined as the ability to perform the role effectively and the ability to influence others to accept a changed role for HR. Hope-Hailey (1997) makes a similar point, noting that the ability to fulfil an architect role was dependent on the perceptions of the importance of people management by other senior managers and directors' interpersonal skills of influencing and negotiating. Another factor is 'corridor power' over key line managers, defined as the ability of HR managers to influence organizational events and decision making. Crucial to this is role-set theory (Katz & Kahn 1978): how the role of HR is conceptualized by others in the organization, especially by line managers. Truss *et al.* (2002) gathered views from HR, from 'top managers' and from employees. They conclude that the organizational context plus the expectations of HR and line management have an impact on the ability of HR to play a strategic role.

Fourth, are there other roles that HR specialists can play? Various typologies of roles have been proposed, whether based on power and degrees of integration (Shipton & McCauley 1993), interventionist versus non-interventionist and tactical versus strategic (Storey 1992) or processes versus people and operational versus strategic (Ulrich 1997). In an empirical testing of Storey's framework, Caldwell (2003) found the Advisor to be most prevalent. With the increased devolution and growing autonomy of divisional and business unit management, 80 per cent of those HR professionals interviewed claimed that 'advisor' was their main role. Typically they enacted their role as internal consultants offering expertise and advice in a persuasive way, rather than in a directive or prescriptive manner. The next most claimed role was that of Change-maker (overlapping considerably with Ulrich's role of Change Agent). Here the skills were in partnering, guiding and facilitating large-scale change. Based on his evidence Caldwell points out that such roles are neither static nor discrete; indeed he highlights several issues of role conflict for the HR professional. He also notes that the four 'types' are too simplistic to capture the dynamic and shifting nature of HR activity. Elsewhere, he specifies four variations on the change-agent role: that of champion, synergist, adaptor, and consultant, each with a different subset of skills and contributions (Caldwell 2001). For all the labels and typologies, the increasing importance of the client-centred advisor role is clear.

This leads to a final question: is there a new potential role for the HR specialist as coach, or even 'therapist'? Employees are being taxed on a personal level like never before, having to deal with unprecedented complexity, uncertainty, paradox, risk and stress. This partly explains the explosion of interest in executive coaching (Bloch 2002), often with a psychoanalytic favour (Arnaud 2003). Recent studies claim that not only are enterprises becoming more boundaryless, the workforce is also exercising more freedom (Arthur & Rousseau 1996). Lifelong loyalties to single enterprises are withering away and job changes come more rapidly as a response to professional development needs. Not only is the pursuit of status *per se* reduced, the concept of status is changed to include the concept of personal learning and development. The ability to construct a case for personal development and career progress is a major issue in the career making. Self-evidently, when such strategies come to be advocated extensively (as they are at career guidance services, in job centres and so on), there is a tendency for the focus to be more inward than external. When traditional boundaries are broken down, and available choices multiply, it is likely that personal crisis or feeling of insecurity occurs (Bauman 2003), and help is needed. The next step towards seeking a coach or psycho-therapeutic help is possibly not far removed. In a private setting this probably explains the explosion of personal counselling. In a corporate context, HR professionals may be expected to play a parallel role in helping employees cope with radically altered psychological contracts, where the 'normal' job agenda is being more and more mixed with the personal development agenda and life–work boundaries are increasingly blurred. The attentive HR professional will look for tools and methods that combine the needs of the organizations for flexible and self-directed staff with the needs of the employees to obtain personal development and progressive learning.

In summary, two scenarios appear to be in play, one striking a positive chord, the other more gloomy. It could be argued that for HR specialists to give away (or have taken away) as much of their expertise as possible to line managers is far from negative, since this way good HR practice is embedded throughout an organization and greater ownership is taken for 'people issues' by those who directly manage staff and know the local context in which policies are to be enacted. Meanwhile HR professionals are released to play an influential role in the formulation of strategic policies and procedures on the one hand, and as in-company consultants and corporate 'therapists' on the other. A more negative scenario is a growing sense of role conflict and professional insecurity for HR specialists as their traditional power base is disaggregated and, for the organization, a gradual dilution of quality and uniformity in its people practices across separate business, national and cultural boundaries.

In this chapter we examine the outcome of the optimistic and pessimistic scenarios in organizations located in three countries. These are not intended to provide a representative picture of the profession across Europe. Rather, the intention is to shed light on different facets of the shifting roles of personnel/HR practice by viewing, in some depth, the business partner role in management development (Norway), the strategic guide/personal counsellor role in managing relocation (UK) and the potential of the psycho-therapeutic role in assessment and development (Denmark). Finally, aided by these cameos of current HR practice, we draw some conclusions at the close of the chapter.

HR as a strategic partner or strategic broker in Norway

In Norway there are long established traditions for *co-operative oriented management*, where the different parties of the labour market (that is the employers as well as the employees) together co-define good management. However, during the late 1990s there has been a noticeable tendency to set aside some of the importance attached to such co-operative management traditions (Byrkjeflot 2002). In recent years management thinking in Norway has become more diverse and to a greater extent influenced by various fads and fashions, like Business Process Reengineering and the Balanced Scorecard (Rolfsen 2000). One of the main reasons behind this development is claimed to be that managers have had to change their introspective focus from the internal issues of their organizations to being proactive and flexible in order to handle more turbulent surroundings, increased competition and globalization (Byrkjeflot 2002).

It is possible to detect two distinct directions in the way the HR role is emerging, and these are illustrated from case studies conducted as part of a wider study of management development in Europe (Mabey & Ramirez 2004). First, it is observable in some organizations that HR's role is becoming more closely linked to the company's strategy than before, a development in accordance with the recommendations found in the literature (Nordhaug *et al.* 1997). This direction is to a certain extent recognizable in a large, Norwegian-owned, internationally operating industrial company (see Box 10.1).

Box 10.1 Global management development: HR as a strategic partner

The company has for several decades run cornerstone companies in a number of communities and has a long history and proud traditions. The HR department in this company is presently responsible for running a worldwide management development programme for approximately 3,000 managers. In an interview the HR manager of the company described two separate purposes of the programme. The first was to perform an evaluation of each manager worldwide. This evaluation was done following the same template across all countries and various divisions of the company. The intention behind it was to make the different managers comparable across countries, divisions and cultures. Corporate expectations of their managers were formulated explicitly in five core elements and further specified in a limited number of key-performing indicators. A challenge, which the HR department was aware of, was to make sure that the performance demands were perceived as guidelines for improvements and not only evaluation criteria as a basis for pay and promotions.

The second purpose of the programme was related to each manager's future needs: his or her development potential and possibilities. The needs of each manager were based on an evaluation of what the company's strategic plans required of skills and knowledge from their managers and where the managers stood in relation to these requirements. The combination of these components of the management development programme formed a document and, it was claimed, this constituted an essential and a significant basis for the company's strategic planning. The programme was, in other words, designed to permit the company to recognize what competencies their managers presently possessed that enabled them to fulfil the current strategy of the company, but also what competencies would need to be developed if the company were to make any strategic changes in the future.

This first case illustrates how the HR department, based on its information and knowledge about the company's human competencies, plays a central role as potential 'strategic partner' in one Norwegian company. Here the HR manager had a place in the top management team that enabled him to participate in the company's strategic discussions and long term planning.

While the HR manager spoke positively of this fomalized MD programme during the interviews, the line managers were much more concerned with the management development found in their day-to-day work and particularly in solving challenging tasks. They were less preoccupied with the formal MD programme, but were still very conscious about their need to develop as managers. The most important development activity, in the line managers' opinion, was performing their jobs, delivering the expected results, learning from experience and growing with the responsibility they were given. As one line manager put it:

> For MD to be useful to me and my job situation, it has to address some issues that I deal with from time to time. Just a lot of too general stuff does not help me, it just steals time and attention from what is really my responsibility: to perform well and deliver results.

Thus there is a noticeable gap between how the HR manager and the line managers percieved the management development processes in their company.

But this example does not provide the complete picture of the HR professional's new role. Alongside the strategic partner role is another and rather opposed direction for the development of the HR professional. To illustrate this alternative direction, we refer to the way management development was managed in another Norwegian company. This is a large electricity producer with approximately 500 employees. The company has a strong engineering culture and – as in the former example – a long tradition of being a well-respected and well-organized company. The role of the HR department in this company is somewhat dual. On the one hand, it is responsible for running a mandatory and comprehensive management development programme, designed to focus on more general leadership issues. Since the programme is mandatory all the managers of the company are involved, which could potentially enable the HR department to have the same central role in this company as described in Box 10.1 above. But, on the other hand, this company has simultaneously decided that when it comes to other management development activities, the HR department has to compete against external deliverers of training and development. Here, the line managers of different departments are free to evaluate the offers from the HR department, compare them to external offers and then choose freely without constraints. So, this company regards HR activities as strategically important, but the HR department is seen more as a strategic *broker* than as a strategic partner. The key issue is to ensure that the managers' development is handled in the best way possible, not necessarily to make use of the internal HR departments' own offerings. The important decisions concerning how employees are developed and trained to enable them to carry out the company's formulated strategy, is left to their line managers.

In other words: instead of viewing it as an important strategic choice to enable the HR department to gain insight and knowledge about the company's management capacities and competencies (and thereby make HR a possible strategic partner), this company chose to consider HR as a valuable, but replaceable supplier of training and development activities. This represents a subtle shift in the role and power base of HR professionals. As before they have to be very sensitive to the various development needs in the company, but now they have more of a facilitation function: advising line managers as to the training options on offer. Alongside this is a 'selling' role; when HR believe that their internal insight and knowledge will be of special value to the developing processes, they have to convince the line managers of their specialist expertise. This arrangement implies to some extent a shift in who are believed to be best qualified to decide what developing activities are most valuable, from the HR department to the line managers. As such, it appears to be a confirmation of the growing Advisor HR role, described by Caldwell (2003): a non-directive internal consultancy, which can be bought in or outsourced as required (Ulrich 1997). Now that they are in direct competition with various external suppliers, the challenge is for HR to develop a new way of thinking.

These examples, taken from two well performing Norwegian companies, acknowledge the value of HR but also illustrate the duality in the new HR roles. Both companies share the same point of departure (HR activities are considered essential) but they choose truly different paths in how they pursue their goals. As yet, there is too little empirical evidence to suggest which path is ascendant in Norway. And, despite their very different approaches, there are still observable similarities that reduce the gap between them. One is related to the fact that the dominant consultant approach in Norway continues to be process oriented (Askvik 1995) as opposed to the *purchase of expertise* model or the *doctor-patient* model (Schein 1988). By process oriented we mean 'a set of activities on the part of the consultant that help the client to perceive, understand and act upon the process events that occur in the client's environment in order to improve the situation as defined by the client' (Schein 1988: 11). This implies that whether internal or external consultants are responsible for the HR activities, a common denominator is the way in which the HR activities are carried out. This is also relevant for the new HR role, since it influences the expectations they face. It can also be argued that the evident process orientation among Norwegian consultants narrows the gap between the two different approaches described here, since the shape of the HR activity is not necessarily very different, whether driven by external HR consultants or the internal HR department. Of more concern is the potential precariousness of the HR professional as their specialist expertise is encroached upon by external providers, their power base is undermined by line managers and their strategic partner role is replaced by that of strategic broker.

Strategic guide and personal counsellor: managing relocation and redundancies in the UK

What evidence do we have that HR is taking up the role of strategic guide and personal counsellor? Here we describe the UK case of a large retailer where HR specialists were called upon to facilitate the relocation of a number of staff, a strategic change which required a number of redundancies (Box 10.2).

It demonstrates how, in one company at least, corporate perceptions of HRM are shifting.

Box 10.2 A new role for HR in a large UK high street retailer

This case concerns a change management project in a major UK retailer company: the relocation of the Finance and HR Shared Service functions to another site. The general perception in the company was that this had been managed successfully, achieving its business plan, with annual savings of £4.5m.

Ostensibly, the HR strategy was 'second-order' strategy, meaning that the primary role of HR in this particular change project was to ensure that 'people issues are consistently kept at the centre of business decision-making' (Barnett *et al.* 1996). This encompassed:

- recruiting the right person to head up both the Shared Service function and the relocation project at the outset;
- supporting that person with the right team, both from a HR and a project manager perspective;
- ensuring that the people issues – availability of a pool of suitably skilled employees – were taken into account when selecting the new location;
- ensuring that the current employees were supported in achieving their preferred options, whether that was redeploying to another role within the organization or taking a redundancy package.

There was clearly an acceptance by line management of their changing responsibilities, particularly with regard to actually making their staff redundant. They expressed more comfort in carrying out this task because they felt well-equipped and prepared by HR to do so. For their part HR were clear that they alone could not conduct individual conversations with sixty people to make them redundant. The line managers saw that they had better knowledge of their teams and that they were therefore better placed to see their own staff. So, provided HR coached, developed and supported the line to carry out this emotionally demanding task, the line were prepared to see this as their accountability and allocate the time to carry out the task, . . .

> . . . Consultation served a useful purpose. It started communication between staff and management, there was lots of dialogue. Lots of anger and frustration were vented early on, this was helpful.
>
> (Senior Line Management)

Continued

> There were positive benefits; it gave people the opportunity to do something about those things they were unhappy with. But was it right for the business? I'd question our legal obligation, is this really the best way? We had unskilled people with no negotiation skills; they couldn't argue with the business case, it was obviously the right thing to do.
>
> (Line Manager)

Devolvement in this particular instance was uncontested. The fact that there was never any real debate about the desire of the line management involved to take accountability for their people, reflects the values and culture of this organization and the historical importance placed on its people.

Although the stated governmental aims of 'consultation' were not necessarily met, the process was perceived to fulfil a useful purpose in that it provided a vehicle for exchanging views between line management and employees, and drew out some of the negative feelings early on, which enabled the whole transition to progress, on a more open footing. It also had a 'cathartic' effect and a positive impact on the level of service provided throughout the transition.

Source: Rudge (2003)

This example illustrates a number of interesting features concerning the changing role of HR specialists.

First, there was evidence that HR were actively seeking out a more strategic role, from involvement in the recruitment of the project leader in the first place, to being a key member of the project team. By helping to implement a specific incremental improvement requiring specialist knowledge and technical expertise, HR was fulfilling the Change Consultant role described by Caldwell (2001: 48). They participated fully in the identification of a location, providing particular expertise with regard to availability of suitable skilled resources, and subsequently drawing up appropriate terms and conditions which would enable the new Shared Services to achieve their aim of reaching the top percentile in terms of costs and efficiencies. This supports the idea of 'negotiated order' and underlines the fact that members of the HR function are not just passive recipients of role expectations but are able to engage actively in processes to alter the nature of their role (Truss *et al.* 2002). There were many references made to how HR wanted to become Business Partners, and how the restructure of the HR group two years ago was designed to achieve that.

Second, the case shows how the devolvement of HR activities to line management can take place effectively, as long as there is the requisite support and coaching from the HR teams and the willingness of line management to take accountability for this. It is perhaps a testimony to the culture of the organization, with its strong history of fairness and regard for its employees that this happened.

Third, HR specialists played an important therapeutic role by offering support for those emotionally and psychologically distressed by the change project. This 'voice mechanism' is one of Delery & Doty's (1996) key strategic HRM practices. It might be asserted that the consultation provided the groundwork for pre-empting any possible industrial action.

Fourth, in terms of the competence of the HR function, it was clear that getting the basics right was essential to gain 'reputational effectiveness' and a prerequisite for moving on from the administrative phase of HR. Perhaps this is an ongoing requirement, whereby the four phases of HR – administrative, welfare, change management and strategic partner, are not linear and additive – and the HR function needs to be continually delivering against each of these. In this case, the welfare aspect was redefined as line management's responsibility. In addition, the very aim of this relocation project for HR and for Finance was to set up a new Shared Services organization, so it will be even more crucial in the future to ensure that the basic administration is carried out efficiently and effectively.

Finally, it can be observed that integration between HR and business strategy took place at lower levels than the Board in this example, a point made about the strategic role of HR by Hope-Hailey (1997). This is where the skills, attributes, and the 'will to become strategic' of the individual practitioners will make a difference. This might go some way to explaining the fact that the local HR teams in the case organization seem to be more highly regarded than the group or corporate function.

Therapeutic practice – a recaptured power base for HR professionals in Denmark?

Earlier we suggested that there is an opportunity for HR professionals to construct and install new and professionally valid ways of working, in short: to re-invent themselves. But what evidence is there that they are taking this opportunity? Some have not spotted the organizational space or, if they have, they may lack the competence and confidence to fill it. Box 10.3 describes ways in which HR practice in some Danish enterprises is moving towards a psychotherapeutic role. The examples are taken from case studies conducted as part of a wider study of management development in Europe (Mabey & Ramirez 2004).

Box 10.3 Legitimizing the use of psychometrics and psychologists in Danish HR practice

A small enterprise in the wholesale business encouraged all its staff members to undertake the Myers Briggs Type Indicator (MBTI) questionnaire, which maps personal work attitudes, preferences and learning styles, prior to an organizational development process. Introducing a testing instrument was not an easy thing to do. Many employees were sceptical, fearing that the test could point out deficiencies and weaknesses that could threaten their job security. Having performed the tests, however, the attitudes have turned away from the negative to the positive. The large majority of the employees feel confident about their test results and see the opportunities in developing the strong features and compensating for the weak ones. This is also true for the managers. The tool is now seen as a dynamic one, with an emphasis on facilitating change rather than 'imprisoning' the individual.

> We are careful not to go too far. For example I know an enterprise where the personnel wears badges with their MBTI letter combination. We would not do that.
>
> (Managing Director)

Since it reveals personal information, the management have decided that the results of the MBTI test should belong to the individual. The manager knows the main letter combination, but where the individual is heading in his/her development is largely a personal matter. The managing director claims that he sees his mission 'to push a bit here and there and in a friendly way to motivate the employees to use their personality preferences to make the most of job chances and career opportunities'.

The intention of the firm is to make an 'enterprise compass', which means a clearer matching between the jobs and the employees. The assumption is that many are placed in the wrong jobs without recognizing this. The benefits for the firm of a better allocation of human resources may seem obvious, but proceeding towards shifts and job changes will require quite a lot of further work. The HR manager's role in the process is to establish events where there is legitimacy for open discussion, for example the annual team building seminars. His role is also to get involved in the process of the annual employee interview, in order to raise questions that arise from the MBTI results. The HR manager gradually spreads narratives that remove the 'dangers' of the tests, and emphasizes stories about employees who have found new tracks where their competences and preferences can be better utilized.

Another enterprise went a step further and offered managers allowances to consult a psychologist. The agenda for the managers' talks with the psychologist was completely open, and there was no reporting to the HR managers or other managers. When interviewing the managers, they appreciate the talks – even more than they expected. The professionalism of the psychologist and the complete anonymous setting was helpful to raise issues such as difficulties of delegating and enhancement of communication with staff. Managers were also free to discuss the balance between work and family life and how to develop personal capacities to cope in a stressful work environment.

> I have a lot of time consuming leisure interests, and often felt that they conflicted with my management job. The psychologist made me reassess the conflict. I renegotiated the work contract, and my job is now part-time. The work relationship has become more straight and unbiased, and I perceive that this is right for me.
>
> (Line Manager)

Here the HR manager, who initiated the offer and found the psychologist, claimed that she herself benefited a lot from psychotherapy. She learned to observe and analyze her own reactions in various situations, and to adapt better. She has also become certificated in nero-linguistic programming (NLP). She finds the tools extremely useful in the everyday contact with staff. Communication is smoother and more efficient, and she feels that she gets a better insight into the motivations of the individual. The use of an external professional in this way is closely connected to the legitimization of the HR role in the organization.

These examples demonstrate a keen interest in psychometric instruments and in issues of personal and psychological development in the Danish cases. To judge from the press on HRM, there is a 'new wave' of experimentation in this field. Furthermore, the Scandinavian countries may be considered as an interesting test bench in a similar way to Volvo's experiments with self-managing groups back in the 1970s. It is possible that the particular cultural circumstances may be more encouraging to this new HRM wave here than in other countries. Hofstede (2001) notes that the Nordic countries were in egalitarian values and pursued democratic organizational models and practices. Power distance is low, so rational and practical solutions found in consensus are favoured. People are co-creators (Trompenaars 1995), and perhaps they want to work on the creation of the organization as well as their own personalities.

Conclusion

We began this chapter by posing a number of questions about the current role and status of the HR professional in European organizations. Undoubtedly, their role is changing, and with the help of recent literature and insights from case examples of organizations in Norway, the UK and Denmark, we have highlighted some important features of this new landscape. Furthermore, it has been pointed out that the key corporate contributions of HR are prescribed, to some extent at least, by the expectations of other organizational players. As Caldwell notes:

> Caught between a past they cannot fully relinquish and a future HR self-image that may ultimately be beyond their reach, personnel and HR professionals may be unable or unwilling to embark on the daunting journey of re-invention that might finally assure them of their professional status, power and value creating role.
>
> (2003: 1003)

So, *if* there were willingness, what might this journey consist of? Amongst a list which is by no means intended to be exhaustive, we close this chapter by proposing three things: the courage to be counter-cultural, the willingness to broker rather than deliver and the readiness to adopt a therapeutic stance.

There is ample evidence that HR professionals are poorly represented on Boards and, even where they are part of the senior management team, their influence is minimal compared to their colleagues (Brewster *et al.* 2004; Mabey & Ramirez 2004). In terms of position and hierarchical status then, they are weak. But this weakness may actually signal an opportunity for unparalleled strength. By virtue of their marginality, HR professionals are able play a more radical and counter cultural role required of an effective OD practitioner. Relatively unconstrained by the operational pressures for delivery that puts pressure on their colleagues to conform, they are well placed to focus less on systems and techniques and more on researching and questioning. In short, if 'post-modern organizations are the paradigm for the next phase of organization development, then it could be the case that human resource managers have a fundamental role to play in organizational transformation' (Shipton & McCauley 1993: 10). Thus in the realm of recruitment, selection and development, for example, there is an opportunity for them to lobby for long-term value over short-term gains and to nurture constructive deviance as against shallow gene-pools of conformist talent. There is, of course, risk in such radicalism, and to play this important OD role requires creating a power base of expertise as against relying on formal authority and the ability to operate as an internal consultant valued by the senior team. Table 10.1 points out what various internal groups expect from HR professionals. In other words: what is their market value and which power base helps them to 'deliver' (see Table 10.1).

Table 10.1 A new market and power base for HR professionals

	Market	*Power base*
Senior team	Must be assured that the inside knowledge of HR is superior to that of other internal or external 'suppliers'	Expertise and consultancy skills seen as indispensable for managing change and large scale people projects
Other managers	Must be convinced that human resources are better championed and allocated with HR than without	HR derive credibility from strategic brokering role and/or being in possession of information monopoly
Employees	Must feel helped in personal career plans and development, which improves their market value and employability	Personal charismatic and/or therapeutic influence to work for privileges of the employees

There are two other ways by which HR professionals may be able to cultivate either a 'market' or a power base for new services. Linked to the first is the possibility of stepping back from day-to-day management and implementation, leaving this to line managers who are ultimately responsible for HR changes and outcomes (Ulrich 1998) and becoming skilled at strategic brokering, understanding intimately the needs of his/her internal clients and also being critically attuned to what the array of suppliers have to offer. To take the example of management development, credibility for HR will be gained by accurate diagnosis of development requirements at different levels of the organization; appropriate matching of these needs to suppliers of training and development (whether internal or external) while avoiding faddish solutions; successfully weaving the development activities within the cultural fabric of the organization; communicating consistently the priority and demonstrating the worth of management development with line managers and senior team alike (Mabey & Ramirez 2004). Again, there are attendant risks. As illustrated by the second Norwegian case above, HR may find themselves dis-empowered by this new role: 'as the line can specify not only the terms of this internal HR involvement but also the extent to which this expertise should be bought in, outsourced or delivered by external consultants' (Caldwell 2001: 48).

Finally, and more speculatively, there is the potentially new role of the HR professional as counsellor or corporate therapist. In some ways, of course, this is not new at all. One of the earliest phases of personnel management, at least in the UK, was that of providing for the welfare of workers and their families (Berridge 1992). To care for their psychological well being is possibly a twenty-first century version of the same motive. Here we only have glimpses rather than extensive evidence of HR professionals fulfilling this role. In this chapter we have noted, for instance, the importance of HR providing an emotional buffer during a painful relocation and the growing use of psychologically driven counselling in Danish management development. Certainly there is increasing recognition of the need for executive coaching and for this to be underpinned by sound psychological methods (Nicholson 2000). And it is interesting to note that the very characteristics of the 'new HR' discussed in this chapter, namely a one-step-removed objectivity from the dominant power nexus (the senior team), a willingness to entertain non-conformity, being non-prescriptive, having high credibility and trustworthiness and the ability to broker to other sources of help, are the very prerequisites of an effective therapist.

There has been much debate in recent years about the diminishing role and influence of the HR professional in European organizations. Doom scenarios abound of HR practice being potentially diluted and the distinctive contribution of the HR professional being irretrievably lost as it is given away to line managers. Others observe that HR is finally being accepted at the 'top table', only to then be tied into business imperatives that overwhelm any moral conscience and counter-cultural contribution. This chapter has explored another way. Three potential roles have been discussed and illuminated with brief cameos of HR practice in northern Europe. Such examples may not be representative or even indicative, but they at least offer some exciting ways forward should HR professionals have the necessary courage to take the risk.

References

Arnaud, G. 2003. A coach or a couch? A Lacanian perspective on executive coaching and consulting. *Human Relations*, 56(9): 1131–1154.

Arthur, M. B. & Rousseau, D. M. 1996. *The Boundaryless Career: A New Employment Principle for a New Organizational Era*. Oxford: Oxford University Press.

Askvik, S. 1995. *Organisasjoner, konsulentbruk og læring, dr. philos thesis submitted at Universitetet i Bergen, Rapport nr 35 (1995)*. Bergen: Institutt for administrasjon og organisasjonsvitenskap.

Barnett, S., Buchanan, D., Patrickson, M. & Maddern, J. 1996. Negotiating the evolution of the HR function: practical advice from the Health Care sector. *Human Resource Management Journal*, 6(4): 49–62.

Bauman, Z. 2003. *Liquid Modernity*. London: Polity Press.

Berridge, J. 1992. Human resource management in Britain. *Employee Relations*, 14: 62–92.

Bloch, S. 2002. Executive couching. *The Economist*, 8 (March): 364 (8284): 8251.

Brewster, C., Mayrhofer, W. & Morley, M. 2004. *Human Resource Management in Europe*. Oxford: Elsevier.

Byrkjeflot, H. 2002. Ledelse på norsk: Motstridende tradisjoner og idealer? In A. Skogstad & S. Einarsen (eds.), *Ledelse på godt og vondt*: 41–61. Bergen: Fagbokforlaget.

Caldwell, R. 2001. Champions, adaptors, consultants and synergists: the new change agents in HRM. *Human Resource Management Journal*, 11(3): 39–52.

Caldwell, R. 2003. The changing roles of personnel managers: old ambiguities, new uncertainties. *Journal of Management Studies*, 40(4): 983–1004.

Delery, J. E. & Doty, D. H. 1996. Modes of theorizing in strategic human resource management: tests of universalistic, contingency, and configurational performance predictions. *Academy of Management Journal*, 39(4): 802–835.

Gratton, L., Hope-Hailey, V., Stiles, P. T. & Truss, C. 1999. Linking individual performance to business strategy: a people process model. *Human Resource Management Journal*, 38(Spring): 17–31.

Guest, D. & Peccei, R. 1994. The nature and causes of effective HRM. *British Journal of Industrial Relations*, 32(2): 219–242.

Hofstede, G. 2001. *Culture's Consequences* (2nd ed.). London: Sage.

Hope-Hailey, V. 1997. A chameleon function? HRM in the 90s. *Human Resource Management Journal*, 7(3): 5–18.

Katz, D. & Kahn, R. 1978. *The Social Psychology of Organisations* (2nd ed.). New York: Wiley.

Larsen, H. H. & Brewster, C., Line management responsibility for HRM: what's happening in Europe? *Employee Relations*, (Special Issue October): 228–244.

Legge, K. 1987. Women in personnel management: uphill climb or downhill slide? In A. Spencer & D. Podmore (eds.), *In a Man's World*. London: Tavistock Publications.

Legge, K. 1996. *Human Resource Management: Rhetorics and Realities*. London: Macmillan.

Mabey, C. & Ramirez, M. 2004. *Developing managers: A European Perspective*. London: Chartered Management Institute.

Nicholson, N. 2000. *Executive Extinct: Managing the Human Animal in the Information Age*. New York: Crown Publications.

Nordhaug, O., Holt Larsen, H. & Øhrstrøm, B. 1997. *Personalledelse – en målrettet strategiprosess*. København: Nyt fra Samfundsvidenskaberne.

Rolfsen, M. 2000. *Trendenes tyranni: produksjon og arbeid i et nytt århundre*. Bergen: Fagbokforlaget.

Rudge, G. 2003. *Adventurous Pioneers or Frustrated Laggards?: The Changing Role of HR in a Major UK Retailer, unpublished MSc project*. London: Dept. of Organizational Psychology, Birkbeck College.

Schein, E. H. 1988. *Process Consultation: Its Role in Organization Development*. Addison Wesley OD Series: Addison-Wesley Publishing Company.

Shipton, J. & McCauley, J. 1993. Issues of power and marginality in personnel. *Human Resource Management Journal*, 4(1): 1–13.

Statt, D. 2000. *Using Psychology in Management Training. The Psychological Foundations of Management Skills*. London: Routledge.

Storey, J. 1992. *Developments in the Management of Human Resources*. Oxford: Blackwell.

Trompenaars, F. 1995. *Riding the Waves of Culture*. London: Nicholas Brealey Publishing.

Truss, C., Gratton, L., Hope-Hailey, V., Stiles, P. & Zaleska, J. 2002. Paying the piper: choice and constraint in changing HR functional roles. *Human Resource Management Journal*, 12(2): 39–63.

Ulrich, D. 1997. *Human Resource Champions*. Boston: Harvard University Press.

Ulrich, D. 1998. A new mandate for human resources. *Harvard Business Review*, 76 (Jan–Feb): 124–134.

Looking beyond:
Societal and economic
macro-trends

Diversity and diversity management: a comparative advantage?

11

MARGARET LINEHAN AND EDELTRAUD HANAPPI-EGGER

Introduction

The workforce in organizations today is becoming increasingly diverse. This development affects the lives of employees and poses numerous challenges for managers. The issues of demographic change specifically relate to the changing nature of the workforce, and in particular to:

- gender – increasing numbers of women entering the labour market;
- ethnic minorities – will be forming an increasing part of the workforce; and
- age – the aging of the working population.

The changing demographic situation will have an effect on organizations and on society. At the societal level, changes will include the costs of caring for the very old and, with longer life expectancy, the increase will mean more demand for medical services. Given the increasing migration rate in Europe, a large number of legal and illegal immigrants now live in European Union countries. A particularly large influx of Muslims and Africans in recent years has been changing the religious and racial composition of these countries. Occupational changes have also occurred over the past decade, for example, Parker (1998) shows by reference to World Bank statistics, that agriculture is still overwhelmingly the dominant occupation for workers in low-income countries. In contrast, however, as Western-based organizations become more global in their employment practices as well as in their marketing activities, the number of people in many of these countries involved in manufacturing and service industries is likely to increase with a corresponding decrease of people working on the land.

From an organizational point of view, which is the main focus of this chapter, much of the work on managing diversity has stemmed from trying to identify what the impacts of the demographic changes for organizations will be and how organizations can prepare themselves for it. Regardless of the cause of the diversity in organizations, the result is that management must deal with the diversity and develop ways to manage it in a productive way. Diversity management makes good business sense as it is a better use of human resources. For example, by discriminating on the basis of gender, race, or disability, managers run the risk of overlooking talented employees. When an organization fails to maximize its full human resource potential valuable resources are wasted through under-utilizing the competences of its employees. Diversity can have a significant impact on organizations, as it provides both opportunities and challenges. Managing diversity can be a source of competitive advantage in the marketplace. Organizations that manage diversity effectively will become known among minorities as good places to work, and in turn these organizations will generally have lower levels of turnover and absenteeism. Managing diversity makes sound business sense as it (i) opens up new opportunities through broadening the customer base; (ii) ensures the selection, training and retention of people from the entire labour market rather than part of it, in order that the organization can attract the best talent; and (iii) increases the important ethical stand of organizations.

Agocs & Burr (1996) identified the expected benefits of diversity management for employees as including:

- decreased conflict and stress;
- enhanced productivity from heterogeneous teams or work groups;
- improvements in morale;
- improvements in job satisfaction;
- improvements in staff retention.

Other researched benefits of good diversity management programmes include: improved organizational performance (Richard 2000); lower levels of absenteeism (Robinson & Dechant 1997); increased creativity and innovation (Elron 1997); and higher quality problem solving (Hubbard 1999).

On the other hand, however, according to Joplin & Daus (1997), diversity in an organization can become a major source of conflict, which can arise for various reasons. Potential avenues for conflict are when an individual thinks that someone has been hired, promoted or fired because of his or her diversity status. Diversity management also requires a shift in thinking. Organizational leaders must engage in a re-education process as dominant groups are likely to experience loss of power and resist new developments. An ever-present issue and one of the biggest challenges in managing diversity is stereotyping. Managing a diverse workforce can often be a difficult task not necessarily because of the real differences that exist between people but because of those that people *believe* exist. Stereotypes abound in society and these are obviously carried into the workplace (Kandola & Fullerton 2001).

Despite the problems and challenges, however, organizations now see workforce diversity as a strategic business initiative, rather than 'just a nice thing to do' (McCune 2001: 183). Consequently, diversity initiatives are now being integrated into human resource management (HRM) policies and procedures because of the potential net benefits. Harris *et al.* (2004), for example, highlight a 'business case' motivation for diversity initiatives. Typical objectives include: being an employer of choice, attracting and retaining talent, developing high-potential employees, increasing productivity and keeping up with competitors. As a result, diversity efforts have to be implemented in recruiting, hiring, training, promoting, and developing *all* workers. Employers also need to integrate their diversity initiatives into the broader, long-term goals and missions of the organization. If employers are genuinely interested in developing successful diversity programmes, they will need to change the culture of their organizations so that diversity is not just supported but valued. It requires incorporating diversity efforts into continuous improvement and total quality management programmes. A key requirement is accountability, where behaviour changes on the job are measured and rewarded when set diversity goals have been achieved. Diversity management is a concept which requires a high commitment from both top management and all employees.

This chapter gives an overview on approaches to diversity and diversity management and it will highlight selected European specifics. The chapter briefly outlines the differences between managing diversity in Europe and the USA. Specifically, it examines how diversity is currently managed in three European countries, namely, Ireland, Austria, and Germany. In managing diversity in Europe, human resource managers now specifically talk about managing issues such as language, cultural contexts, and of having the capacity to identify and use alternative cultural styles and behaviour to achieve business goals. The chapter illustrates that diversity initiatives are beginning to be integrated into HRM policies across Europe, but, as yet these policies and practices are not well integrated into overall organizational policies. Loughran's (2004) research recommends that organizational culture, HR processes, and people management competencies should be combined in order to deliver the benefits of managing diversity strategically.

Defining diversity and diversity management

In many organizations the conversation continues to centre around the issue of what diversity actually is. Cox (2001: 3) defines diversity as 'the variation of social and cultural identities among people existing together in a defined employment or market setting'. With respect to the business dimension, diversity management deals with creating conditions that 'minimize its potential to be a performance barrier while maximizing its potential to enhance organizational performance' (2001: 4).

Of course, other definitions of managing diversity exist, too. For example, Thomas (1990: 112) suggests that managing diversity 'means enabling every member of your workforce to perform to his or her potential. It means getting from employees, first, everything we have a right to expect, and, second, if we do it well – everything they have to give'.

Kandola & Fullerton (2001: 8) propose:

> The basic concept of managing diversity accepts that the workforce consists of a diverse population of people. The diversity consists of visible and non-visible differences which will include factors such as sex, age, background, race, disability, personality and work-style. It is founded on the premise that harnessing these differences will create a productive environment in which everybody feels valued, where their talents are being fully utilised and in which organizational goals are met.

Loughran's (2004: 21) definition is:

> The workforce consists of visible and invisible differences. Managing diversity is founded on the premise that harnessing these differences will create a productive environment in which everybody feels valued, where their talents are fully utilised and in which organizational goals are met.

Diversity has to be considered as being different from discrimination, although the concept of diversity is often used when discussing discrimination. Diversity is about variety and differences whereas discrimination means treating people differently through prejudice referring to social dimensions. Diversity also has to be considered as being different from equal opportunities and not as a new label for an old concept. Equal opportunities have traditionally been a concept which sought to legislate against discrimination. This means that equal opportunities programmes focus on providing people from 'problem groups' with the same chances as others representing the 'normal' groups. This perspective in some sense reduces diversity dimensions and stresses the importance of assimilation. From an organizational context, equal opportunities were often seen as mainly the concern of personnel and human resource managers. Managing diversity, however, is seen as the concern of *all* employees, especially managers within an organization. The term managing diversity highlights the importance of difference, and suggests a view where difference is welcomed and is perhaps even to be celebrated (Ross & Schneider 1992).

Diversity management in the USA and Europe

Most of the research on managing diversity and implementing diversity initiatives has taken place in the USA. In the late 1990s, for example, the International Labour Organization surveyed workplace anti-discrimination diversity training programmes in fourteen countries. The survey was only completed in three countries – the United States, the UK, and the Netherlands because of difficulties in other countries to cite examples of workplaces where such training existed. It is interesting to observe how the concept of diversity management stemming from the USA has to be adapted to the European context. As a management technique, managing diversity has been pioneered by the subsidiaries of US firms in Europe (e.g. Intel, Hewlett Packard, Apple), although there was a strong need for national adaptation. In Europe, it is still unclear as to how well diversity management programmes are implemented in organizations.

Stuber (2003) highlights selected differences between USA and European diversity approaches. Even though diversity measures are assessed as being important for internal as well as for external affairs, organizations in Europe focus mainly on internal improvements and are less active in setting externally oriented measures such as marketing strategies. As Europe is a multi-lingual area, the meaning of cultural plurality and the multi-lingual setting are considered as being essential for successful diversity policies. Since the legal framework of an anti-discrimination policy is not yet well developed in Europe, the force of establishing a broad, normative diversity understanding in organizations is less than in the USA. Consequently, the main focus of European organizations is on the economical advantages of diversity management.

The management of diversity in Europe has also been indigenously developed in contexts where structures need to respond to:

- increased demographic complexity;
- inward migration;
- the large number of women in the labour market;
- cultural complexity resulting from increasingly freer movement of labour within the European Union.

Diversity management has gained ground in socio-economic environments where management has had to respond to change and also to the increasing impact of equality driven legislation and recognition of rights under the European Social Charter. The notion of diversity in the labour force, and the consequent need for changing enterprises to manage and develop diversity approaches in Europe is necessary because of institutional reform and the adoption of a single European market. Management of diversity in European terms has been centrally linked to the question of enforcement of the principle of equality among citizens and the prohibition of discrimination on a wide range of grounds. In most European Union member states, however, there remains a gap between the legal prohibition of discrimination and the actual outcomes for traditionally disadvantaged groups. In all countries, legal proof of discrimination tends to be very difficult.

Generally, it is clear that HRM practices not only vary according to their geographical location, i.e. USA, Asia, Europe, Africa, and South America (Beardwell *et al.* 2004; Sepheri 2002) but, in Europe there are many national variations. This is particularly evident in the case of managing diversity. The importance of diversity management stems in large part from the demographic shifts that are already underway in Europe's labour force. These changes mean that there are increasing numbers of ethnic minorities and women entering the workplace, and that there is an aging population. The basic premise of managing diversity is that if organizations are to manage this heterogeneous workforce effectively they have to find flexible ways of operating to accommodate the needs, desires, and motivations of different people to the benefit of all. All this points to an increasing internationalization of markets and the way organizations operate. This also means that organizations will have to deal with managing diversity not only in their own countries but also in others, and have people from their overseas operations working together on projects. In order to illustrate some of these concerns, we have selected three countries Ireland, Austria, and Germany to give an overview of some of the characteristics which are specific to each of these countries in managing diversity.

The situation in Ireland

The European politics on diversity have had a particular impact in Ireland. Here the currently fastest growing economy in Europe has had to contend with rapidly evolving labour market conditions and expectations. The pace of change has been mirrored by some of the most extensive equality driven legislation and monitoring structures in Europe. In addition, the Irish concept of equality has diverged dramatically from the original European one – which focused primarily on gender – to embrace a wide range of other social categories.

In recent years Ireland's demographics have rapidly changed and led to a country that has become increasingly multi-cultural. The Central Statistics Office reported that net immigration in 2002 was 47,500. Thirty-nine per cent were returning Irish nationals, 15 per cent were from Britain, 13 per cent were from the rest of the European Union countries, 6 per cent from the USA, and 27 per cent were from the rest of the world. Less than five years ago no more than 1,500 immigrant workers applied for work permits to work in Ireland. Today, despite restrictions on the number of permits issued to employers for non-nationals, 46,000 permits were issued by the Department of Enterprise, Trade and Employment to employers to hire workers from outside the European economic area. In addition to immigrants being a vital source of labour to fill the looming labour market gaps FAS (the Irish state training and employment authority) see older women, i.e. those aged 45 and over, as another critical source of supply.

For decades, Irish management resisted change in defence of the traditional and hierarchical structures that served them well in the past. By the 1970s, when Ireland joined the European Union, change was inevitable because of the concepts of equal pay and employment equality being enshrined in law (Merriman 1999). Many people were convinced of the need for employment equality, but in an economy in recession, it was difficult to prove the 'business case'. Progress was difficult to achieve, but more and more employments broke traditional moulds, because women succeeded in the educational field, in professions, and the 'marriage bar' was revoked. The marriage bar required that women leave paid employment on getting married. Such a requirement emerged in many countries, including Ireland, in the 1930s in response to high unemployment. It applied mainly to women's white-collar occupations, in both the public and the private sector, rather than to lower-level industrial or service occupations. In many countries the marriage bar waned in the 1950s when labour shortages became widespread; in Ireland, where labour surpluses have been larger and more long-standing than in most countries, it persisted until the 1970s – except for primary teachers, for whom the marriage bar was lifted in 1957 in response to a temporary shortage of teachers. The marriage bar was abolished in the public sector in 1973, and discrimination in employment on grounds of gender was made generally illegal in 1977. These changes brought a new dynamism and balance to the workplace.

Diversity management practices in Ireland: a survey

Although workforce diversity has rapidly become an important new issue for Irish managers to deal with, there is a distinct lack of research on the topic of diversity within an Irish context. This has resulted in a lack of evidence to prove that when diversity is used as a business strategy, to its full potential, it does impact on an organization's bottom line. One in ten of the current Irish population between the ages of 25 and 34 is described as a foreign-national. A recent study which was conducted by Talbot & Cullen (2004) with nine Irish and multinational organizations aimed to ascertain why businesses perceive diversity as being important to their success and to develop a picture of the diversity initiatives that have been implemented. Structured interviews were undertaken with identified diversity experts in each company and two web-based questionnaires were produced. The first of these were completed by the nine diversity experts and the second was issued to 100 staff in companies participating in the research.

The results of the research illustrate that staff believed that the strongest rationale for undertaking diversity initiatives stemmed from 'good personnel/HR practice' which might imply that these initiatives are driven exclusively by HR, rather than from an overall organizational perspective. Interestingly, the majority of diversity experts believed the main driving force behind diversity initiatives was the fact that they were part of company values, but none believed that these initiatives were driven by 'moral reasons'. The research unearthed concerns about the clarity of the diversity objectives among staff – while 78 per cent of the organizational diversity experts stated that their organization had a diversity statement, 70 per cent of staff members were not aware of this. In addition, there was some disparity between diversity experts and staff opinions regarding the most successful diversity initiatives in place within their respective companies. More than half stated that they did not understand the term 'diversity'. Seventy-four per cent of staff responded that they had received no diversity training and 64 per cent stated that they did not understand their role in the management of diversity. The research also revealed that while the majority of organizational diversity experts believe that diversity initiatives contribute to a company's financial performance, only 37 per cent of staff thinks that it plays such a strategic role. In summary, the research indicated that there is scope to develop a better understanding of the benefits to be gained by managing diversity more purposefully. To achieve this, however, diversity must not be driven solely by the legislative obligations placed on business today. Managers must regard diversity as a genuine strategic business opportunity and manage it at all levels within an organization.

Significant barriers, however, remain. The glass ceiling difficulties noted in the literature have been replicated in Irish conditions. Women are significantly under-represented at senior managerial levels. Despite women's high level of participation in the workforce, female CEOs are in a remarkably small minority in Ireland's top 1,000 companies. There are only ten women chief executives in the *Business & Finance* top 1,000 companies, and there is only one in the top ten (Corcoran 2002). Demand for childcare has escalated with the economic boom and demand for labour. Yet, there is no state or public system of childcare. The cost of childcare remains prohibitive and the quality is capable of significant variation in view of the lack of enforced national standards. Those with low incomes can seldom afford the childcare available or cannot access it at all. Without adequate state provision these women are left further behind (IBEC 2002).

Concluding remark: Ireland

The awareness that Ireland is now a multicultural and diverse society is widely accepted. What is not clear is how this relates to conceptual clarity, understanding of historic cultural differences and mechanisms of change in the labour market itself. Legislation can prevent more blatant forms of discrimination. In a society where legislation itself has often reinforced discrimination, a more fundamental challenge to models of diversity management and inclusion may be needed. Promotion of tolerance that works in the interest of all social stakeholders will require significant investment in work-based learning, innovative management training systems and person-centred strategic planning to inculcate principles of diversity. While anti-discrimination legislation has produced conformance much remains to be done in the area of education and positive programmes that promote a vigorous and multidimensional socio-economic entity.

The situation in Austria

Even though Austria has a long tradition of immigration – which means it has always been a meeting point of diverse people – public awareness does not match this fact. The dynamics of immigration was heavily connected with economic and political issues. Employees from other countries, for example, were attracted to Austria in times of economic growth in the 1960s and also after the fall of the Iron Curtain and the war in Yugoslavia in the early 1990s. Due to different legal frameworks regarding Austrians and non-Austrians, discrimination became a crucial phenomenon in Austrian society. This situation, however, has changed since Austria joined the European Union in 1995; therefore, there is now more legal equality between Austrians and people from other European Union members. Nevertheless, for people from non-European Union member countries the problem of legally legitimized inequality remains.

Similar to Ireland, the recent enlargement of the European Community has significant consequences for Austria. Moving from a peripheral position to a central one opens up new aspects of diversity, mainly because of the freer movement of labour (at least after the first seven years). It is anticipated that migration from the east to the west, in particular to Austria and Germany, will continue to take place. Barfuß (2002) estimates that about 335,000 people per year will move from the countries of middle and eastern Europe to Western countries. After ten years this will decrease to 150,000 migrants. This means that changes in the Austrian labour market will emerge not only because of general factors such as globalization, aging workforce etc., but because of the enlargement of the European community. Fassmann & Hintermann (1997) have shown that, in particular, highly educated and motivated migrants are likely to move. From those who are willing to migrate 23 per cent consider Austria as an attractive country, two thirds of them are men, one third are women, three quarters are younger than forty years of age (1997). The main economic reasons for willingness of people from Eastern European countries to migrate are higher income, better career chances, better working conditions, better qualifications, and further education opportunities (Fassmann & Hintermann 1997). Consequently, diversity management will be a crucial factor in organizations, as the workforce becomes more diverse.

Overall, Austria is an immigration country and recent developments will increase diversity in Austrian society. Diversity in organizations, however, cannot be reduced to managing migrants and people with cultural differences stemming from ethnicities. This would neglect diversity among other groups. Diversity management needs to include other social categories such as gender, education, religion etc. A brief overview on various modes of diversity management in Austrian companies will be outlined below.

Diversity management practices in Austria: cases and trends

As already mentioned it is an interesting phenomenon that Austria is an immigration country even though it is not generally perceived as such. Consequently, there are various different ways of handling diversity in organizations. Recent data show that there is a bias in the employment policy of companies: people with a migration background are often positioned at the lower end of the hierarchy which means that such employees suffer from psychological and physical strain due to bad working conditions (Biffl 2003). The Austrian Labour Market Service (AMS 2003) reported that the number of people older than 45 hired between 1994 and 2003 increased by 52.9 per cent. From 2002 to 2003, 3.3 per cent more people older than 45 were hired. This shows that there is a slight upswing in the willingness of companies to hire older people. Regarding disabled people, the number of hired persons decreased by 3.7 per cent. It becomes clear that diversity management is challenged by such observations. In Austria, it can be seen that different concepts of diversity management are implemented. It is necessary, therefore, to classify the various activities in Austrian companies along the social categories such as gender, age, disability etc. This is particularly important as there is no empirical survey on the state-of-the-art of diversity management in Austria.

- Family-friendly policies
  There is already a strong awareness of the necessity to promote women in companies. One important measure to allow for work–life balance is a family friendly policy. Although this addresses women as well as men with parental duties, it is strongly perceived as a promoting women measure. In order to create an incentive for companies, annual nationwide competitions are organized to reward companies with family-friendly policies (see OECD 2003) or even with 'best place to work'-awards.
- 50+ generation
  Facing severe demographic changes, in particular, the aging of the workforce, leads to changes in organizational cultures regarding the specific demands of older employees. As already mentioned above, the number of employees older than 45 increased by more than 50 per cent in comparison with earlier years. This can be taken as a sign that companies are responding to the aging workforce. This dynamic is supported by initiatives undertaken to restrict access to early exit schemes (see European Foundation for the Improvement of Living and Working Conditions 1999).

- Promotion of women

  In order to encourage women, in particular, to choose non-traditional jobs, various initiatives have been introduced. Starting from access to information (e.g. in schools) to the implementation of the 'girl's days' (in which daughters accompany their parents to their work places) and finally implementing mentoring programmes, networks and/or specific programmes for women.

Concluding remark: Austria

Generally, it can be stated that in Austria the long existing social partnership leads to a strong co-operation between public institutions and private companies. In terms of diversity management this means that public administration offers a variety of financial incentives to encourage companies to establish diversity management measures, e.g. the City of Vienna started the 'FemPower' Call, where companies could apply with projects in which highly qualified women were involved. Furthermore, the relevance of gender mainstreaming for public administration implies consequences for private organizations also. By binding public funding to gender mainstreaming the private sector is continuously confronted with issues of equal opportunities. A similar development could and should probably take place with diversity management.

As already mentioned, until now there is no adequate awareness of the importance of diversity management as a company-wide concept in Austrian companies. In addition, diversity management in Austria is focused mainly on gender and age. Sexual orientation, ethnicity, religion and even disability are not adequately considered yet. Even though in the Austrian subsidiaries of multinational companies diversity management is better implemented than elsewhere, most of the small and medium-sized companies are not facing the necessity of diversity management. This is because these firms are not seeing the advantages but rather the cost of diversity management. Clearly more empirical research is needed in order to 'translate' diversity management into their language.

The situation in Germany

Besides the social and political developments in Europe, such as the fall of the Iron Curtain and the enlargement of the European Community, the re-union of Germany in 1989/1990 challenged traditional understandings of diversity, nationality, and culture due to higher east–west migrations. Generally diversity in Germany is treated in a similar way to Austria. A publication of the Viennese '*Europaforum*' (2002) points out that in those countries a strong 'exclusive' model is observable. This means that public awareness of immigration is negative and this perception is difficult to overcome. National origin is perceived as substantially important. To become an Austrian or a German citizen is very difficult for immigrants and is not seen as a starting point of integration, but rather as a final reward of a long process. As Fassmann & Münz (2002) point out, Germany is essentially affected by the migration consequences of the European Union enlargement. Thirty-seven per cent of the population of Eastern Europe with strong migration tendencies would choose Germany as a destination due to expected better jobs and a better social security system. The majority of people living in Germany with non-German backgrounds are Turkish.

Nevertheless, general demographic developments such as increasing life expectations, the aging workforce, and low fertilization rates also influence the situation in Germany. As Engelbrech (2003) points out, there is still a slight upward trend in workforce demand, which cannot be met from 'traditional' segments of the workforce. Consequently staff have to be recruited to a greater extent from women and people with migration backgrounds. For example, when the demand for computer experts increased, Germany consciously started immigration initiatives and tried to attract people from India. Even though this initiative was heavily discussed it can be seen as a sign to recognize that specific economic circumstances require more diversity. As the Micro Census Germany (2003) shows there are several trends influencing the future of employment. More women are employed in comparison to previous years, even though there is still a gender-specific bias in various industries. The age of the workforce is also a trend to be aware of in Germany. In 2003 only 20 per cent of employees were younger than 30 years. The 45+ generation increased from 11 per cent (1991) to 13 per cent (2003). Generally, it can be observed that the public discussion on immigration or in general diversity is heavily interwoven with economic issues. Obviously, these trends have consequences for managing human resources in organizations, and in particular, dealing with a diverse workforce.

Diversity management practices in Germany: changes and trends

The above sketched historical developments together with the German tradition leads companies to base their management practices on a so-called 'Leitkultur' (leading culture). This means that in companies dominant value systems are present and are maintained without any critical reflection on which exclusion mechanisms they create. This situation, however, has begun to change over the last few years. Krell (2004) notes that in Germany equal opportunity laws are concerned with specific diversity categories such as gender, ethnicity, religion, sexual orientation, and language. In the private sector there are laws forbidding discrimination. Due to this, diversity management in Germany is mainly discussed in private companies, although there are also some examples of organizations in the public administration in which diversity management initiatives have been introduced. The relevance of diversity management in companies originates from the general trend in demographic changes which forces organizations to consider employees coming from other diverse groups. Besides the economic arguments of cost and loss in productivity, a positive aspect for diversity management is also mentioned, namely to be viewed as an attractive employer.

Krell (2004) highlights various studies done in Germany showing the specific aspects of diversity management in German companies. In particular, similar to Ireland, international companies such as Ford, Motorola, and Daimler Chrysler have introduced diversity management concepts into their German subsidiaries. German private companies increasingly have begun to react to these new requirements (e.g. Lufthansa, Deutsche Bank etc.). Finally, German public administration, which is similar to that of Austrian public administration, is supported by public funding and several projects on diversity management have been initiated.

Concluding remark: Germany

Diversity management in Germany marks a change in management practices. As a first step many companies are identifying specific measures, addressing specific groups (or referring to specific diversity dimensions) and trying to satisfy these requirements. Included among these measures are programmes promoting women (family-friendly policies, flexible work arrangements, mentoring programmes etc.), taking the 50+ generations into account (analyzing job requirements, changing further education politics and so on), and programmes focusing on the integration of employees with migration backgrounds. There are also some initiatives to change companies' policies to treat homosexual partnerships on a par with heterosexual partnerships. Belinszki's (2003) observation of diversity management, based on a qualitative analysis of five German subsidiaries of international companies, is that diversity refers mainly to core dimensions such as gender, ethnicity, age, disabilities, and sexual orientation.

A severe barrier for diversity management, however, stems from the lack of awareness in middle management. Thus education and training is important, in particular, regarding economic legitimization. Depending on the organizational context the implementation of diversity management is either organized centrally or decentralized as part of other activities managed locally. The next step will be to link the single measures and to come up with all-inclusive concepts of diversity management. In other words, to reach a new understanding of organizational culture where diversity is an integral part.

Some lessons for European human resource management

European-based managers are now facing the increasing necessity of managing diversity in their organizations. Empirical investigations of European companies show that there is a specific understanding of diversity management which was introduced mainly by subsidiaries of multinational companies. These diversity management measures, however, tend to be concentrated on internal activities, for example, recruiting, selection, and promotion of employees. Externally oriented business activities such as marketing, and customer retention still play a lesser role in the European setting. This suggests that diversity management is considered part of HRM. Furthermore, most diversity policies focus on specific diversity dimensions, such as gender and age, while aspects such as ethnicity, disability, sexual orientation, and religion are largely neglected. As illustrated, in the three country examples, diversity management focuses on specific measures such as family-friendly policies, promoting women programmes, and 50+ generation initiatives. Ethnic minorities are becoming a group of growing importance, disability is a less considered topic. The establishment of diversity management as an overall strategy has not yet reached any of the three countries examined. In Austria, the tradition of the social partnership leads to a rather non-controversial co-operation between public administration and private industries pushing issues such as gender mainstreaming. This probably will also happen with diversity management. In Germany, there are bigger national companies implementing diversity management and consequently function as best practice examples. In Ireland, the economic growth offers an important field for diversity management.

Generally, it can be stated that diversity management in Europe, as exemplified by the cases of Ireland, Austria, and Germany, is not yet understood as an overall company strategy. There are single measures implemented, but the organizations are far from establishing diversity efforts in all business fields. It seems to be more an attempt to deal with demographic changes (such as aging, migration etc.) in order to prevent decreasing productivity than seeing diversity management as a new chance to increase productivity.

Kandola & Fullerton (2001) suggest that managing diversity must pervade the entire organization, if it is to be successful. They propose a MOSAIC vision, which summarises the key characteristics of the diversity-oriented organization. MOSAIC is an acronym for **M**ission and values, **O**bjective and fair processes, **S**killed workforce: aware and fair, **A**ctive flexibility, **I**ndividual focus, and **C**ulture that empowers. In highlighting these key characteristics it is clear that the focus becomes that of ensuring all individuals within an organization can maximize their potential, regardless of any groups they may belong to. In summary, diversity management is an organizational concept addressing all functional areas as well as all people in organizations. Diversity management is based on the idea of celebrating differences as a source for increasing productivity. Diversity management stresses the importance of decreasing the power of dominant groups and establishing more egalitarian settings. The issues of globalization, ethics in business and workforce diversity underpin the human resource function and the human resource manager needs to raise the subjects in the many areas associated with the employment of people. But furthermore the area of marketing in terms of market shares and customer retention will also play a growing role in the future. This is still a definite gap in the European context.

Overall, it can be stated that diversity management should lead to positive economic effects for organizations. An example of one aspect of diversity, i.e. gender, can be taken to illustrate that the return on equity as well as the total return to shareholders correlates positively with the quota of women in top management. 'In four out of five industries, the companies with the highest women's representation on their top management teams experienced a higher total return to shareholders than the companies with the lowest women's representation' Catalyst (2004).

Of special concern to HRM is ensuring that individuals selected for employment are moulded into the type of employees who can abide by the organization's corporate culture (Pascale 1985). The ultimate purpose of this moulding process is to change the values of those selected to match the value system subscribed to by the organization's corporate culture (Higgins 1991). Cross-cultural research suggests that HRM models neglect the potential impact that diversity might have on organizations (Laurent 1983). The research further suggests that human resource managers are of the opinion that a strong corporate culture moderates the effect of diverse values that individuals bring to the workplace. The assumption is that employees, even if they are from different ethnic, cultural or racial backgrounds, leave their socially instilled values at the doorway as they enter the workplace. If they do not, the assumption is that the prevailing corporate culture will neutralize potential influences that their values might have on the organization's value system. Subsequently, new employees are expected to respond to situations within the organization in ways that are consistent with the prevailing value system (Hopkins 1997).

In the coming years, it is predicted that publicly quoted companies will have to engage in triple bottom line reporting. Together with traditional 'cash' capital, these organizations will be expected to report on their 'social' and 'natural' capital. This means reporting on what they are doing to be effective in terms of corporate social responsibility and managing diversity (Loughran 2004). Diversity management is particularly applicable in the twenty-first century, where there has been a change of emphasis from personnel management to HRM.

References

Agocs, C. & Burr, C. 1996. Employment equity, affirmative action and managing diversity: assessing the differences. *International Journal of Manpower*, 17(4): 30–45.

AMS 2003. *Austrian Labour Market Service, Annual Report 2003*. http://www.ams.or.at/neu/ams_gb_2003_V.pdf [11.11.2004, MET 9.00].

Barfuß, K. M. 2002. Globale migration: triebkräfte, wirkungen und szenarien aus ökonomischer Sicht. In U. O. The board of the Institute for Migration Research and Intercultural Studies (ed.), *IMIS-Beiträge 19/2002.*

Beardwell, I., Holden, L. & Claydon, T. 2004. *Human Resource Management: A Contemporary Approach* (4th ed.). Harlow: Prentice Hall/Financial Times.

Belinszki, E. 2003. Die Praxis von Diversity Management. Zusammenfassende Betrachtung von Best Practice Beispielen. In E. Belinszki, K. Hansen & U. Müller (eds.), Münster: LIT Verlag.

Belinszki, E., Hansen, K. & Müller, U. 2003. *Diversity Management. Best Practices im Internationalen Feld.* Münster: LIT Verlag.

Biffl, G. 2003. *Socio-economic determinants of health and identification of vulnerable groups in the context of migration: the case of Austria. WIFO Working Papers,* 206.

Catalyst 2004. *The Bottom Line: Connecting Corporate Performance and Gender Diversity.* http://www.catalystwomen.org/knowledge/titles/files/full/financialperformancereport.pdf [6.4.2005, MET 11.00]

Cox, T. J. 2001. *Creating the Multicultural Organisation.* San Francisco: Jossey-Bass.

Elron, E. 1997. Top management teams within multinational corporations: effects of cultural heterogeneity. *Leadership Quarterly,* 8(4): 393–412.

Engelbrech, G. 2003. Diversity und Chancengleichheit. Eine neue Herausforderung erfolgreicher Personalpolitik. In E. Belinszki, K. Hansen & U. Müller (eds.), *Diversity Management. Best Practices im Internationalen Feld.* Münster: LIT Verlag.

Europaforum 2002. *Migration und Integration, Teil 1: Von Integration zu Diversität, Vienna,* http://www.europaforum.or.at/data/media/med_binary/original/1074260863.pdf, downloaded 1.12.2004 [9.00 MET].

European Foundation for the Improvement of Living and Working Conditions 1999. *Active Strategies for an Ageing Workforce, Conference Report,* http://www.eurofound.ie/publications/files/EF9962EN.pdf (21.11.2004, MET 13.00).

Fassmann, H. & Hintermann, C. 1997. *Migrationspotential Ostmitteleuropa,* ISR-Forschungsberichte. Heft 15. Institut für Stadt- und Regionalforschung, Vienna.

Fassmann, H. & Münz, R. 2002. EU enlargement and future east–west migration in Europe. In I. I. O. F. Migration (ed.), *New Challenges for Migration Policy in Central and Eastern Europe.* Geneva, Vienna: IOM, UN.

Harris, H., Brewster, C. & Sparrow, P. 2004. *International Human Resource Management.* London: Chartered Institute of Personnel and Development.

Higgins, J. M. 1991. *The Management Challenge.* New York: Macmillan.

Hopkins, W. E. 1997. *Ethical Dimensions of Diversity.* London: Sage.

Hubbard, E. 1999. Diversity and the bottom line: facts, figures and financials. *Diversity Factor,* 7(4): 29–33.

IBEC 2002. *Women in Management in Irish Business.* Dublin: IBEC.

Joplin, J. R. W. & Daus, C. S. 1997. Challenges of leading a diverse workforce. *Academy of Management Executive,* August: 32–44.

Kandola, R. & Fullerton, J. 2001. *Diversity in Action: Managing the Mosaic.* London: CIPD.

Krell, G. 2004. *Chancengleichheit durch Personalpolitik. Gleichstellung von Frauen und Männern in Unternehmen und Verwaltungen. Rechtliche Regelungen-Problemanalysen-Lösungen* (4th ed.).Wiesbaden: Gabler Verlag.

Laurent, A. 1983. The cultural diversity of Western conceptions of management. *International Studies of Management and Organisation,* 13: 75–96.

Loughran, J. 2004. What is managing diversity? *People Management,* 2(2): 20–23.

McCune, J. C. 2001. Diversity training: a competitive weapon. In M. H. Albrecht (ed.), *International Human Resource Management: Managing Diversity in the Workplace.* Oxford: Blackwell Publishers.

Merriman, B. 1999. Managing diversity in Ireland: implementing the Employment Equality Act, 1998. In J. Fullerton & R. Kandola (eds.), *Managing Diversity in Ireland: Implementing the Employment Equality Act, 1998*. Dublin: Oak Tree Press.

Micro Census Germany 2003. *Leben und Arbeiten in Deutschland, Ergebnisse des Mikrozensus 2003*, Statistisches Bundesamt, http://www.destatis.de/presse/deutsch/pk/2004/mikrozensus_2003i.pdf downloaded 30.11.2004 [22.00 MET].

OECD 2003. *Babies and Bosses – Reconciling Work and Family Life, Vol. 2, (Austria, Ireland and Japan, 2003)*. http://www.oecd.org/document/37/0,2340,en_2649_37457_28932069_1_1_1_37457,00.html [12.02.2005, 22:00 MET]

Parker, B. 1998. *Globalization and Business Practice: Managing Across Boundaries*. London: Sage.

Pascale, R. T. 1985. The paradox of culture: reconciling ourselves to socialization. *California Management Review*, 27: 26–41.

Richard, O. C. 2000. Racial diversity, business strategy and firm performance: a resource based view. *Academy of Management Journal*, 43(2): 164–177.

Robinson, G. & Dechant, K. 1997. Building a business case for diversity. *Academy of Management Executive*, 11(3): 21–31.

Ross, R. & Schneider, R. 1992. *From Equality to Diversity – A Business Case for Equal Opportunities*. London: Pitman Publishing.

Sepehri, P. 2002. *Diversity and Managing Diversity in internationalen Organisationen: Wahrehmungen zum Verstandnis und okonomischer Relevanz*. Munschen/Mering: Rainer Hampp Verlag.

Stuber, M. 2003. Die Umsetzung von Diversity in Europa. In E. Belinszki, K. Hansen & U. Müller (eds.), *Diversity Management. Best Practices im internationalen Feld*. Münster: LIT.

Talbot, J. & Cullen, J. 2004. *Understanding Diversity Management in Ireland: A Survey of Management Practices*. Dublin: IMI Centre for Management Research.

Thomas, R. R. 1990. From affirmative action to affirming diversity. *Harvard Business Review*, March–April: 107–117.

12

Virtualization: boundaryless organizations and electronic human resource management

RÜDIGER KABST AND STEFAN STROHMEIER

Introduction

There is increased awareness, in particular in the business press but also in the academic literature, of a novel management phenomenon called virtualization, virtual organizations, or virtual HR. In particular in the early 1990s articles on virtualization first made the headlines of well-known business magazines like *Business Week* (Byrne *et al.* 1993), *Harvard Business Review* (Handy 1995), or *HR Magazine* (O'Connel 1996). The first book on *The Virtual Corporation* by Davidow & Malone was published by HarperCollins in 1992. Since those days numerous articles on virtualization have appeared (for reviews see, for example, Lepak & Snell 1998 or Scholz 2004).

It is said that virtualization may provide for a response to the current pressures for more flexibility, efficiency, and competitiveness. It is even suggested that virtualization may serve as something like a miracle cure or panacea for a modern organization. So what is behind this new phenomenon? How and when does virtualization yield benefits? Is virtualization a universal phenomenon or do we see divergent (local) practices across borders?

Whereas the delineation of virtualization, as with most new management phenomena, may still be under discussion, two major dimensions of virtualization can be distinguished: institutional and functional (Scholz 2004). From an institutional point of view, organizations show an increasing tendency to co-operate whereby leaving the traditional boundaries of the firm. In the past, hierarchical organizations tended to differentiate within their corporate boundaries, today virtual organizations extend beyond their boundaries to establish collaborative structures with suppliers, competitors, or external actors in general. From a functional point of view, information technology changes the way HR is handled in the organization. Internet as well as intranet provide new and more efficient mechanisms to organize HR related workflows. Already today, organizations rely heavily on electronic human resource mangement (e-HRM).

Addressing the two dimensions of virtualization separately, we show key characteristics, conceptual arguments and practical examples of HRM in boundaryless organizations and of electronic HRM. The set-up of the chapter is divided into sections and is as follows:

Boundaryless organisations introduces virtualization in respect to boundaryless organizations. Two aspects of virtualization in boundaryless organizations are discussed: HRM in international joint ventures and outsourcing of HR tasks. The theoretical underpinning of virtualization in boundaryless organizations is layed out contrasting transaction cost and neo-institutionalist arguments. A case study concludes the section on virtualization in boundaryless organizations.

Electronic HRM introduces virtualization in respect to e-HRM. Electronic HRM is delineated by discussing its concept, applications, and outcomes. Convergence or divergence of e-HRM practices are addressed briefly in order to set up the ground for international comparative analysis. A case study concludes the section on virtualization in respect to electronic HRM.

Conclusion concludes the discussion on virtualization by summarizing key arguments and integrating the two dimensions of virtualization.

Boundaryless organizations

Compared to traditional hierarchical organizations an increasing number of firms are partnering with others to expand their strategic scope. These firms are often referred to as virtual or boundaryless organizations (Powell 1990, Miles & Snow 1992, Davidow & Malone 1992, Ashkenas *et al.* 1995). Boudaryless organizations allow external knowledge to be accessed through partnering with other organizations. Contractual relationships are manifold thus affecting HR in two different, however, interrelated aspects. First, on the organizational level new forms of interfirm co-operation (e.g. joint ventures) emerge that cause novel challenges for the qualification and transfer of employees over organizations' boundaries, mostly over national boundaries. Second, HR departments in general are becoming more virtual in nature, increasing their reliance on external providers to perform part, if not all, of these HR activities (Lepak & Snell 1998). Both aspects of boundaryless organizations (interfirm co-operation and outsourcing) are discussed in the following section in order to set the field for a theoretical underpinning of boundaryless organizations.

Interfirm co-operation: international joint ventures (IJVs)

On the organizational level, interfirm co-operations, most popular joint ventures, received particular attention in the HR literature. Joint ventures allow parent companies to realize synergies that neither company would be able to generate alone. Most often one parent company brings in the technical expertise or an existing product and the other company provides for the sales knowledge and structure. As a typical example, a company intends to enter a new foreign market for its existing products, however, does not process the knowledge and foreign sales-structure to sell these products abroad. Thus the foreign company aligns with a domestic company that provides for the necessary complementary knowledge. Other set ups, like two technology companies joining together to develop new products or two machine tool companies forming a joint venture to realize cost synergies are further examples showing the motives for joint venture formation.

HRM for international joint ventures brings about challenges to existing HR practice. Starting with the pioneering studies of Flick (1972), Peterson & Schwind (1977), and others, early systematic overviews of HR problems by Shenkar & Zeira (1987, 1990) or more recent ones by Schuler (2001) suggest that joint ventures bring about new tasks to HRM, especially in respect to expatriate management. These HR challenges include: (a) Staffing friction: most parent companies wish to place their own expatriates in key positions in the joint venture on the assumption that whoever has the most people in charge will control the organization, or at least its key functions; (b) Blocked promotions: local managers of IJVs are frequently frustrated by the lack of promotion opportunities to key jobs, since senior positions are reserved for foreign parent or host parent transferees; (c) Exile syndrome and reentry difficulties: managers are often reluctant to join an IJV because they are afraid to interrupt their career back home. Further they tend to promote their parent interests of the venture itself; (d) Split loyalty: appointees who were recruited by the host or foreign parent tend to remain loyal to that parent rather than shift their loyalty to the IJV because they usually expect to work for that parent following the end of their assignment; (e) Compensation gaps: each parent company has an established compensation policy and these compensation policies usually differ, that is different employee groups receive different compensation packages. In addition, each employee group has a different perception about which compensation package is most desirable; (f) Blocked communication and incomplete information: parent companies hesitate to pass information (e.g. technology) to anyone other than their own representatives in the venture. They worry that such information will be used by the IJV itself or the other parent(s), whom they may perceive as competitors; (g) Limited delegation: many parent firms try to maintain control over the IJV by strictly limiting the scope of decision-making authority. This is especially true when the parent depends on the IJV for scarce and vital resources; (h) Blurred organizational culture: especially in the early stages of a joint venture's life, its culture tends to accept those of the parent firms; thus the IJV may lack its own culture. Furthermore, the higher the number of transferees in key positions, the more difficult it becomes for the venture to develop its own distinctive culture which reflects and complements its particular environment.

It is obvious that most HR challenges are connected with transferring parent company expatriates into the international joint venture. As we know from international HRM, expatriate management per se is no easy task. However, compared to wholly owned subsidiaries, expatriate management for joint ventures reiterate the problem as many parent companies, as a matter of principle, favour dominant control over the joint venture. This basic attitude, however, may be one of the fundamental reasons for serious HR problems and therefore volatility of the joint venture. Schaan (1988: 4) illustrates this attitude by citing an executive manager as follows: 'We do not enter joint ventures unless there is no other way of taking advantage of a business opportunity. We like to have full control over our operations. We always have majority ownership'. In agreement with the above daily wisdom the dominant strategy for many companies consists of sending as many expatriates into key joint venture positions as possible.

Key to a successful international joint venture or a well-functioning expatriate management is the insight that it is not maximum control via transferees that is needed, but, an efficiency oriented situational control, which most of the time is quite less elaborated, supports a smooth and successful joint venture.

External providers: outsourcing

While the interest in virtualization has primarily focused on the firm as a whole, a parallel transformation has been occurring with the HR department. Companies are rethinking how to organize the HR function to make it more flexible while still providing a full complement of HR services. In an attempt to meet these objectives, many HR departments are becoming more virtual in nature, increasing their reliance on external providers to perform HR activities that have traditionally been conducted in-house (Lepak & Snell 1998; Klaas et al. 1999; Kabst & Matiaske 2001; Matiaske & Mellewigt 2002).

Outsourcing, generally defined as outside resource using, was first introduced in the context of IT services. General Motors' acquisition of EDS in the mid-1980s and the subsequent transfer of all information systems support to EDS or the choice of IBM, DEC, and Businessland as external providers for the overall communication systems of Eastman Kodak at the end of the 1980s are examples for the first publicly announced cases of IT outsourcing (Dirlewanger 1992; Szyperski 1993).[1] Not surprisingly, the 1990s were marked by an academic as well as practitioners' discussion of the outsourcing phenomenon mainly focused on IT services. However, nowadays organizational practice as well as academic discussion is not bound to outsourcing of IT services any more, but it is widely understood that outsourcing has become an overall organizational issue detached from a single functional area (Grover *et al.* 1996).

Outsourcing can help firms minimize costs by externalizing HR tasks that do not contribute directly to a firm's competitive advantage, thereby enabling HR departments to focus on value-creating activities (Lepak & Snell 1998; Carrig 1997). Rather than investing significant resources to establish and maintain an in-house capability to provide an HR service that may be needed infrequently or for only a short period of time, firms may turn to external providers.

HR outsourcing, however, is not undisputed. The risk of losing essential company-specific know how and skill has proven to be one of the critical issues. As Greer *et al.* (1999) pose the question: 'Does outsourcing of HR activities spell doom for the HR department?' In some instances, HR outsourcing has been shown to reduce costs by providing economies of scale, increasing incentives and accountability, and increasing access to specialized expertise. In other instances, outsourcing has been found to limit the development of distinctive HR competencies and sophistication and to create inefficiencies because contractors lacked firm-specific knowledge and engaged in opportunistic behaviour (Klaas *et al.* 1999). Questions that need to be answered are: Which factors determine which HR activities to outsource? Furthermore the relationship between excellence and outsourcing needs to be addressed. Might outsourcing be part of the effort towards excellence of the HR activities?

Clearly, our understanding so far is limited. Cost-motives for outsourcing dominated the discussion in the early 1990s. However, outsourcing motives have become much more diverse in recent years, including motives to improve the performance and excellence of the HR function (Greer *et al.* 1999). Thus not only are HR tasks that can be performed at lower cost by external providers increasingly outsourced, but also HR tasks that are not performed to the quality needed by the internal HR departments (due to economies of scale, knowledge, etc.). Thus outsourcing may also enhance the HR value chain as well as support the development of HR as a business partner and strategic contributor to the organization's goals (Greer *et al.* 1999). HR departments are increasingly responsive to both internal and external customers, and must look for ways to improve the quality and responsiveness of their services. Outsourcing may offer HR an option to satisfy competing demands for improved service and responsiveness at a reasonable cost (Greer *et al.* 1999). Thus outsourcing is not only a question of whether someone else can perform the job cheaper than you, but also a question of whether someone else can perform the activity better than you.

The theory of the boundaryless organization: dominated by efficiency calculus?

The theoretical starting point of studies analyzing boundaryless organizations is mostly rooted in transaction costs economics (Williamson 1975, 1985, 1996). Over the past thirty years, transaction cost economics has emerged as a predominant theoretical explanation of boundary choice. This institution-economic foundation is obvious, not least because of its focus on the market-hierarchy-continuum and its close link to the classic 'make-or-buy' decision (Picot 1991).

Transaction cost economics belongs to the New Institutional Economics school of thought which has set itself the objective to explain the structure, behavioural effects, efficiency, and change of economic institutions. New Institutional Economics developed from dissatisfaction with a lack of realism of neo-classicism, and claims to expand neo-classical microeconomics on the one hand, and on the other hand to partly refute it, as it does not accept institutions such as markets and organizations as fact, but pursues the question of efficiency of institutions (Coase 1937; Williamson 1975). In its analysis of institutions its basic question focuses on which kinds of transactions in which institutions of governance can be organized at the relatively lowest cost. For this reason Williamson (1981, 1985) calls transaction cost economics a 'comparative institutional analysis', which considers alternative organizational forms of economic activities in the light of efficiency aspects. Williamson states that the level of production and transaction costs necessary for a certain governance structure vary systematically with (1) certain characteristics of the transaction and (2) certain characteristics of the governance structure. Thus the transaction cost approach is a micro-analytic instrument that can explain the development of mechanisms of governance and serve as a basis for the formation of contractual relations. Following Commons (1931), the transaction constitutes the basic unit of microeconomic analysis in transaction cost economics.

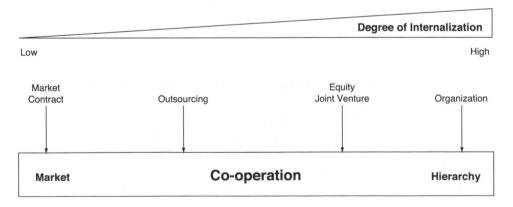

Figure 12.1 Boundaryless organizations between market and hierarchy

Source: Author's own creation

Transaction cost economics is based on three assumptions that characterize the behaviour of the actors: bounded rationality, opportunism, and foresight (Williamson 1999; 2000). With these assumptions transaction cost economics purposely moves away from the concept of neo-classicism. Instead these assumptions should make allowances for human nature as we know it and represent an important step closer to reality. The behavioural assumptions are of fundamental significance when contractual problems occur. In addition Williamson (1985) identifies three transaction characteristics that are influential in carrying through and organizing a transaction. These are: the extent of asset specificity, uncertainty in connection with the transaction, and the frequency a transaction is repeated. However, asset specificity is the central determinant for the existence of transaction costs and consequently for the choice of governance structure. (Williamson 1985; Picot 1991). Williamson (1985: 56) states: '[A]sset specificity is the big locomotive to which transaction cost economics owes much of its predictive content . . . the absence of asset specificity [would] vitiate much of transaction cost economics'. Goods and services can be produced either by general-purpose or by specific-purpose technology, whereby for the latter non-trivial specific investments are made (Williamson 1985.) Specificity comes about therefore through the use of specific-purpose technologies or, in more general terms, from investments that are made for certain transactions and which outside this particular transaction would mean loss of value or would not be able to be put to any use at all. The degree of specificity increases with the level of the quasi-rent to be appropriated, in other words with the sum of the difference of the values in the proposed transaction and its next-best utilization. Thus specific investments cause a special dependency relationship in which the identity of the transaction partners is essential.

In order to transfer the transaction cost argument to boundaryless organizations we will shortly sketch the main theoretical discussion put forward when analyzing international joint ventures and outsourcing from an efficiency perspective.

The dominating motive for entering into a joint venture is that the planned objective cannot be carried through alone, or only with difficulty, and that the co-operation within the framework of a joint venture through the combination of necessary proprietary assets promises the greatest benefit. It enables each parent company to tap protected assets that are essential for the proposed field of activity. The sum of the utilization of individual assets of the parent companies is on its own less than the utilization of the combined whole in the joint venture. Alchian (1984) also points out the synergy effects of such a co-operation. The group that emerges is termed a coalition. Coalition-specific investments are defined as investments of which the value is higher in the coalition than in an alternative governance mode. If specific assets are transferred to the joint venture, however, the danger of opportunistic behaviour on the part of the other parent company cannot be ruled out.

Thus the transfer of specific assets from the parent company into the joint venture triggers the danger of opportunistic behaviour on the part of the joint venture partner, and this is to be met with corresponding safeguards. These safeguards need not necessarily be directed toward the control of the joint venture as a whole, they can be targeted toward the protection of those specific assets that have been deployed. Staffing key positions of the joint venture with assignees of the joint venture parent companies represents a mechanism of selective control. By posting its own expatriates in critical positions the parent company can steer the diffusion of its specific assets. Thus a joint venture parent company's need for control can be satisfied if specific R&D assets that have been transferred are protected by filling the position of the R&D manager with one of its own expatriates, thus creating a protection to counter opportunism. The transferred specific investments are protected, without necessarily having to control the joint venture as a whole, in other words without affecting the need for protection of the joint venture partner. By controlling selected activities both parent companies can look after the necessary protection of transferred specific assets in an efficient conflict-reducing manner. Thus transaction cost economics aims for an efficient (and not maximum) degree of control, reducing direct labour costs as well as HR problems discussed above.

Transaction cost analysis in respect to outsourcing again underlines the risk of opportunism. When firms rely on outside suppliers, they are relying on market contracting as a form of governance. When firms rely on internal employees, they are relying on hierarchy as a form of governance (Williamson 1985). Transaction cost economics argues that firms attempt to choose governance structures that minimize total transaction costs associated with the focal transaction. Contractual hazards may arise from opportunistic behaviour by external providers upon whom the organization has grown dependent. Examples of this sort of opportunistic behaviour include introducing excessive price increases at contract renewal, charging excessively for adjustments or add-ons during the contract period, and reducing service quality in areas where outcomes are not thoroughly specified (Klaas *et al.* 1999).

Transaction-specific investments, when referring to HR work, called human asset specificity, are the decisive decision criteria in this context. The specificity of human capital raises transaction as well as production costs of outsourcing. Outsourcing is either not possible because of the specificity of human capital, or causes comparatively higher transaction costs due to the necessity of training the external service provider. In addition, the disclosure of proprietary information would increase the risk of opportunistic behaviour by the external party. Behaviour uncertainty, caused by team production, increases contractual hazards.
Thus outsourcing, from a transaction cost rationale, may only be efficient in cases of low human asset specificity and low behaviour uncertainty.

The theory of the boundaryless organization: more than just efficiency?

In recent years, however, transaction cost reasoning for boundaryless organizations has been confronted by widespread criticism. It is argued that transaction cost theorists are unable to explain the success of organizational practices that is rife with inefficiency. Hence, transaction cost theory has been criticized for overemphasizing efficiency and ignoring social context variables (Granovetter 1985). Considering an international comparative lens and extending the reasoning suggested by Roberts & Greenwood (1997) and Barringer & Milkovich (1998), transaction cost economics may be complemented with arguments from institutional theory in order to enhance the understanding of how different institutional environments and pressures influence boundary choice.

Institutionalists view organizations as open systems that are shaped by the environment they are embedded in (Meyer & Rowan 1977; DiMaggio & Powell 1991). In order to increase their chances of survival, organizations do not only have to be efficient but they have to be legitimated. By adding institutional constraints, we shift the underlying rationale from efficiency optimizing towards efficiency satisfying. Organizations strive for efficient designs, however, they are biased in favour of designs that are legitimated within their institutional environment.

Transaction cost economics and institutional theory offer seemingly contradictory interpretations of organizational phenomena. In the words of Granovetter (1985), transaction cost economics provides an undersocialized account whereas institutional theory offers an oversocialized perspective. However, transaction cost and institutional perspectives are not necessarily in conflict, but are complementary elements of a constrained-efficiency framework (Roberts & Greenwood 1997: 347).

Neo-Institutionalist approaches to the study of HRM provide a useful framework for understanding the problems of the transferability of HRM over organizational fields and national boundaries (Geppert et al. 2004).

The American neo-institutionalist school, mostly labelled new institutionalism, refers to authors like Meyer & Rowan (1977), Zucker (1987), or DiMaggio & Powell (1983) and views organizations as open systems that are shaped by the environment in which they are embedded. In order to increase their chances of survival, organizations do not only have to be efficient but they have to be legitimate. Legitimacy can be acquired by adopting structural elements that socially constructed environments regard as appropriate. Thus the formal structure of an organization reflects the societal perception of rational design. In order to survive, organizations need to adapt management practices to societal expectations leading to structural equivalence of organizations. Three mechanisms of isomorphism can be distinguished: coercive (pressures from the environment), mimetic (pressures from reference organizations), and normative (pressures from professional associations).

The European neo-institutionalist school, mostly labelled as the 'business systems' approach, pre-dominantly refers to the works of Whitley (1999), Hall & Soskice (2001) and Albert (1991). Whitley argues that differences in institutional environments (divergent capitalisms), in particular on a supranational level, need to be considered in a more systematic fashion. Depending on the institutional frame of a particular economy, a customized national business system evolves. Historically grown institutional traditions and systems of a society determine the nature of the firm, non-ownership mechanism of co-ordination, and work organization.

Thus expanding transaction economics reasoning by neo-institutionalist arguments allows the boundary choice to be analyzed in respect to international joint ventures or outsourcing, not solely from an efficiency calculus, but taking into consideration mimetic pressures from the organization, which in general explain the spread of new management phenomena (like interfirm co-operations and outsourcing) in organizational fields. Business systems approach in particular focuses on the particularities of every single business environment highlighting the differences in HR practices across borders. Neo-institutionalism allows divergence to be searched for in HR practices across borders instead of hunting for convergence due to mimetic pressures in industries.

Case study example: Kingkraut Ltd

Kingkraut Ltd was founded in 1996 in Manchester by a British and a German machine tool company both owning 50 per cent of the voting rights. The parent companies joined in order to realize synergies, in particular the technological expertise of the German and the sales and local expertise of the British company. The goal was to enter new markets in a generally saturated market for machine tools in Europe.

However, soon after foundation the shared equity joint venture became a disappointment, missing out on synergies as well as generating less turnover and even losses. Mistrust, conflicts resulting from differences in national and corporate culture, and unclear decision competencies prevented the joint venture from realizing the intended synergies as open communication and dissemination of needed knowledge was greatly hindered. The excessive placement of gatekeepers from the parent companies in key management positions in the joint venture, in particular the twin staffing of the CEO-position with both an expatriate from the German parent and an expatriate from the British parent was identified to be the main cause for the unsatisfactory business development. The experience has shown that both CEOs had different business policies, leading to severe frictions for employees and customers as well as low efficiency of the overall joint venture operations.

As a result the foreign assignment policies of the parent companies were reexamined and the dual staffing of the CEO-position was eliminated. Just one expatriate, coming from Britain, was appointed as new CEO of the joint venture. The German parent

Case Example

company agreed to refrain from appointing the CEO-position, however, it was then able to transfer an expatriate heading the R&D and production activities of the joint venture. In addition, cultural training programmes were initiated to overcome differences between home, host, and third country employees. In respect to performance appraisal and compensation, unique joint venture policies were established utilizing autonomous decision making of the joint venture. Each expatriate was provided with a formal career plan before their joint venture assignment in order to decrease dependency of expatriates on a single parent company.

Another problem concerned the global HR policy of the German parent company which required the utilization of external providers for the recruitment process of new employees. The German parent company outsourced its entire recruitment activities in order to reduce costs. From the perspective of the German parent the outsourcing decision was clearly justified. The German parent had a turnover rate of below 1 per cent and a generally stagnating market. Recruitment was no concurrent task but was undertaken rather seldom. In addition, potential employees had to be recruited for standard jobs provided for by vocational training in Germany reducing information asymmetries and qualification uncertainty. The implementation of a recruitment outsourcing policy for Kingkraut Ltd, however, ended in frictions both in regard to cost and qualification. The institutional environment in Great Britain, especially those with turnover rates of 10 per cent and more and no standardized vocational training, make outsourcing of the recruitment process seem less favourable. Both from efficiency as well as institutionalism perspective, Kingkraut Ltd would have been better off leaving the recruitment process in house.

Electronic human resource management

Having discussed the institutional dimension of virtualization above, the functional dimension of virtualization, based on information technology and applied to HRM, is introduced in the next chapter.

The term 'electronic Human Resource [Management]' (e-HR[M]) is widely used today. Without doubt, the term originated in the development of practical HRM; a prominent example is the recruiting of employees via the Internet (Lievens and Harris 2003). Since e-HRM is a reasonably new development in managing human resources, little is known on this subject. Hence, e-HRM is subsequently delineated by emphasizing the crucial aspects and controversies that are associated with e-HRM. In addition, an example of practical e-recruiting in Europe is given, so as to deepen the insights in e-HRM. Leaning on both, the delineation and the example, two main conclusions for HRM are drawn.

Delineation of e-HRM

Concept of e-HRM: well-defined term or catchphrase?

Even though the term e-HRM is widely used there are hardly any explicit definitions (see, as an exception Lengnick-Hall & Moritz 2003, 365). Hence, it seems unclear, whether e-HRM is just another ambiguous and short-lived catchphrase or a well-defined and lasting concept. So as to avoid any ambiguity, the following definition of e-HRM can be established:

> e-HRM is the, as a rule, spatially segregated, both technically networked and technically supported, shared performing of HRM tasks through at least two human or technical actors.

The criterion of *spatial segregation* demonstrates that the actors involved are, as a rule, not in the same place, as, e.g. an applicant and a recruiter with an application over the Internet. Spatial segregation here is not to be understood as a compulsory criterion, since there may be networked actors working in the same room.

Technical networking, however, is a criterion that must be met. Information technology (and the increasingly converging communications and media technologies) enables actors to be technically networked irrespective of their working in the same room or on different continents. Shared organized HR processes can thus be separated both in terms of space and time.

The criterion of *technical support* requires that the technology applied will assume, beyond the mere networking of actors, the performing of certain parts of a task either in a fully or partly automated mode. This additional requirement excludes simple e-mail or similar contacts from turning into a minimal variety of e-HRM.

The interrelated criteria of *shared tasks* and *at least two actors* point out that the sharing of work processes between several actors is a necessary requirement. This and the way in which processes are shared, i.e. the concrete process organization, are at least in part dictated by the technology employed.

The criterion *performing of HRM tasks* demonstrates that e-HRM is essentially geared towards work processes in HRM, i.e. recruiting, development, compensation etc. Thus, a well-defined concept of e-HRM is feasible.

Additionally, it seems of special interest whether e-HRM is a widely accepted practice or a mere concept of HRM. Due to the scarce and fragmented empirical research in e-HRM (see Avolio *et al.* 2000; Lievens & Harris 2003 for reviews) our knowledge on the adoption of e-HRM rests mainly on surveys of consulting organizations (Watson Wyatt 2000 and 2002; Towers Perrin 2002; iLogos Research 2003; Cedar 2004) and an escalating host of 'experience reports' (e.g. Mecham

2001). Although sometimes scientifically questionable, the surveys in particular show the ongoing international growth of e-HRM, indicating that both the number of organizations adopting e-HRM and the depth of applications within organizations are continually increasing. Due to its advanced adoption e-HRM is described as 'mainstream' in the developed countries (Cedar 2004, 1) at present.

Thus, despite of the lack of empirical studies, e-HRM should no longer be treated as a mere idea, but as matter of fact.

Purpose of e-HRM: substitute or addendum?

Concerning the HR tasks there is fundamental congruence between conventional and electronic HRM: e-HRM, of course, has to recruit, develop, compensate etc., too. Therefore, concerning the basic purpose of e-HRM the question arises, whether it is a substitute or just an addendum to conventional HRM. If e-HRM is to be seen as a substitute, it will replace conventional HRM practices, if it is to be seen as an addendum, it will supplement conventional HRM practices. Hence, it is of interest, whether e-HRM can be extended to *all* HR tasks or, whether, for technical or other reasons, it has to be limited to certain areas and certain support levels of HRM.

The answer depends reasonably on the required level of support from information technology. If a more modest level of support is satisfactory, then basically *all* HR tasks can be technically supported. Meanwhile, this also applies to 'qualitative' tasks such as an assessment or leadership that could formerly not be technically supported. Corresponding to this, electronic versions of practically all HRM tasks are discussed, e.g. e-recruiting (Lievens & Harris 2003), e-assessment (Konrad & Sarges 2003), e-performance monitoring, respectively e-appraisal (Stanton & Barnes-Farrell 1996), e-compensation, respectively e-benefits (Stifler 2001; Simon & Mattle 2002) e-development, respectively e-learning (Schaper & Konradt 2003) or e-leadership (Avolio *et al.* 2000). Hence, basically all HR tasks *can* be performed in the form of e-HRM. If the requirements for technical support are raised, though, depending on the level of requirements, more differentiated answers will be necessary.

Thus, e-HRM is not a mere addendum but a partial substitute to conventional HRM.

Applications of e-HRM: web-focused or web-exceeding?

e-HRM utilizes applications of information technology obligatory in a twofold manner: first, these applications are necessary to connect normally spatial segregated actors and enable interaction between them. Here, information technology serves as a medium with the aim of integration and co-ordination. Second, these applications support diverse actors by partially substituting and complementing them in fulfilling tasks. Here, information technology serves, in addition, as a device of task fulfilment. Since the Internet is the ever-present global technical network, it accomplishes the first purpose of connecting and co-ordinating spatially segregated individuals in a virtually perfect manner. Hence, central applications of e-HRM are actually web-based. This holds especially true for diverse (manager-, employee- or applicant-) self service-applications (e.g. Zampetti & Adamson 2001a, 2001b), portal-applications (Watson & Fenner 2000) or web-based training (WBT)-applications (e.g. Liaw & Huang 2002). e-HRM therefore shows a strong web-affinity. Consequently, the terms 'Internet-' or 'web-based HRM' (e.g. Walker 2001) are widely used synonymous with e-HRM. But there are also applications in e-HRM which do not necessarily depend on web technologies. In particular, human resource information systems (HRIS) (e.g. Rampton *et al.* 1999) and (the HR-modules of) enterprise resource planning (ERP) systems (e.g. Norris *et al.* 2000) can network actors by means of their general multi-user capability. In the same way, general computer supported co-operative work (CSCW)- and workflow-applications (e.g. Basu & Kumar 2002) are at least not necessarily web-based. However, sharp delimitations between these application categories are problematic since practical applications increasingly combine the properties and functionalities of different categories. Particularly, the previously not web-based HRIS- and ERP-applications more and more include self-service and portal functionalities and hence become at least partially web-based.

Thus, e-HRM shows a strong and increasing web focus, but is, however, not exclusively restricted to the web.

Actors of e-HRM: conventional or novel?

Actors of e-HRM are all those who perform HR tasks in a technically networked and supported way. Conventionally, two internal and two external actor categories are primarily responsible for HRM: of course, above all, the actors of the HR management, respectively of the HR department, are accountable for HR tasks. In addition, the internal category of *management,* consisting of line managers with personnel responsibility, participate within the framework of decentralization in HRM. Both categories are facultatively supported by external *consultants,* e.g. concerning the recruitment of experts or executives. As a fourth collective category *administration* comprises the manifold external HR-relevant actors or institutions, such as banks, public employment agencies, labour courts, health insurances, etc. In interaction with internal offices these actors take over (certain parts of) HR work, e.g. the recruitment of labour through a public employment agency. These four conventional actor categories are, of course, also key actor categories of e-HRM. However, they are complemented and to some extent substituted by two novel actor categories of e-HRM. With the assistance of employee self-service systems and employee portals the *employees* themselves, as the conventional 'target group' of HRM, become an actor category who fulfills parts of the HRM tasks. (To a certain degree the actors of line management and HR, in addition, belong to the employee category, if they are subject to HRM as individuals employed by the company.) The same holds true for the external *applicant* category. In contrast to conventional HRM, in e-HRM applicants assume their own active role in HR work, even though their job is limited to certain aspects of recruiting and selection. Hence, employees and applicants are 'empowered' in e-HRM and thus constitute novel actor categories.

Since at least two technically networked actors *interact* in order to perform a HRM task a variety of initially twenty-one possible interaction segments of e-HRM can be distinguished. Each segment, such as *applicant-HR* or *HR-management,* constitutes one specific variety of interaction. When further ordering these categories according to internal and external actors, the segments can be grouped into three major areas (see Figure 12.2).

Certainly, the internal interactions between management, HR department, and employees in the *first area* constitute the core activities of e-HRM. In addition to the actors' technical networking and support, a substantial contrast to conventional HRM lies in the fact that now the employees themselves perform (parts of) HRM. The separation of internal actors into management, HR, and employee therefore is necessary to better understand crucial e-HRM-phenomena such as controlled decentralization, virtualization, etc.

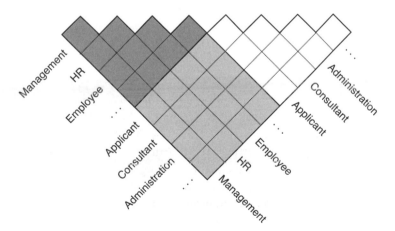

Figure 12.2 Actors and interactions of e-HRM

Source: Author's own creation

The interactions in the *second area* go across the company. Here, the range of tasks is performed by external applicants, consultants or administrative institutions and the internal actors management, HR and employees.

Without exception, the *third area* contains company–external interactions so that one can doubt whether this is part of e-HRM at all. However, in the categories *administration* and *consultant* so-called intermediary actors can be located who connect other actors following the pattern actor–intermediary actor. For example, an Internet job board as an intermediary actor connects an applicant with the HR department. This shows that e-HRM can also consist of external interactions. Generally, segments can be found that are unorthodox in HRM and seemingly do not make sense, such as *applicant–applicant* or *employee–applicant*. However, this should not lead to an inconsiderate elimination of these segments. Indeed, for example, in the *employee–applicant* segment first examples for the development of ('virtual') actor communities (Rheingold 1993) can be found with an exchange of employment conditions of certain companies etc., leading to severe consequence for the HRM (see for a 'legendary' example the 'greedy associates'-phenomenon delineated by Taras & Gesser 2003). Even though this clearly does not mean e-HRM, these are certainly developments of particular relevance to e-HRM. As a matter of principle, such currently unconventional interactions should not be excluded from the discussion of e-HRM, irrespective of the clearly differing relevance of individual segments of interaction.

The depiction of six explicit actor categories certainly names the major but, by no means, all actors of e-HRM. Linked to the internationally varying role of employee representatives, for example, the internal category *works-council* and the external category *union* can gain relevance. Thus, e-HRM incorporates conventional *and* novel actor categories.

Ontology of e-HRM: real or virtual?

Akin to the title of this chapter, the concept of 'virtual HRM' builds a further synonym of e-HRM (e.g. Lepak & Snell 1998; Strohmeier 1998). 'Virtual' often is appreciated as a kind of antagonism to 'real'. However, since the concept is seldom delineated, it remains unclear, what 'virtual HRM' actually means. In order to elucidate virtual HRM one has to split the actors and organizational units of e-HRM on the one hand, from the tasks or functions of e-HRM on the other: the actors and units *can be* virtual in some circumstances, while tasks or functions are definitely not virtual. Due to their real existence actors and organizational units of e-HRM often are real. If an applicant submits an application to a recruiter via the Internet, without doubt two real actors carry out real actions. However, there are technical applications like the above mentioned self-service systems that can completely replace real actors or even units. Such a technical actor is virtual in the sense of 'apparent', 'pretended' or 'not real', since the actor is not an acting human or unit, but merely technically modeled after the actor's job function, thus 'pretending' in this aspect the existence of a human.

As a result the patterns of e-HRM interaction are to be distinguished in terms of whether the interaction is taking place between real, real and virtual or, as a special case, exclusively between virtual actors. Virtual, however, are only the actors or units. The tasks carried out by such virtual actors as well as the results are necessarily real in the sense of not only 'apparent' and not only 'pretended' (Strohmeier 1998). If we understand HRM to be the tasks and not the corresponding actors or units, then the term 'virtual HRM' is somewhat misleading. e-HRM is real HRM.

Thus, the mere organizational dimension of e-HRM *can* partially be virtual, while the functional dimension is definitively not.

Variety of e-HRM: convergence or divergence?

Due to the comprehensive potentials of information technology there is a host of design options for e-HRM. Consequently, with reference to the international convergence or divergence of HRM practices (McGaughey & De Cieri 1999) the reinforcement of cross-cultural differences, hence the *divergence* of e-HRM practices, seems to be the most plausible scenario. However, due to two reasons the opposite seems to be realistic. First, packaged e-HRM solutions increasingly overtake the previous use of custom developed solutions as the platform for e-HRM (Cedar 2004: 28–31). Yet, packaged software usually possesses customizing properties, i.e. the possibility to adapt data structures, functions etc. to individual needs. Nonetheless the use of generally standardized software like that of the e-HRM market leaders SAP, PeopleSoft-Oracle or ADP (Cedar 2004: 30–31) leads, at least as a general rule, to comparable practices within the user organizations. Second and more important, there is an e-HRM inherent urge to standardize practices to some extent. Since networking and interaction of spatial segregated actors on a technical basis is a central feature of e-HRM, the basic compatibility of applications and practices is a necessary prerequisite. If, for example, payroll is partially outsourced in an *HR-consultant* interaction the basic payroll practices and applications of both actors ought to be compatible to ensure a successful collaboration. Due to this general requirement, the 'HR XML Consortium' was founded in 1999 as an international non-profit organization with the central aim of *standardizing* e-HRM related data structures, and therefore, subsequently the corresponding e-HRM processes (Scholz 2003; HR XML Consortium 2005). This confirms the urge towards an international compatibility of e-HRM practices and demonstrates why divergence is not a plausible assumption for e-HRM. Since technology is a macro-level variable (McGaughey & De Cieri 1999: 238) and the sparse empirical hints of cross-cultural differences in individual perceptions of these technologies on the micro-level (e.g. Harris *et al.* 2003) there is no negative impact on the convergence proposition.

Thus, within the complex convergence-divergence dynamics the increasing application of e-HRM is a macro-level force towards HRM similarity, and therefore *convergence*.

Outcomes of e-HRM: opportunities or risks?

A crucial but for the most part unanswered question relates to the possible and factual outcomes of e-HRM. At the outset, it has to be stressed that the so called 'technological determinism' is an inadequate kind of thinking and theorizing about e-HRM outcomes (Ropohl 1982). Electronic devices used in HRM are not just causal antecedents of spatio-temporal invariable effects, like cost reduction etc., which can be easily examined. Rather, they provide actors with a wider range of usage potentials. Outcomes then are dependent both on the range of the provided potentials and on the specific kind of usage of these potentials by the actors. Hence, a broader spectrum of e-HRM outcomes including chances *and* risks is to be expected. On the opportunity side aspects like cost reductions and efficiency gains, which enable a more strategic perspective of HRM can be considered (Lengnick-Hall & Moritz 2003: 369). On the risk side, it has to be emphasized that e-HRM projects are costly and by no means failure proof. Other risks may rest in the fact that the reallocation of the HR task to managers, external consultants, applicants and employees and the corresponding information systems will, on the one hand be an additional burden to the internal actors, and, on the other hand result in an urge to reduce HR staff (Strohmeier 1998). Despite some initial results of the above mentioned surveys, e.g. a more strategic role of HR (Cedar 2004: 14) or a reduction of HR staff (Cedar 2004: 17) due to e-HRM, a thorough empirical programme is necessary to elucidate the provided potentials, the actual usage, and the resulting outcomes of electronic devices in HRM.

Thus, beyond the often far reaching promises of consultants and software vendors there are risks beside the opportunities of e-HRM, both of which are not thoroughly assessed at present.

Case study: e-recruiting in France, Germany, and the UK

E-HRM practices within Europe can be demonstrated by the e-recruiting activities of a MNE in France, Germany, and the UK (see Hesse 2003). As a leading MNE in the sector of media and entertainment the group comprises 76,000 employees in 56 countries. The group is differentiated into six divisions, each comprising a multitude of single corporations acting as independent profit centres. Due to an explicitly decentralized management style, the HRM practices differ, more or less, throughout the single corporations and countries. By concentrating on e-recruiting the example does not present a comprehensive e-HRM approach, it serves, however, appropriately as an illustration of the above discussed dimensions of e-HRM.

The general *purpose* of the project was to establish a comprehensive, enterprise-wide recruiting device, featuring the special functions of image building, recruiting of external individuals, as well as recruiting and career development of internal employees. Due to the huge effort of conventional 'paper based' applications and an ever increasing number of applications on the one hand, and expectations towards general improvements on the other, replacement of conventional recruiting procedures was an explicit objective of the project.

In general, the approach is based on four interconnected *applications*, a corporate website for recruiting, an internal job board, an 'entry system' for fresh employees, and, as a core system, an application management system. All systems possess a web-based front end and are a part from the application management system, realized as portals with self-service features. The corporate website is used for image building and attracting external applicants. Comfortable, personalized tools support the applicants, for example, getting comprehensive information, electronically applying for a job, tracking the application status, or getting in touch with corporate or profit centre recruiters. The web-based entry system supports new employees after a successful application during their first weeks by providing central information, FAQs, etc. The internal job board is both accessible via Inter- and Intranet and supports employees in applying for internal jobs, as well as recruiters in searching for internal candidates. Finally, the corporate application management systems supports corporate and profit centre recruiters, e.g. in posting job offers, administering the applications, searching and selecting adequate applicants and integrating external Internet job boards such as 'monster.com'. Since there is an in-house software division, all systems are realized as internal solutions. The application management system, however, has become a packaged solution offered to external customers. All applications are continuously improved, e.g. by a matching-algorithm that supports the pre-selection of applicants at present.

As expected, HR-professionals and applicants are the main *actor* categories of the approach. However, with the internal job board and the integration of external Internet job boards managers, employees, and consultants also recurrently participate. At present, approximately 300 HR professionals and 2,000 managers are permanent internal users.

continued

Since there are built-in self-service features in the applications, recruiting units and actors have become partially 'virtual' in the above mentioned way.

In this actually divergent HR environment the 'convergence forces' of e-HRM can be demonstrated to some extent. The project started in Germany and within one year the approach was introduced in all German HR departments. Since the US constitutes an important market, within the second year the approach was introduced there, before it was transmitted to France and the UK. The single country versions show slight differences. Besides the differing languages these are mainly due to varying national legislation. The age of an applicant, for example, is crucial information for German recruiters, however, in the US this information is not permitted due to equal employment opportunity legislation. Beside this, there is a push towards integration and convergence. In order to use possible cross-country synergies, e.g. the identification of redundant applications of an applicant in different countries or, for example, the transfer of an adequate, but in country A not needed applicant to country B, the systems have to use similar processes based on a common database. Additionally, the compatibility to the external job board consultants is necessary. The similarities of e-recruiting in France, Germany, the UK, and beyond therefore exceed their differences.

The *outcomes* proved to be in a comprehensive manner very successful. For example, there were considerable improvements in recruiting time cycles, superior and more internal candidates, cost reductions, and so on. In general, internal calculations show a pay off of investments within only one year. Hence, lest drawing an overly positive picture of e-HRM, it has to be stressed, that the example was chosen due to its 'best practice' character.

Conclusion

Virtualization is a novel management phenomenon facilitated by technology, global competitiveness, and imitation of best practices. Thus the emergence of virtualization underlines how isomorphism is leading to the implementation of common practices. Electronic HRM as the functional dimension of virtualization constitutes a typical example of how technology facilitates the spread of similar practices on an international scale largely independent of differences in institutional settings. Interfirm co-operation and HR outsourcing as aspects of the boundaryless organization also constitute results of global isomorphism, however, in contrast to e-HRM, are more significantly influenced by the national business system. Practices stemming from boundaryless virtualization are spread internationally, but its kind of implementation is mediated by forces stemming from the national business environment.

Whereas we made a distinction between the institutional and the functional dimension of virtual HR in our article, of course, both dimensions of virtualization are not independent of each other but iterate each other. Or, as Lepak and Snell (1998. 216) put it, virtualization constitutes 'a network based structure built on partnerships and typically mediated by information technologies to help the organization acquire, develop, and deploy intellectual capital'. Thus information technology is both a determinant and an outcome of boundaryless organizations.

Note

1 When studying the outsourcing literature, two different definitions of outsourcing can be found: internal and external outsourcing. Internal outsourcing implies the taking out of services to equity-related companies, e.g. the case of General Motors. In contrast, external outsourcing means the use of external providers that are legally and economically independent, e.g. the case of Eastman Kodak (Matiaske & Mellewigt 2002).

References

Albert, M. 1991. *Capitalisme contre Capitalisme*. Paris: Éditions du Seuil.

Alchian, A.A. 1984. Specifity, specialization, and coalitions. *Journal of Institutional and Theoretical Economics*, 140(1): 34–49.

Ashkenas, R., Ulrich, D., Jick, T. & Kerr, S. 1995. *The Boundaryless Organization: Breaking the Chains of Organizational Structure*. San Francisco: Jossey-Bass.

Avolio, B. J., Kahai, S. & Dodge, G. E. 2000. E-leadership: Implications for theory, research and practice. *Leadership Quarterly*, 11(4): 615–668.

Barringer, M. W. & Milkovich, G. T. 1998. A theoretical exploration of the adoption and design of flexible benefit plans: A case of human resource innovation. *Academy of Management Review*, 23 (2): 305–324.

Basu, A. & Kumar, A. 2002. Workflow management issues in e-business. *Information Systems Research*, 13(1): 1–14.

Byrne, J.A., Brandt, R. & Port, O. 1993. The virtual corporation. *Business Week*, 8 (February 1993): 36–40.

Carrig, K. 1997. Reshaping resources for the next century – lessons from a high flying airline. *Human Resource Management*, 36: 277–289.

Cedar Consulting 2004. *Workforce Technology Survey*. Baltimore: Cedar Publishing.

Coase, R. H. 1937. The nature of the firm. *Economia*, 4(4): 386–405.

Commons, J. R. 1931. Institutional economics. *The American Economic Review*, 21: 648–657.

Davidow, W. H. & Malone, M. S. 1992. *The Virtual Corporation. Structuring and Revitalizing the Corporation for the 21st Century*. New York: HarperCollins.

DiMaggio, P. J. & Powell, W.W. 1983. The iron cage revisited: institutional isomorphism and collective rationality in organizational fields. *American Sociological Review*, 48: 147–160.

DiMaggio, P. J. & Powell, W. W. 1991. Introduction. In W. W. Powell & P. J. DiMaggio (eds.), *The New Institutionalism in Organizational Analysis*. Chicago: University of Chicago Press, 1–38.

Dirlewanger, W. 1992. Outsourcing – Quell der Hoffnung? *Zeitschrift für Kommunikations- und EDV-Sicherheit*, 8: 187–195.

Flick, S. E. 1972. The human side of overseas joint ventures. *Management Review*, 61(1): 29–42.

Geppert, M., Matten, D. & Schmidt, P. 2004. Die Bedeutung institutionalistischer Ansätze für das Verständnis von Organizations- und Managementprozessen in multinationalen Unternehmen. *Berliner Journal für Soziologie*, 14(3): 379–397.

Granovetter, M. S. 1985. Economic action, social structure and embeddedness. *American Journal of Sociology*, 91: 481–510.

Greer, Charles R., Youngblood, Stuart A. & Gray, David A. 1999. Human resource management outsourcing: The make or buy decision. *Academy of Management Executive*, August 1999, 13(3): 85–97. [website: http://www.epnet.com]

Grover, V., Cheon, M. J. & Teng, J. T. C. 1996. The effect of service quality and partnership on the outsourcing of information systems functions. *Journal of Management Information Systems*, 12(4): 89–116.

Hall, P. A. & Soskice, D. 2001. *Varieties of Capitalism: The Institutional Foundations of Comparative Advantage*. New York: Oxford University Press.

Handy, C. B. 1995. Trust in virtual organization. *Harvard Business Review*, 73(3): 40–50.

Harris, M. M., van Hoye, G. & Lievens, F. 2003. Privacy and attitudes towards Internet-based selection systems: A cross-cultural comparison. *International Journal of Selection and Assessment*, 11(2/3): 230–236.

Hesse, G. 2003. *E-Cruiting bei Bertelsmann*. In G. Hertel & U. Konradt (eds.), Human Resource Management im Inter- und Intranet, Göttingen. Hogrefe: 72–91.

HR-XML Consortium 2005. *Mission statement*, retrieved 01/01/2005. http://www.hr-xml.org/channels/about.cfm

iLogos Research 2003. *Global 500 Website Recruiting*. 2003 Survey. San Francisco.

Kabst, R. & Matiaske, W. 2001. Outsourcing und Professionalisierung in der Personalarbeit – Eine transaktionskostentheoretisch orientierte Studie. *Zeitschrift für Personalfor- schung*. Special issue: Neue Formen der Beschäftigung – neue Personalpolitik. 16: 247–269.

Klaas, B. S., McClendon, J. & Gainey, T. W. 1999. HR outsourcing and its impact: The role of transaction costs. *Personnel Psychology*, 52(1): 113–136.

Konrad, U. & Sarges, W. (eds.) 2003. *E-Recruitment und E-Assessment*. Göttingen: Hogrefe.

Lengnick-Hall, M. A. & Moritz, S. 2003. The impact of e-HR on the human resource management function. *Journal of Labour Research*, 24(3): 365–379.

Lepak, D. P. & Snell, S. A. 1998. Virtual HR: strategic human resource management in the 21st century. *Human Resource Management Review*, 8(3): 215–234.

Liaw, S.-S. & Huang, H.-M. 2002. How web technology can facilitate learning. *Information Systems Management*, 19(1): 56–61.

Lievens, F. & Harris, M. M. 2003. Research on Internet recruiting and testing. Current status and future directions. In C. L. Cooper & I. T. Robertson (eds.), *International Review of Industrial and Organizational Psychology*, 18: 131–165.

Matiaske, W. & Mellewigt, T. 2002. Motive, Erfolge und Risiken des Outsourcings – Befun de und Defizite der empirischen Outsourcing-Forschung. *Zeitschrift für Betriebswirt schaft*, 72: 641–659.

McGaughey, S. L. & De Cieri, H. 1999. Reassessment of convergence and divergence dynamics: implications for international human resource management. *International Journal of Human Resource Management*, 10: 235–250.

Mecham, K. 2001. How Microsoft built a cost effective HR portal. *HR Focus*, 8: 4–5.

Meyer, J.W. & Rowan, B. 1977. Institutionalized organizations: formal structure as myth and ceremony. *American Journal of Sociology*, 83: 340–363.

Miles, R. & Snow, C. 1992. Causes of failure in network organizations. *California Management Review*, 34: 53–72.

Norris, G., Hurley, J. R., Hartley, K. M., Dunleavy, J R. & Balls, J. D. 2000. *E-Business and ERP: Transforming the Enterprise.* New York: John Wiley & Sons Ltd.

O'Connel, S. 1996. Virtual HR: an economic reality. *Human Resource Management Magazine,* March: 37–40.

Peterson, R. B. & Schwind, H. F. 1977. A comparative study of personnel problems in international companies and joint ventures in Japan. *Journal of International Business Studies,* 8(1): 45–55.

Picot, A. 1991. Ein neuer Ansatz zur Gestaltung der Leistungstiefe. *Zeitschrift für betriebswirtschaftliche Forschung,* 43. Jg.(12): 336–357.

Powell, W. 1990. Neither market nor hierarchy: network forms of organizations. *Research in Organization Behavior,* 12: 295–336.

Rampton, G. M., Turnbull, I. J. & Doran, J. A. 1999. *Human Resource Management Systems.* 2nd ed. Toronto: Carswell.

Rheingold, H. 1993. *The Virtual Community. Homesteading on the Electronic Frontier.* Cambridge and London: MIT Press.

Roberts, P. W. & Greenwood, R. 1997. Integrating transaction cost and institutional theories. Toward a constrained-efficiency framework for understanding organizational design adoption. *Academy of Management Review,* 22(2): 346–373.

Ropohl, G. 1982. *Zur Kritik des technologischen Determinismus.* In Rapp, F. & Durbin, P. T. (eds.), Technikphilosophie in der Diskussion, Braunschweig and Wiesbaden. Vieweg, 3–17.

Schaan, J. L. 1988. How to control a joint venture even as a minority partner. *Journal of General Management,* 14(1): 4–16.

Schaper, N. & Konradt, U. 2003. *Personalentwicklung mit E-Learning,* In G. Hertel & U. Konradt (eds.), Human Resource Management im Inter- und Intranet. Göttingen: Hogrefe: 274–293.

Scholz, C. 2003: *Datenaustausch in webbasierter Personalarbeit über XML.* In: Scholz, C. & Gutmann, J. (eds.), Webbasierte Personalwertschöpfung. Theorien – Konzeption Praxis. Wiesbaden: Gabler: 207–222.

Scholz, C. 2004. *Virtualisierung der Personalarbeit.* In E. Gaugler, W. A. Oechsler & W. Weber (eds.), Handwörterbuch des Personalwesens. (3rd edn). Stuttgart: Schäffer & Poeschl: 1979–88.

Schuler, R. 2001. HR issues and activities in IJVs. *International Journal of Human Resource Management,* 12(1): 1–52.

Shenkar, O. & Zeira, Y. 1987. Human resources management in international joint ventures: directions for research. *Academy of Management Review,* 12(3): 546–557.

Shenkar, O. & Zeira, Y. 1990. International joint ventures: a tough test for HR. *Personnel,* 1: 26–31.

Simon, S. H. & Mattle, W. G. 2002. Rethinking online benefits. *Compensation and Benefits Review,* 34(3/4): 80–84.

Stanton, J. M. & Barnes-Farrell, J. L. 1996. Effects of electronic performance monitoring on personal control, task satisfaction, and task performance. *Journal of Applied Psychology,* 81: 738–745.

Strohmeier, S. 1998. Reengineering, artificial intelligence and virtualization: Innovations in information technology and chances for Human Resource Management. In W. Weber, M. Festing & R. Kabst (eds.), Proceedings of the 6th Conference on International Human Resource Management, Paderborn.

Szyperski, N. 1993. Outsourcing als strategische Entscheidung. *Online,* 2: 32–41.

Taras, D. G. & Gesser, A. 2003. How new lawyers use e-voice to drive firm compensation: The 'greedy associates' phenomenon. *Journal of Labor Research,* 24(1): 9–29.

Towers Perrin 2002. *HR on the web: 2002 HR Service delivery survey report.*

Walker, A. J. (ed.) 2001. *Web-based Human Resources. The Technologies and Trends That are Transforming HR.* New York: McGrawHill.

Watson Wyatt 2000. *The Net Effect: eHR™ and the Internet.* Washington: Watson Wyatt.

Watson Wyatt 2002. *eHR™: 2002 Survey Report.* Washington: Watson Wyatt.

Watson, J. & Fenner, J. 2000. Understanding portals. *Information Management Journal,* 34(3): 18–21.

Whitley, Richard 1999. Competing logics and units of analysis in the comparative study of economic organization. *International Studies of Management & Organization,* 29(2): 113–127. website: http://www.epnet.com.

Williamson, O. E. 1975. *Markets and Hierarchies.* New York: Free Press.

Williamson, O. E. 1985. *The Economic Institutions of Capitalism.* New York: Free Press.

Williamson, O. E. 1996. *The Mechanisms of Governance.* New York: Free Press.

Williamson, O. E. 1981. The economics of organisation: The transaction cost approach. *American Journal of Sociology,* 87(3): 548–577.

Williamson, O. E. 1999. Strategy research: governance and competence perspectives. *Strategic Management Journal,* 20: 1087–1108.

Williamson, O. E. 2000. *Why law, economics, and organization.* Working Paper, University of California at Berkeley.

Zampetti, R. & Adamson, L. 2001a. Web-based manager-selfservice. In A. J. Walker (ed.), *Web-based Human Resources. The Technologies and Trends That are Transforming HR.* New York: McGrawHill, 24–35.

Zampetti, R. & Adamson, L. 2001b: Web-based employee-selfservice. In A. J. Walker (ed.), *Web-based Human Resources. The Rechnologies and Trends That are Transforming HR.* New York: McGrawHill, 15–23.

Zucker, L. G. 1987. Institutional theories of organization. *Annual Review of Sociology* 13: 43–464.

Conclusion

13 European HRM: on the road again

HENRIK HOLT LARSEN AND WOLFGANG MAYRHOFER

European HRM – the two-fold rationale

The emerging nature of the HRM concept

As we have stressed from the outset, the rationale behind this book is two-sided. The book deals with a generic concept – human resource management (HRM) – which has forced its way into management research and practice during the last decades, and we apply this concept to Europe, a continent with very specific, albeit diverse institutional, historical, political, and economic characteristics. Regarding the first issue, that is, HRM, this concept was introduced as a much needed and refreshing managerial discipline more than twenty years ago in the US. The concept has travelled to Europe and had a very significant impact on the way in which private and public organizations deal with their human resources. When the HRM concept reached the shores of Europe in the 1980s and 1990s, it appeared in a somewhat paradoxical shape. On the one hand, many US-concepts and tools were deliberately taken to the heart of European HR managers in an authentic, 'unspoiled' way. Part of the fascination had to do with the fact that the pa[...] US flavour was preserved, rather than washed out. Many fads, quick-fi[...] universal, normative HR 'theories', often founded on anecdotal evid[...] this category. The underlying philosophy was: 'If it works in the[...] work (perhaps even better) in Europe', and many US manag[...] on road shows to European conference centres with stan[...] HRM-flavoured Big Macs and Chicken McNuggets. [...] was heavily influenced by – and copied intentiona[...] practice. Obviously, European subsidiaries of [...] of (and were often also forced to, in fact) [...] and procedures into their national HR[...]

On the other hand, one also saw a reaction *against* importing HRM wisdom uncritically from the US. After all, the concept of situational leadership, a US invention, by the way, has stressed for almost four decades the need for adapting and tailoring any managerial method to the specific contextual conditions. The argument is that a HRM practice (and other organizational interventions) will only take deep roots and flourish if it matches with the specific features of the situation. Logically and specifically, this means that US HRM-thinking and -methods will only be of practical use in European organizations if they are conditioned to national and local cultures. In addition, US-based HRM theory and, in particular, concrete HRM systems/practice have been exposed to a somewhat fierce critique from European academics. This critique has been fuelled by a paradigmatic, ideological perspective, emphasizing that HRM is a Trojan horse. What appears to be new methods of developing and empowering people and increasing their commitment and flexibility is underneath a discreet and cunning way of manipulating and monitoring human beings for the benefit of the employer. Obviously, when one adds to this critique the fact that a US-born management principle is imported into Europe in a somewhat 'one size fits all' way, it must create a heated debate in academic circles and, to a lesser extent, among HR practitioners.

The distinctiveness of Europe as an organizational and labour market environment

As mentioned above, be... of HRM being the first rationale, the emph... onale for publishing a book on ...used explicitly on European and factor is the European Union, ...mber states and the four major d entrepreneurship – within the f individual and organizational s legal levels, is also , but there is a general trend ...al types and characteristics ...ve analyzed three major ...l organizations – all

...particular ...tools and ...ence, fell into ...US, it will also ...ement gurus went ...dardized menus of ...this way, European HRM ...n this way, US mainstream HRM ...ly – US corporations had a good chance ...importing US HRM-thinking, systems ...M practice.

– and subsequently the ...nstitutional context, its characteristics, the ...surement of HRM ...nomic macro-trends,

In the following we will highlight the major findings and consequences of these four major themes.

Looking outside: the institutional context

An analysis of the institutional context inevitably includes referring to the European Union as a core collective actor. Within Europe, the EU is one – if not *the* – major change driver affecting individuals, organizations, and nation states. First, the European Union provides a historically unique context within which organizations and individuals act. Six decades after the end of the Second World War, all those European parties who confronted each other in the most deadly and destructive conflict of recent history are (with the exception of Russia) both an integral and official part of the ambitious European project or are taking serious steps to get officially included. Among others, doing business across European borders has clearly been made easier. The four freedoms have inevitably changed how businesses are set up and run. Second, the perceived success of the EU at least in economic terms, taking tangible measures such as per capita income or GDP as a frame of reference, has made the EU highly attractive. Hence, most European countries currently outside the EU are taking serious steps to get officially included or at least to profit through various forms of partnerships. Third, the efforts of the EU to create a common frame of reference in terms of legal regulations led to an interesting situation where EU-regulations and national regulations and practices, respectively, sometimes complement and sometimes are at odds with each other. Fourth, beyond the legal aspect, the EU takes serious measures to create a common frame of reference of thinking. Building bridges, understanding each other and each other's differences, providing opportunities to connect to each other and allow cross-national interactions are at the core of a number of EU efforts. For example, programmes such as SOCRATES, Leonardo da Vinci or TEMPUS not merely support, among others, the exchange of people within Europe. They also create an informal network of understanding and contacts and lead to a greater insight into different ways of living. Likewise, funding various large scale research efforts not only produces and distributes knowledge, but softly enforces an exchange of viewpoints, common understanding and linking resources across countries.

European HRM and its uniqueness cannot be understood without referring to the developments because of activities of the EU. Let us take just a few examples from different areas. The legal environment relevant for HRM has drastically changed over the past two decades with EU legal regulations providing a new framework. They cover areas as diverse as gender mainstreaming, employee relations or regulations about hiring workforce from abroad. In addition, through the EU an additional level in the system of industrial relations has emerged. Pan-European networks of employers' associations and trade unions, or European works councils constitute actors that European HRM, especially in organizations operating across

European borders, have to take into account. The increased mobility of the workforce and, consequently, its changing competency profile allows European HRM a different approach to foreign assignments. Various EU programmes supporting the exchange of people from primary school up to the university level constitute the basis for this. The EU has also changed the legal regulations for the contract award processes. Under specific conditions, invitations for tenders have to be announced Europe-wide. Consequently, the contract award process has to follow certain steps. For European HRM, this opens up a completely new line of training and quality control issues.

Deregulation partly linked to the efforts of the EU to create a single market and partly linked to global tendencies of reducing competitive barriers. At the surface level, the situation seems to be quite straightforward: the EU as well as international institutions such as the WTO undertake serious efforts to open up national markets through deregulating national environments. However, national interests as well as various interest groups such as trade unions sometimes do have conflicting interests due to the clientele they are representing. The tension between flexibility tendencies promoted by a coalition of EU institutions and employers' association and security concerns voiced by trade unions, some political parties and non-governmental organizations such as ATTAC provide a typical example of a development with clear relevance for European HRM. The various regulations with their great complexity and the need to take into account sometimes conflicting views about these issues are a core characteristic for the specific institutional environment that is an integral part of European HRM. Far from the mono-dimensional notion of organizations and their HRM being rather autonomous actors who have a relatively unrestricted space of potential action, the flexibility-security debate illustrates the heavy interdependence between European HRM and its external environment and the high density of regulations the European HRM faces.
In addition, no uniform answers emerge in Europe. As the example about handling the flexibility-security nexus in Belgium, France, and the Netherlands shows quite convincingly, similar problems are solved in quite different ways due to different national preferences and necessities. Consequently, this leads back to another characteristic of European HRM: being similar and different at the same time as expressed in the cluster view of HRM in European countries.

Looking inside: embeddedness in the organization

As it was mentioned in Chapter 1, the internal institutional setting has a strong impact on HRM processes and outcomes in an organization. Hence, when designing or choosing between different HRM methods and systems, organizational characteristics should be taken into consideration. Parallel to this, HRM research should incorporate and make explicit the organizational context, in which the research is done, and in those organizational settings in which it is applicable. Unfortunately, this is not always done, which is a serious shortcoming when considering the vast range of organizational types in which HRM is found. In Chapters 5–7 we analyzed three very different, but significant – and for Europe important – organizational types, i.e. multinational corporations, small and medium enterprises (SMEs), and not-for-profit organizations.

The three organizational types are characterized by distinctive and very different missions, visions, and values. This is particularly the case for not-for-profit organizations, whose entire existence is based on support – not only from external stakeholders, but also from the employees. The need for integrating the HR strategy to the overall corporate strategy is very pronounced, because the 'product' of the organization is often intangible, immaterial, ideological, and derived from the overall objectives and values of the organization. In addition, the employees may not be formally employed by the organization (receiving a proper salary and being subject to traditional employment conditions), but volunteers who are unpaid or only receiving symbolic financial benefits.

What is desirable and/or actual management behaviour also varies with the internal situational characteristics of the organization. In SMEs, for instance, managerial positions are quite often filled by founders and/or owners. Their management behaviour is entrepreneurial and typically tied to the field of functional expertise which was the rationale behind the establishment of the organization in the first place. The managerial behaviour is very visible to staff in an SME, and the employees 'read' this behaviour and regard it as the expression of organizational values and goals.

The structural characteristics of an organization include whether there is a proper HR function or not. As discussed in Chapter 6, most SMEs have no formal HRM function, which makes it paradoxical that most of the studies and writings about HRM assume that there is such a HRM function. In SMEs, line manager responsibility for HRM is not just a *supplement* to whatever a proper HR function is doing, as is often seen in larger organizations. As SMEs very rarely have a HRM function in the first place, the only provider of HR tasks and the locus for HR responsibility is hence the line manager(s).

An important feature of HRM is the way knowledge and information floats across organizational boundaries. A typical example is knowledge sharing in MNCs, where recent research shows that traditional, hierarchical lines of communication are increasingly supplemented or replaced by reverse communication or communication between subsidiaries directly. Focusing exclusively on the strategic HRM orientation of the parent company is inadequate. There is an increasing resource dependence of the parent company on its subsidiaries, and this poses new HRM challenges and provides new answers, e.g. centres-of-excellence, outsourcing, new types of expatriation, acquisitions etc.

Looking at oneself: the roles and contribution of HRM

One of the features European HRM inherited from the US origin of the discussion was the actual terminology, i.e. combining the three words, human, resource, and management. In many European countries the HRM terminology was translated into the local language, in some cases so 'effectively' that the three components could hardly be found in the local tongue. In other countries it was found so difficult – or undesirable – to find such a one-to-one translation that the original English-language term was introduced into the country and language. Regardless of whether one or the other solution was chosen, an intensive debate among researchers and practitioners in the various countries often followed. Where do we (want to) put the emphasis: *human* resource management, human *resource* management or human resource *management*? On the whole, most attention has been attached to the word *resource*, and as we have seen in the previous chapters (in particular Chapters 8 and 9), there is a strong interest in assessing the economic or financial implications of HRM. *As* the (generic) concept was initially called HRM, *as* the resource aspect was exported from the US to Europe, and *as* most countries chose *not* to 'lose' the resource word on the way, there is, so to speak, an arranged marriage between HRM and various subdisciplines under the umbrella of economics/finance. You raise the level of ambition – and it obliges – to call the field Human *Resource* Management, and it has been a favourite discussion topic among European HRM scholars whether the use of the word *resource* is a compliment to human beings as it is seeing resources as invaluable, scarce, precious treasure which is difficult to imitate and should preferably be used in a refined form *or* – opposite – the word resource takes the uniqueness and the dignity out of human beings. Regardless of which side is on, the word resource opens a gateway to measurement, as it is mainstream thinking and practice in finance and accounting to measure resources. HR costing and accounting, intellectual capital, and so on, are examples hereof.

The resource-based approach to HRM – being one of the most developed, devoted, and determined theoretical directions within HRM research – has a twenty-year record in measuring human behaviour. There may be several reasons for the fact that this approach has not travelled very well over the Atlantic. One reason is the reluctance or resistance towards the very quantitatively and statistically oriented research methodology among (some) European scholars. Similarly, quantitative assessment systems such as performance appraisal, evaluation of managers, 360 degree feedback or psychological tests etc. have been met with a very suspicious and antagonistic attitude in some European cultures and work organizations. With the increasing intrusion of HRM-thinking in European research and practitioner communities, this scepticism has weakened and in many cases even been turned into an acceptance of quantitative assessment of HR features as a monitoring device for the HR profession. Hence, it is not only because of what has been called the arranged marriage between HRM and finance/accounting above that there has been a pressure for measurement of human behaviour. This pressure also comes from inside the HR profession and has been used as a self-defence mechanism to 'prove', legitimate or justify the need for investment in human resources.

Thus, European organizations have – despite the hesitance described above – gradually taken a much more positive approach towards measurement. Reflecting the realization that the language of business is money and the quite often deeply felt perception that the HR and corporate strategy should be integrated, HR practitioners and (some) researchers have stressed the need to express the activities and outcome of HR in the 'currency' which is being used as strategic decision makers, i.e. the executives of the organization. We have presented a series of data from the Cranet survey, showing the understanding, but not always implementation of integrating HR professionals in the strategy development. The rhetoric is in place, so to speak, but the actual synergy between HR and corporate strategy is certainly not always achieved.

This dilemma bridges the roles of the HR professionals. In Chapter 10 various HR roles were discussed: OD consultant, strategic broker, and individual therapist. This came out of an ascertainment that HR professionals have traditionally found it difficult to get into the executive circles and be an active player in the formulation of corporate strategies. However, perhaps the need to have a significant impact on the organization should be pursued by other methods. The chapter argues, at least, that what is called the daunted journey of re-invention of the HR field could be achieved by 'the courage to be counter-cultural, the willingness to broker rather than deliver and the readiness to adopt a therapeutic stance'. The theoretical discussion as well as the practical implementation of various ways of organizing HRM activities certainly gets an interesting twist by introducing such significantly different perspectives on the role of HRM and its agents or practitioners.

Looking beyond: societal and economic macro-trends

Under this heading diversity/diversity management and virtualization were discussed as essential themes relevant in European HRM. Given the core characteristics of European HRM outlined in the first chapter of this book, the findings in these chapters have a number of consequences for European HRM.

First, European HRM faces distinct problems in terms of the diversity of the workforce and its management. Clearly going beyond a mere male-female or ethnicity divide, the existence of a great number of dimensions that create diversity in the workforce make the task – but, of course, also the possible rewards – of managing this diversity especially demanding. The workforce is characterized by a large number of differences in terms of religion, ethnicity, cultural heritage, national and local cultural patterns, and nationality/citizenship. While in some European countries, e.g. England, such a situation has a long tradition and has been part of the picture of HR work for a long time, in other countries this is a rather new situation. Hence, for European HRM maybe it is not so much the 'absolute amount' of diversity, but the speed and relative change towards a 'truly' diverse workforce which poses a number of problems. For example, in terms of recruitment and selection, the recognition of diversity as a legitimate and partly legally required dimension of decision making requires a thorough check of recruitment guidelines and procedures. In another example, the frequency of work groups which are highly diverse in a number of possible dimensions such as culture, nationality, language, and religion, bring along all the problems – but, again, of course also all the potential benefits – linked with culturally mixed teams.

Second, in terms of diversity and diversity management, European countries are clearly moving in the same direction. Especially the EU countries and those countries which are moving closer to the EU see an increase in workforce diversity. An increasingly international workforce even in indigenous companies or the efforts of the EU to protect and support minorities by ensuring equal treatment regardless of gender, sexual orientation, and ethnicity, show an increasing awareness regarding these issues. For European HRM, such developments constitute important parts of the picture.

Third, Europe provides a fertile ground not only for different types of organizations beyond the profit world as has been shown above. High competitive pressures, small regional distances, a great proportion of highly skilled persons in the workforce, good infrastructure and the need to link European and non-European operations are supporting factors for the prominence of new organizational forms and virtual elements in HRM. On the one hand, this gives rise to 'new' theoretical concepts or 'old' concepts applied in a new way dealing with questions about HRM in new organizational forms and virtualization. On the other hand, virtualization leads to blurring organizational boundaries. In network organizations, for example, it is even more difficult than in 'normal' organizations to draw the 'inside/outside' distinction or make internal differentiations. In addition, virtualization and electronic HRM allows the integration of – from a European perspective – remote parts of an organization in other regions of the world into one picture. Consequently, the label 'European' denoting a specific region, institutional context and set of tasks can become misleading. If, for example, electronic learning management systems in an organization are used not only across Europe, but also beyond, it might be increasingly difficult to talk about European HRM. In this sense, virtualization might be regarded as a factor contributing to the dissolving of a specific European 'flavour' of HRM.

Travelling on a long and winding road

In a sense, the message of the present book can be summarized in the following paraphrase: 'On a clear day, you can see European HRM'. We have identified a number of distinctive, unique features of European HRM and related these to the generic HRM concept as this was coined in the US in the 1980s. We have interpreted the distinct European flavour of the HRM concept by incorporating a range of contextual factors, we have seen how HRM unfolds in various organizational types, we have analyzed the measurement of HR processes, and we have bridged HRM with organizational performance. By doing so, we hope to have illustrated the significance of a European-based HRM concept which can guide researchers and practitioners in dealing with human resource issues in European organizations. Despite these virtues, a number of future challenges for the field remain.

First, while European HRM can ride on the wave of the original US-based HRM concept, it inevitably will suffer from the many inherent contradictions in the very same concept. Despite twenty years of rigorous research, there is still much dispute over the HRM concept, whether it is just Personnel Management in new wrapping, and/or whether it is good in the first place. Chapter 10 summarized some of this critique: marginality in management decision making, inability to defend the boundaries of the HR expertise, lack of ability to document business contribution, and difficulties in describing the mutuality between the individual and the organization. The very same chapter, however, provided a potential way out of these problems.

Second, even before the smoke settles and some consensus regarding the content of the (European or generic) HRM concept may eventually be achieved, critical voices claim that HRM has reached the 'Best before' date. The argument is that HRM rests on a traditional view of organizations as being tangible, physical, and hierarchical entities. This does – consequently – not take into account newer conceptualizations of organizations as being enacted, socially constructed, dynamic, and often irrational.

Third, the European dimension is in itself complex and contradictory. We claim that 'there is such a thing as European HRM' at the same time as we stress the diversity, multiplicity, and cultural embeddedness of the HRM practice. National cultures provide a context for – and give a particular flavor to – HRM. What works well in one culture may not work in another culture and may even be looked down upon because it violates cultural values or norms. We have emphasized present and new member states of the EU as an example of contextual differences and the power of a magnetic field of convergence and divergence in HRM practice.

We propose, however, to regard these issues as starting points for future developments in the field rather than actual shortcomings of the European HRM concept. The multiplicity and complexity of European HRM issues does not imply that it is meaningless to discuss European HRM as a theoretical construct and as an applied discipline. Rather, it stresses the need for a contingency approach to European HRM theory and practice. The disadvantage of this is that universal solutions to HRM problems are rare. The advantage is that the field is stretched simply because extreme attention to contextual and other characteristics of a given situation is needed in order to analyze it – not to mention coming up with recommendations for how to deal with specific European HRM problems.

The sky is the limit for European HRM, we would be tempted to say as a closing remark – had we not been familiar with the old European wisdom about Icarus growing exhilarated about his opportunities and following this dictum instead of choosing the middle ground between the sea and the sun . . .

Index